Database Projects

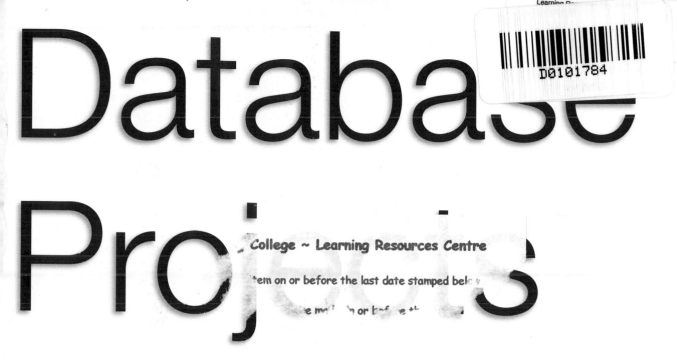

College ~ Learning Resources Centre

...em on or before the last date stamped bel...

in Access for Advanced Level

Julian Mott and Ian Rendell

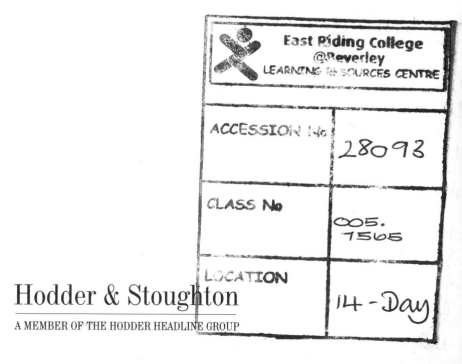

Hodder & Stoughton
A MEMBER OF THE HODDER HEADLINE GROUP

The authors would like to thank the following people for their assistance: Phil Webster, Nicola Joiner, Jane Mott and Helen Royall.

Orders: please contact Bookpoint Ltd, 130 Milton Park, Abingdon, Oxon OX14 4SB. Telephone: (44) 01235 827720. Fax: (44) 01235 400454. Lines are open from 9.00–6.00, Monday to Saturday, with a 24 hour message answering service.

British Library Cataloguing in Publication Data
A catalogue record for this title is available from the British Library

ISBN 0 340 738057

First published 2001

Impression number 10 9 8 7 6 5 4

Year   2007 2006 2005 2004 2003 2002

Typeset by Pantek Arts Ltd, Maidstone, Kent.

Printed in Great Britain for Hodder & Stoughton Educational, a division of Hodder Headline Plc, 338 Euston Road, London NW1 3BH by J.W. Arrowsmith, Bristol.

Contents

Introduction   v
How to use this book   vii
Ideas for projects   ix

Part One – The Development of a System
1 The Pass-It Driving School   1
2 Getting started   3
3 Setting up the tables   9
4 Entering the data   22
5 Defining the relationships   35
6 Select queries   39
7 Further queries   47
8 Setting up multi-table queries   56
9 Setting up forms using the Form Wizard   64
10 Working in Form Design View   70
11 Taking form designer further   81
12 Setting up reports   98
13 Further reports   111
14 Macros   121
15 Adding a switchboard   125
16 Using SubForms   135
17 Setting up search and sort options   150
18 Calculations in reports   155
19 Using action queries   166
20 Finishing touches   175

Part two – Documenting a system
21 Documenting a system   193

Part three – 50 Access tricks and tips   229

Part four – Appendices   255
1 Access glossary   255
2 Access toolbars   261
3 Keyboard shortcuts in Access   264
4 Coursework specifications and requirements of the
different exam boards   267

Index   289

Introduction

Aims

The book is aimed primarily at students studying the A/S and A levels in ICT offered by AQA, OCR and Edexcel. The book offers advice and support materials for the practical component of the specification, making candidates aware of analysing, designing, implementing, testing and evaluating solutions to problems using the advanced features of a software package.

The book, however, could also prove useful for students studying A/S and A levels in Computing where a software package solution to an ICT system can be offered as an alternative approach to a programming solution.

The materials and approach used in the book might also be applicable to students on many courses in further and higher education where a study of databases through Microsoft Access is necessary.

Advanced features of Access

The following advice is intended only for guidance. Teachers should use this in conjunction with the Specification and Examiners' Reports to ensure the correct features are being used appropriately.

Use of these features alone does not guarantee high marks. It is down to how the student uses them to solve an ICT problem and documents the solution. A level projects in Microsoft Access are likely to include some of the following features:

- simple input masks and data validation;
- select and parameter queries;
- data entry using fully customised forms;
- list boxes or combo boxes to facilitate data entry;
- output fully tailored to user requirements;
- macros to automate commonly used features;
- a switchboard;
- subforms to display information in related tables;

- options to run action queries;

- forms and reports based on multi-table queries;

- customised reports with use of logos, headers and footers to show grouped data and calculated totals;

- fully customised menus.

Students are expected to go beyond implementing a single table database. Solutions should be relational and used in a relational manner.

Solutions do not need to be over-complicated. Three or four tables are sufficient at this level. Referential integrity should be enforced.

Students are expected to work towards the production of fully automated and customised solutions that hide the software from the user. Wizards should be seen as the starting point on which students would develop their solution.

As more and more records are added, data will build up. The clearing down of old data must be considered. For example, in a school library system how long will details of loans be stored?

Students should also consider the cyclic nature of their solutions. For example, how will the library system handle those pupils in years 11 and 13 at the end of the school year? Procedures at the end of the year, start of the season or end of term might be considered and reflected in solutions.

Programming and the use of Visual Basic are not usually within the spirit of the specifications or the systems promoted in this book. The chosen software package should drive the solution and not Visual Basic code. However students may wish to enter modules with code from routines researched and found in books or other media but this must be acknowledged at all times.

■ Access 97/2000 issues

Access 2000 is not fully compatible with Access 97 but all the materials in this book are compatible with both versions.

Access 97 files can only be opened in read-only format in Access 2000. Access 97 files can be converted to the later format in Access 2000 by clicking on:
Tools, Database Utilities, Convert Database, To Current Access Database Version...

Access 2000 files cannot be opened in Access 97 and need to be converted to Access 97 format. This can be done in Access 2000 by clicking on:
Tools, Database Utilities, Convert Database, To Prior Access Database Version...

Enter the name of the database that you want to create and then click on **Save**.

Access 2000 does offer a number of new features that are clearly listed under Microsoft Help but the materials in this book work in both Access 2000 and Access 97.

The Database Window is slightly different in Access 97 and in Access 2000 as can be seen on page 7.

How to use this book

The book assumes students have a working knowledge of Windows and Windows based software. Students will have been introduced to databases via the National Curriculum or the study of ICT at Key Stage 3 and Key Stage 4. It is expected that students will be familiar with the concept of files, records and fields and will have practical experience of simple searching and sorting techniques.

It is also assumed that students will have studied the design of relational databases through a theory component in their course of study.

The book can be used as a formal teaching aid by lecturers or students can work independently through the self-study chapters in class or away from the classroom.

Part One takes the student through the development of a system with each chapter building on the range of features in Access. The system is based around a driving school, is fictitious and has been designed to incorporate as many features as is possible for demonstration purposes only. The chapters are best worked through in sequence.

Chapters 1 to 15 set up a working system, using features which might be expected from students at this level. Chapters 16 to 20 show how to develop this system further.

Part Two covers the major issues in documenting coursework projects and offers pointers, hints and examples of good practice.

Part Three offers a range of useful tips and features in Access to support the units and should provide interesting reading. These could be used as further activities for students. It is hoped that they can be the starting point for finding out even more about Access.

A note to students and lecturers

It is important to note that the system used in the text is not being put forward for a particular grade at any level. The system is fictitious and is aimed at showing the student the potential of Microsoft Access and how software features can be incorporated to produce a working ICT system.

All boards provide exemplar materials, support and training. It is vital that students in conjunction with their tutors are guided by the specifications.

The documentation of ICT solutions at this level follows the systems life-cycle approach of analysis, design, implementation, testing and evaluation. Again though different specifications and different solutions will have a different emphasis.

A word of real caution. Students must on no account copy materials in text books and submit them for examination. Moderators, examiners and the exam boards are very aware of published exemplar materials. You will be penalised severely.

■ Choosing a coursework project

Don't try to do everything. Using every single feature of Access would almost certainly lead to a very complicated and contrived project. It is better to choose a problem which involves some of the advanced features rather than all of them in the solution.

Don't try to do too much. It is easy to be over-ambitious. Computerising the payroll, income tax, national insurance and pension records of a county council or producing a stock control system for a multinational company is unrealistic at this level. It is best to stick to something that you know you can achieve.

Don't try to do too little. However, the opposite is also true. A shopping list or a list of friends' birthdays would be too simple at this level. If you can set the system up in a few lessons, it is likely the project chosen does not have enough scope.

Do try to find a real user. It is best to choose a real problem with a real end-user. The user could be one of your parents or a friend or neighbour. They could be a member of staff in your school or college. Having a real user does make analysis, testing and evaluating your solution all the easier. *For some courses, such as the AQA A level major project, a real end-user is essential*.

■ Ideas for projects

Car hire

A car hire company wants to store details of customers, cars for hire, pricing structure and future bookings. The system might produce timetables for cars on hire, details of car availability, reports on when a particular car has been hired and invoices for customers.

UCAS applications

A school's head of sixth form wants to store records of application by year 13 students for courses at universities, including applications and offers. The system might produce full information on any student, full lists of applicants, details of who has not yet applied, details of offers and details of students who have not yet had an offer. The system would offer on-line access to student records for the head of sixth form and print weekly update reports.

The school library

A school library wants to store details of pupils, reference books, books that can be borrowed and loans. The system might produce details of books currently on loan, details of books that are overdue, reports on which books are available, reports on when a particular book has been borrowed and letters for pupils reminding them that a book is overdue.

Sports club membership

A sports club wants to store membership details electronically. The system might produce membership lists, details of who has and who hasn't paid their subscriptions and send out letters to members about meetings. The system could also store details of bookings of the club's facilities such as squash courts or fitness equipment but potentially there are two separate systems here.

Work experience placements

A school wants to store details of work experience placements including names of pupils, employers, who is going to which employers and any special details. The system might produce details of which pupils will not be in school on a certain day, lists for staff, details of which pupils can be visited and when including a contact name, pupils who have not yet got a placement finalised and individual letters to employers and pupils telling them of arrangements.

Stock control

A fast food outlet wants to computerise its stock control. The system might store details of current stock levels, deliveries and today's sales. It might produce sales reports and stock reports, update stock levels automatically and produce orders for new stock.

ICT inventory

A school ICT department wants to keep an inventory of all its hardware on computer. The system might store details of hardware including purchase date, serial numbers, repairs and maintenance details, location and guarantee expiry. It might produce reports for internal audit, health and safety, service records and repair and maintenance history for each hardware item.

The driving school

A driving school wants to store details of lesson bookings including names of students and instructors. The system might produce timetables for all instructors for all days, details of when an instructor is available for a lesson, print records of students and produce membership cards.

School assessment records

A school wants to store details of pupil assessment records including names, teachers, marks, subjects and dates. The system might produce full results for any assessment, full information on any pupil, chart progress in a subject, compare performance in different subjects and print an automatic report for parents.

The dry-cleaning shop

A dry-cleaning company wants to store details of customers, items deposited for cleaning and charges for customers. The system might produce reports on what items have been brought in today, reports on when a particular customers has used the shop, show sales figures day-by-day or week-by-week and produce invoices for customers.

School options

A school wants to store details of the option choices for year 9 pupils, including names of pupils, options available, and who has opted for which subjects. The system might produce details of how many pupils have opted for each subject, produce pupil lists for each subject, produce subject lists for each pupil and reports on pupils who have not yet made their choices.

Shoe repair shop

A shoe repair shop wants to store details of shoes brought in for repair, type of repair needed, as well as names and contact details of customers. The system might produce reports on work in hand, work completed, allocate collection tickets to customers, store sales details and produce invoices for customers.

School play seat booking

A school wants to produce tickets for its school play on computer and store details of the tickets sold for the various performances. The system might include what seats are available, the times and dates of performances, the cost of tickets, which ones have been sold. It should be able to produce up to the minute reports on sales and income and produce diagrams to show which seats have not been sold for each performance.

Hotel room availability

A local hotel wants to set up an automated booking system. The system will store details of customers, rooms available, prices and bookings. Rooms must not be double booked. The system might produce reports on bookings, room availability and customer invoices.

Hairdressers' salon

A small hairdressers needs to be able to store appointment details. The system will store details of customers, stylists, requirements and bookings. Times for each booking must reflect the needs of the stylist. The system might produce reports on bookings and availability.

Local garage

A garage wants to store details of repairs electronically. The system will store details of customers, cars, MOT testing, servicing and repairs and bookings. The system might produce timetables for this week, reports on garage availability and customers for whom a service or MOT is due.

Sandwich shop

A sandwich shop takes orders from customers every morning, makes the sandwiches and delivers them to local shops, offices and factories. They want an electronic system to store details of orders, and provide reports on what sandwiches must be produced, ingredients needed and delivery lists.

Watch repairer

A watch repairer who runs his own business wants more accurate reports on repairs to be carried out. He wants to store details of customers, watches to be repaired and charges for customers. The system might produce reports on what items have been brought in today and show sales figures day-by-day or week-by-week.

Project timetable

A project timetable helps you ensure that the work-load is spread evenly throughout the project period, allowing for other factors such as module tests in ICT and other subjects, holidays and half-terms, workloads in other subjects etc. You should break your project up into sub-tasks and draw up the timetable at the start and try to stick to it. If you don't you can end up with too much to do at the last minute. This means that deadlines cannot be met and the final sections are rushed and only get low marks.

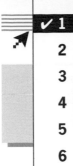
The Pass-It Driving School

The system covered by this book is based on a local driving school. The driving school caters for many students in the surrounding villages. The school has a number of full time and part time instructors.

When a student starts a course of lessons they are issued with a membership card and allocated an instructor. Students can book lessons through their instructor or by phoning the driving school office. Students usually book lessons of one or two hours though they can book longer sessions if they wish.

The school offers different types of lesson – introductory, Standard, Pass Plus or the Driving Test. Fees are charged depending on the type of lesson booked. The driving school organises the practical and theory test for the students and if successful the students can go on to a Pass Plus course.

The system will have four related tables Student, Instructor, Lesson Type and Lesson. Details are given in Table 1.1 on page 2.

The system will allow the user to book, cancel and cost driving lessons. Details of all students and their test dates will be stored enabling quick access and easy editing. Contact details for instructors working for the school will also be stored.

A range of search options will allow the user quickly to locate details of students and/or lessons. Full reporting menus will be implemented with options of weekly or daily lesson timetables for specified instructors. Student and Instructor reports will also be offered.

Further options will include the automatic

- issue of membership cards;

- increase or decrease of lesson price ranges;

- processing of students who leave the school after passing their test;

- filing of lessons.

All user interfaces will be fully customised with user-friendly menus.

Student Table	Instructor Table	Lesson Table	Lesson Type Table
Student ID	Instructor ID	Lesson Type	Lesson Type
Title	Surname	Student ID	Cost
Surname	Forename	Instructor ID	
Forename	Address 1	Date	
Address 1	Address 2	Start Time	
Address 2	Address 3	Length Of Lesson	
Address 3	Address 4	Collection Point	
Address 4	Home Tel No	Drop-Off Point	
Tel No	Mobile No	Lesson Type	
Date of Birth			
Sex			
Theory Test Date			
Passed Theory Test			
Practical Test Date			
Passed Practical Test			
Pass Plus Req			
Issued Card			

Table 1.1

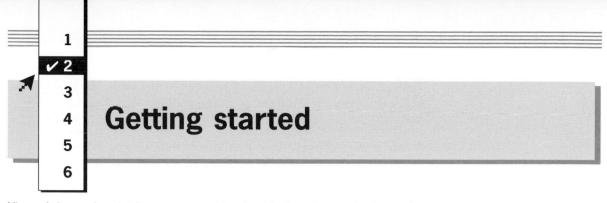

Getting started

Microsoft Access is a database management system. It allows the user to store and manipulate data.

The main components of an Access database are:

- tables
- queries
- forms
- reports
- macros
- modules

Access 2000 has a Pages component, allowing data to be saved in web format.

■ Tables

Access stores data in tables. A table is organised in rows (called records) and columns (called fields).

For example in a student table a row would store the information about one particular student. This is called a record. Each column would contain details about each student such as forename, surname etc. These are called fields.

Library No	Surname	Forename	Sex	Year	Form
4	Askham	Mathew	Male	7	S
5	Hunt	Gregory	Male	13	R
6	Smith	Robert	Male	11	T
7	Smith	Joanna	Female	11	T
8	Mather	Daniel	Male	10	H
9	Sumpton	Michael	Male	12	T
10	Hunt	David	Male	13	O
11	Johnson	Samantha	Female	9	N
12	Haywood	David	Male	11	N
13	Williams	Emma	Female	13	J
14	Lewis	Caroline	Female	9	N
15	Higginbotham	Simon	Male	12	O

Record: 12 of 108

Figure 2.1

Typically a system will consist of more than one table. For example in a school library the database might be made up of a student table, a book table and a loan table. The student table is shown in Figure 2.1.

Access is often referred to as a relational database package. Relationships can be defined between tables and used to support the searching and processing of data. A relational database will have at least two tables that are linked together.

■ Queries

A query is a way of asking questions about the data in your tables according to certain criteria. The user may wish to display a list of appointments for a particular day or output customers who owe payments. In the example in Figure 2.2 a query has produced a list of students in Year 11. This is known as a **Select Query**.

Library No	Surname	Forename	Sex	Year	Form
6	Smith	Robert	Male	11	T
7	Smith	Joanna	Female	11	T
12	Haywood	David	Male	11	N
36	Harris	David	Male	11	P
39	Holden	Lisa	Female	11	S
54	Simpson	Emma	Female	11	N
55	Kirkhope	Scott	Male	11	H

Record: 1 of 14

Figure 2.2

You will notice that there are 14 records in the output from this query. In the original table there were 108 records. 14 of the 108 pupils are in Year 11.

Queries in Access offer a powerful processing tool. Later you will meet action and parameter queries. Queries can also be used to take data from more than one table and perform calculations on data.

■ Forms

Forms are used mainly to display the records in a table in a user friendly way. Through a form you can enter and edit records more easily.

Forms are fully customisable. You can add buttons and controls, edit the appearance and include images (see Figure 2.3).

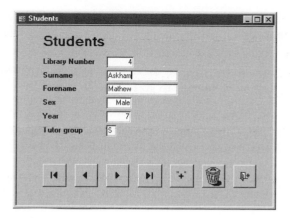

Figure 2.3

Reports

Reports are used to print information from your database. They provide professional looking output from a table or query. They can be fully customised and can display summary information (see Figure 2.4).

Students

Library Number	Surname	Forename	Sex	Tutor group
4	Askham	Mathew	Male	S
5	Hunt	Gregory	Male	R
6	Smith	Robert	Male	T
7	Smith	Joanna	Female	T
8	Mather	Daniel	Male	H

Figure 2.4

Macros

A macro is a set of one or more actions that perform a particular operation. You can use macros to add buttons to print a report, open a form and other commonly used tasks. Macros help you to automate and customise your system fully.

■ Modules

Modules are procedures written in Visual Basic for Applications (VBA) allowing the system developer to go further. The use of VBA is beyond the scope of this book.

Starting Access

To start Access click on **Start**, **Programs**, **Microsoft Access**. The Microsoft Access dialog box appears as shown in Figure 2.5.

Figure 2.5

From here you can either open an existing database, create a new database or use a range of pre-defined databases.

The databases you have most recently used appear in the lower half of the dialogue box.

The Database Window

When you open an Access database the **Database Window** is displayed. The **Database Window** is the control centre of your application

In Access 2000 the Database Window appears as shown in Figure 2.6.

In Access 97 the Database Window looks very similar to that shown in Figure 2.7.

Figure 2.6

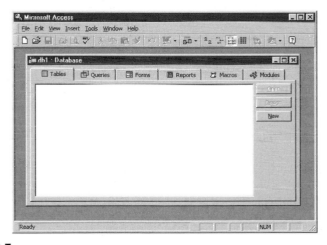

Figure 2.7

The Database Window operates in a very similar way whichever version of the software you use.

From the Database Window you can access any of the components in your database by clicking on the object tabs. For example, in both the screen shots above the **Tables** tab is selected ready to create a new table.

You would also click on this tab to open an existing table or edit an existing table.

Similarly by clicking on the **Queries**, **Forms**, **Reports**, **Macros** or **Modules** tabs, you can open, edit or create queries, forms, reports, macros or modules.

The Database Window Toolbar

Figure 2.8

◢ **Open** allows you to open a table, query or form.

◢ **Design** allows you to enter Design View to edit a table, query, form, report or macro.

◢ **New** allows you to set up a new table, query, form, report or macro.

◢ **Delete** allows you to delete an object in the Database Window (Access 2000 only).

◢ The remaining icons offer display options in the Database Window (Access 2000 only).

Toolbars

The toolbars in Access change dynamically depending on which mode you are working in.

For example, if you are designing a table, there is a **Table Design** toolbar as in Figure 2.9.

Figure 2.9

If you are viewing a form, there is a **Form View** toolbar. If the toolbar is not on the screen, click on **View**, **Toolbars** and choose from the menu (see Figure 2.10).

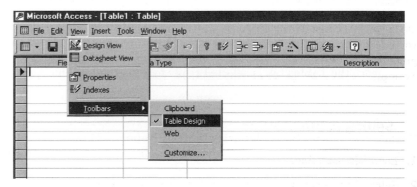

Figure 2.10

Setting up the tables

In Chapters 3 and 4 you will learn how to set up the tables that are needed to store the data for the *Pass-It* Driving School. The Driving School system is based on four tables.

 Student

 Instructor

 Lesson

 **Lesson Type**

In this chapter you will set up the **Student Table**. In Chapter 4 you will enter the data and set up the remaining tables.

There are two stages to designing a table:

1. Define the field names that make up the table and declare the data type for each.

2. Set the field properties for each field name.

Defining the field names and data types

Access needs to know the name of each field in each table and what sort of data to expect. For example in the Student table, the student's telephone number might have as its **Field Name** Tel No. You also need to tell Access whether the **Data Type** is number, text, date/time, currency etc. In this case it is text.

Setting the field properties

Once you have named the table and defined each field with its data type, you can control the fields further by setting **Field Properties**. These properties tell Access how you want the data stored and displayed. For example a date could be displayed 19/06/94, 19th June 1994 or 19-Jun-94.

Setting up the Student table

1. Load **Microsoft Access**.

2. Select **Blank Access Database** and click on **OK** (see Figure 3.1).

Figure 3.1

The **New Database Window** appears as in Figure 3.2.

Figure 3.2

3. Name the file **Drivingschool** and click on **Create**.

The Database Window loads. This is the control centre from which you can design tables, queries, forms, reports and macros. See Figure 3.3.

Figure 3.3

Remember: The database window will look slightly different in Access 97.

4. Click on **Tables** (it should already be selected) and click on **New**

The New Table window will appear. See Figure 3.4.

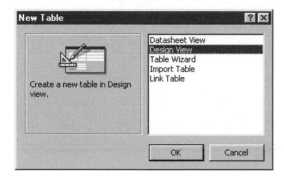

Figure 3.4

5. Click on **Design View** and click on **OK**.

The **Table Design** Window appears as shown in Figure 3.5.

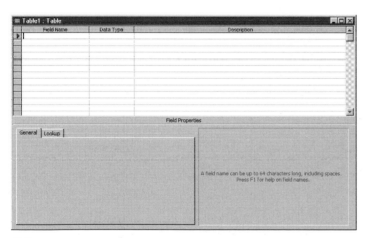

Figure 3.5

Once you are in Table Design view you can start entering the details of the fields needed in the table.

Defining the Field Names and Data Types

1. Enter the first Field Name **Student ID** and press TAB or RETURN to move to the **Data Type** field.

After entering the Field Name you will notice Field Properties are displayed in the lower half of the window, we will enter these later.

2. Click on the drop down and select **AutoNumber** (see Figure 3.6).

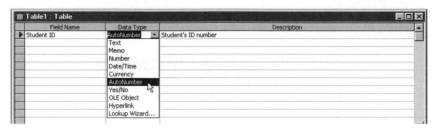

Figure 3.6

3. In the Description Field enter Student's ID number. This is optional and only for information.

4. Complete the Field Names and Data Types as shown in Table 3.1 for the Student table.

Field Name	Data Type
Student ID	AutoNumber
Title	Text
Surname	Text
Forename	Text
Address 1	Text
Address 2	Text
Address 3	Text
Address 4	Text
Tel No	Text
Date of Birth	Date/Time
Sex	Text
Theory Test Date	Date/Time
Passed Theory Test	Yes/No
Practical Test Date	Date/Time
Passed Practical Test	Yes/No
Pass Plus Req	Yes/No
Issued Card	Yes/No

Table 3.1

5. Set the Student ID field to be the key field by clicking on the row selector for this field and clicking on the **Primary Key** icon of the **Table Design** toolbar or click on **Edit**, **Primary Key**. A small picture of a key appears to the left of the Field Name (see Figure 3.7).

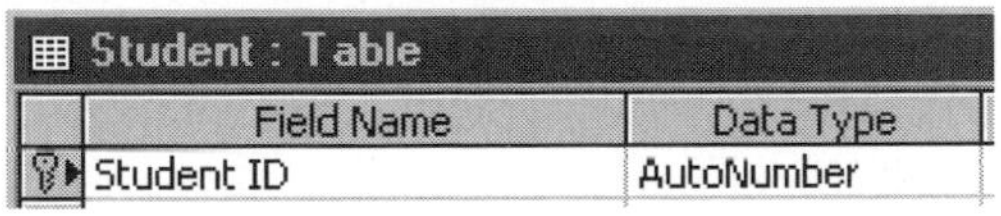

⊞ Student : Table	
Field Name	Data Type
⚷▶ Student ID	AutoNumber

Figure 3.7

Your Table Design Window should appear as in Figure 3.8.

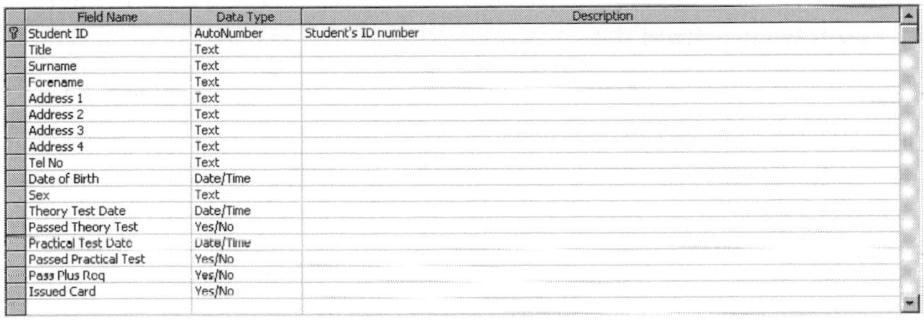

Field Name	Data Type	Description
⚷ Student ID	AutoNumber	Student's ID number
Title	Text	
Surname	Text	
Forename	Text	
Address 1	Text	
Address 2	Text	
Address 3	Text	
Address 4	Text	
Tel No	Text	
Date of Birth	Date/Time	
Sex	Text	
Theory Test Date	Date/Time	
Passed Theory Test	Yes/No	
Practical Test Date	Date/Time	
Passed Practical Test	Yes/No	
Pass Plus Req	Yes/No	
Issued Card	Yes/No	

Figure 3.8

6. Save the table by closing the window or by choosing **File**, **Save**. The **Save As** dialogue box will appear. Name the table **Student**.

Naming tables

> **Note**
>
> When saving tables some Access users like to start the name with tbl, e.g. **tbl student**. They would start queries with qry, forms with frm, reports with rpt and macros with mcr. You may wish to consider using this naming convention.

Editing the table structure

If the **Table Design** toolbar is not already on the screen insert it by clicking **View**, **Toolbars**, **Table Design** (see Figure 3.9). Details of the functions can be found in the Appendix.

Figure 3.9

During the course of setting up the table it is probable you will make a mistake or decide to make a change to your table's structure. You have a number of editing options available.

Inserting a field

Click on the row selector of the field below the insertion point.

Press the INSERT key on the keyboard or click the **Insert Rows** icon on the toolbar.

Deleting a field

Click on the row selector of the field to delete.

Press the DELETE KEY on the keyboard or click the **Delete Rows** icon on the toolbar.

Moving a field

Click on the row selector of the field you wish to move.

Click again and drag to its new position – a black line marks the insertion point.

Changing the primary key field

You can only have one primary key. If you have set the wrong field as the primary key, remove it as follows:

Click on the row selector of the correct field.

Click on **Edit**, **Primary Key** or click the **Primary Key** icon on the toolbar.

Setting the field properties

When you click on a field in Design View its field properties are displayed in the lower half of the window.

We will go through each field in the Student table and set its field property including input masks where appropriate.

Student ID

1. From the Database Window click on **Tables**, select the **Student** table and click on **Design**.

2. The Student ID field should be the one selected. If not, click in the row selector for Student ID.

3. In the Field Properties set **Field Size** to **Long Integer** (it probably already is). See Figure 3.10.

General	Lookup	
Field Size	Long Integer
New Values	Increment
Format	
Caption	
Indexed	Yes (No Duplicates)

Figure 3.10

Title

The Title field can only have the values Mr, Mrs, Miss and Ms.

We can use the **Lookup Wizard** whenever we want to restrict the data entered into a field to certain values.

1. Click on the **Title** field name. (See Figure 3.11).

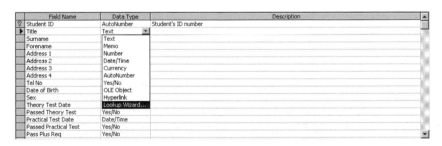

Field Name	Data Type	Description
Student ID	AutoNumber	Student's ID number
Title	Text	
Surname	Text	
Forename	Memo	
Address 1	Number	
Address 2	Date/Time	
Address 3	Currency	
Address 4	AutoNumber	
Tel No	Yes/No	
Date of Birth	OLE Object	
Sex	Hyperlink	
Theory Test Date	Lookup Wizard...	
Passed Theory Test	Yes/No	
Practical Test Date	Date/Time	
Passed Practical Test	Yes/No	
Pass Plus Req	Yes/No	

Figure 3.11

2. In the Data Type column click on **Lookup Wizard** (see Figure 3.12).

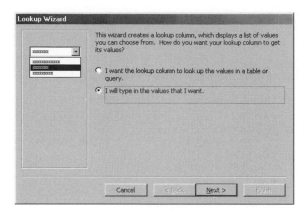

Figure 3.12

3. Click on **'I will type in the values that I want.'** and click on **Next** (see Figure 3.13).

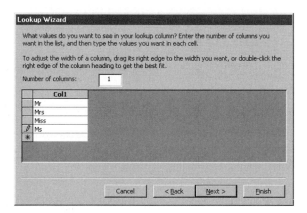

Figure 3.13

4. Enter Mr, Mrs, Miss and Ms into the column, press TAB to move to the next row (see Figure 3.14).

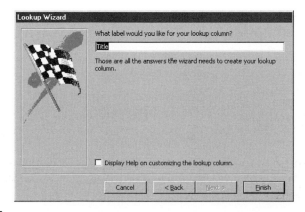

Figure 3.14

5. Click on **Next** and then click on **Finish**.

6. In the Field Properties set the Field Size to 6 (see Figure 3.15).

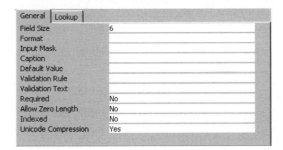

Figure 3.15

7. If you click on the **Lookup** tab you will see the screen shown in Figure 3.16.

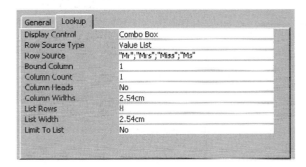

Figure 3.16

When you wish to enter data into this field a combo box (drop-down box) will give you the choice of Mr, Mrs, Miss or Ms.

Surname, Forename, Address 1 and Address 2

1. Select the Field Name Surname and set the Field Size to 20, repeat for Forename.

2. Select the Field Name Address 1 and set the Field Size to 30, repeat for Address 2.

Address 3

The Pass-It Driving School is based in Derby. It is likely that students will live in Derby. It will save time if we set the default value for the Address 3 field to Derby.

1. Click on the **Address** field.

2. In the Default Value box of the Field Properties, enter Derby Access inserts speech marks around the text.

3. Set the Field Size to 20 (see Figure 3.17).

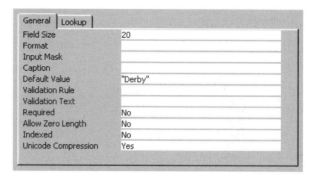

Figure 3.17

NB. More information on Default Values can be found at the end of Chapter 4.

Address 4

The **Address 4** field is the student's postcode.

1. Click on the **Address 4** field name.

2. Set the Field Size to 10.

3. Click on the **Format** property box and enter > as shown in Figure 3.18.

This will convert any lower case letters entered into upper case e.g. de34 2qy will become DE34 2QY. Later you will see how to set an Input Mask to make entering post codes easier.

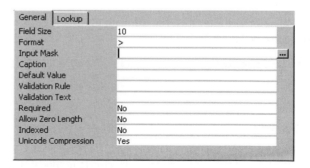

Figure 3.18

Tel No

Select the Field Name **Tel No** and set the Field Size to 15.

NB. Telephone numbers cannot be a number field as they are likely to include a space or brackets.

Date of Birth

The student table uses three Date/Time fields. We will use the **Short Date** format for each e.g. 19/06/94.

1. Select the **Date of Birth** field.

2. Click on the **Format** box in the Field Properties.

3. A drop down list appears. Choose **Short Date** (see Figure 3.19).

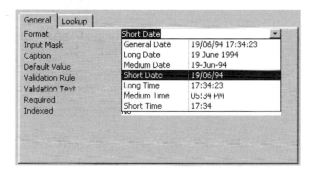

Figure 3.19

It is also possible to use the Input Mask wizard to set a placeholder —/—/— for each date entered.

4. Click in the Input Mask property box and click the three dots icon at the end of the row or the **Build** icon on the **Table Design** toolbar, you will be asked to save your table first. The Input Mask Wizard window is shown as in Figure 3.20.

5. Select the **Short Date** option and click on **Next**.

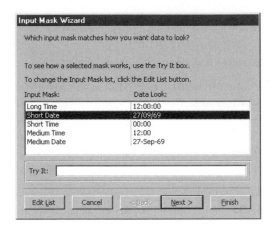

Figure 3.20

6. A choice of placeholders is offered. Click on **Next** and then click on **Finish** (see Figure 3.21).

The field properties are set as shown in Figure 3.22.

7. Repeat this for the other two Date/Time fields, **Theory Test Date** and **Practical Test Date**.

NB. More information on Input Masks can be found at the end of Chapter 4.

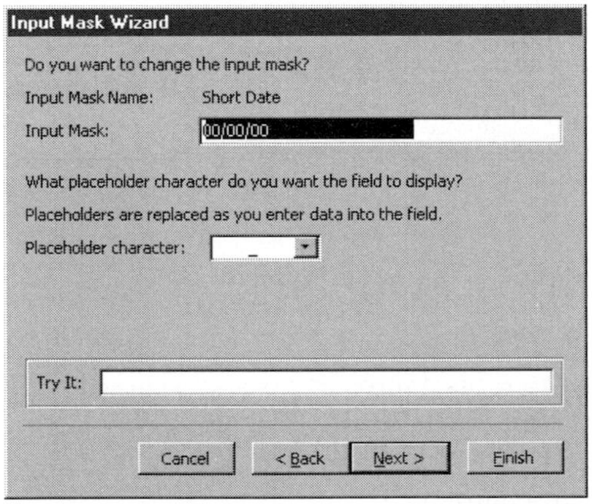

Figure 3.21

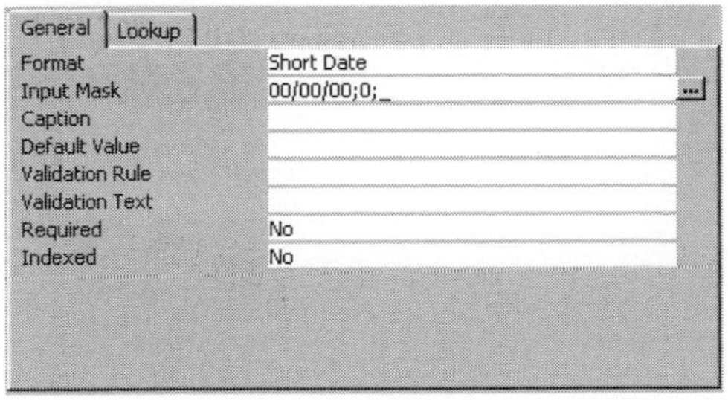

Figure 3.22

Sex

The Sex field can only have the values M and F. We can use the Validation Rule box in the Field Properties only to allow M or F.

1. Click on the **Sex** Field Name.

2. In the Validation Rule box enter **M or F**.

3. In the Validation Text box enter **Sex must be either M or F**.

This is the error message that will appear if the user tries to enter anything other than M or F into this field. The field properties will appear as shown in Figure 3.23.

It is of course equally possible to have used the Lookup Wizard for this field property and limit the choices to M or F.

NB. More information on Validation Rules can be found at the end of Chapter 4

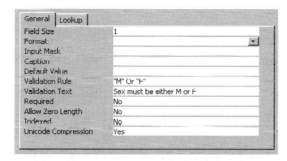

Figure 3.23

4. Save your table.

Passed Theory Test, Passed Practical Test, Pass Plus Req and Issued Card fields

All the above fields have already been set to **Yes/No** field types and no further field properties are required.

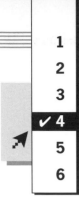

Entering the data

In this chapter we are going to enter the data into the Student table and set up the remaining tables needed to complete the system.

There are two modes for working with tables. So far we have worked in **Design View**.

Design View is used to set up new tables, to edit the structure and to define validation checks and input masks.

To enter new data you have to switch to **Datasheet View**.

In the Database Window select the **Student** table and click **Open** on the toolbar to open the table in **Datasheet View** as shown in Figure 4.1.

☐ File Edit View Insert Format Records Tools Window Help							_|𝗑|𝗑
Student Id	**Title**	**Surname**	**Forename**	**Address 1**	**Address 2**	**Address 3**	**Address 4**
▶ (AutoNumber)	▾					Derby	

Figure 4.1

You can switch between modes by selecting **View**, **Design View** from the menu

► Entering data into the Student table

Enter details of the first student Robert Brammer as given in Figure 4.2. Use TAB or ENTER to move between fields.

Student ID	Title	Surname	Forename	Address 1	Address 2	Address 3	Address 4	Tel No	Date of Birth	Sex	Theory Test Date	Passed Theory Test	Practical Test Date	Passed Practical Test	Pass Plus Req	Issued Card
1	Mr	Brammer	Robert	10 Plymouth Drive	Stenson Fields	Derby	DE28 9LO	01332 885304	27/07/81	M	12/05/00	Yes	12/06/00	Yes	No	No

Figure 4.2

You will notice a number of features as you enter the data.

 The Student ID which is an Autonumber field is entered automatically

The Title field has a drop down box set up by the lookup table wizard (see Figure 4.3).

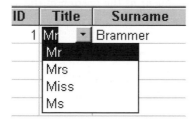

Figure 4.3

Data entered into the Sex field is validated and any invalid entries rejected (see Figure 4.4).

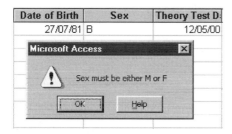

Figure 4.4

Placeholders appear in the fields where you have set input masks to make data entry easier.

Enter data into Yes/No fields by ticking the check box for Yes and leaving unchecked for No (see Figure 4.5).

Student ID	Surname	Forename	Theory Test Date	Passed Theory Test
1	Brammer	Robert	12/05/00	☑
2	Jenkins	Steven	14/05/00	☑

Figure 4.5

When you have entered the last field in a record a blank record appears underneath to enter the next record. Don't worry if your table finishes with a blank record. Microsoft Access will ignore it.

When a new record is created, the Address 3 field is set to Derby. This can still be edited.

Data is saved as soon as it is entered. Adjust the column widths by dragging out the column dividers.

Navigation buttons appear at the bottom of the screen allowing you to scroll through the records (see Figure 4.6).

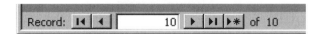

Figure 4.6

Useful keys for entering data

Key	Action
TAB key, ENTER or right arrow	Move to next field
SHIFT + TAB key or left arrow	Move to previous field
Down arrow	Move to next record
Up arrow	Move to previous record
HOME	Move to start of field
END	Move to end of field

Undo

Press ESC to quit editing a record.

Use the **Undo** icon to undo the last action. You can only undo **one** action.

Deleting records

To delete a record, click on the record selector and press DELETE.

Complete the Student table by entering the following data as shown in Figure 4.7.

Student ID	Title	Surname	Forename	Address 1	Address 2	Address 3	Address 4	Tel No	Date of Birth	Sex	Theory Test Date	Passed Theory Test	Practical Test Date	Passed Practical Test	Pass Plus Req	Issued Card
1	Mr	Branner	Robert	10 Plymouth Drive	Stenson Fields	Derby	DE28 9LO	01332 885304	27/07/81	M	12/05/00	Yes	12/06/00	Yes	No	No
2	Mr	Jenkins	Steven	37 Woodfield Close	Etwall	Derby	DE49 5PQ	01283 539264	14/05/83	M	14/05/00	Yes	15/12/00	No	No	No
3	Miss	Fowler	Sarah	19 Sea View Road	Mickleover	Derby	DE34 8NT	01332 293751	05/06/82	F	12/04/00	Yes	05/08/00	Yes	No	No
4	Mr	Beswood	Michael	25 Lundie Close	Allestree	Derby	DE45 5AF	01332 752410	15/02/82	M	22/07/00	Yes	24/10/00	No	No	Yes
5	Miss	Williams	Charlotte	21 Church Street	Littleover	Derby	DE33 8RD	01332 293184	30/03/81	F	23/06/00	Yes	17/12/00	No	Yes	Yes
6	Mr	Windsor	David	86 Milford Road	Allenton	Derby	DE5 4PT	01332 389144	18/04/82	M	02/07/00	Yes	31/10/00	No	No	Yes
7	Mrs	Trueman	Mary	156 Station Road	Allestree	Derby	DE45 9HS	01332 347810	27/10/81	F	07/02/00	Yes	28/09/00	No	No	Yes
8	Ms	Spencer	Victoria	73 Mayfield Road	Sterson	Derby	DE23 9VB	01332 832004	20/12/80	F	16/08/00	Yes	03/10/00	No	Yes	Yes
9	Mr	Watson	Greg	7 Derwent Close	Etwall	Derby	DE49 8HU	01283 552994	17/05/81	M	21/06/00	Yes	21/12/00	No	Yes	Yes
10	Ms	Jones	Lucy	183 Uttoxeter Road	Allenton	Derby	DE5 2GN	01332 668228	28/05/82	F	31/03/00	Yes	10/09/00	No	No	Yes

Figure 4.7

Closing the table

When you have finished entering the data, close the table by clicking on the Close icon. You will return to the database window with the name of the table highlighted (see Figure 4.8).

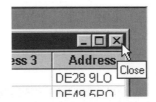

Figure 4.8

 Setting up the Instructor table

You now need to set up a second table called Instructor to store the details of the instructors. Set it up with the structure as shown in Figure 4.9.

Field name	Data type	Other information
Instructor ID	AutoNumber	Set as Primary Key field
Title	Text	Lookup table values: Mr, Mrs, Ms, Miss Field Size 6
Surname	Text	Field Size 20
Forename	Text	Field Size 20
Address 1	Text	Field Size 30
Address 2	Text	Field Size 30
Address 3	Text	Default value = 'Derby' Field Size 20
Address 4	Text	Field Size 10 and set Format to >
Home Tel No	Text	Field Size 15
Mobile No	Text	Field Size 15

Figure 4.9

Save the table as **Instructor** and switch to Datasheet View mode to enter this data (see Figure 4.10).

Instructor ID	Title	Surname	Forename	Address 1	Address 2	Address 3	Address 4	Home Tel No	Mobile No
1	Mr	Jones	Doug	57 Swanmore Road	Etwall	Derby	DE65 6LU	01283 122541	07720 521478
2	Mr	Batchelor	Arnold	13 Gairloch Close	Etwall	Derby	DE34 5FG	01283 552147	07980 352145
3	Mr	Smith	Andrew	5b Sunrise Road	Littleover	Derby	DE45 4ED	01332 521452	07980 525214

Figure 4.10

 ## Setting up the Lesson Type table

The third table will be the **Lesson Type** table, storing details of the lessons and the cost of each lesson. The structure is shown in Figure 4.11.

Field name	Data type	Other information
Lesson Type	Text	Set as Primary Key field Field Size 25
Cost	Currency	

Figure 4.11

Save the table as **Lesson Type** and enter the data as shown in Figure 4.12.

Lesson Type	Cost
Introductory	£12.00
Pass Plus	£17.00
Standard	£15.00
Test	£25.00

Figure 4.12

 ## Setting up the Lesson table

The fourth table will be the **Lesson** table. This is the table that links all the other tables together and stores details of lessons booked with the driving school. Its structure is shown in Figure 4.13.

Field name	Data type	Other information
Lesson No	AutoNumber	Set as Primary Key field
Student ID	Number	Long Integer
Instructor ID	Number	Long Integer
Date	Date/Time	Format: Short Date and set Input Mask
Start Time	Date/Time	Format: Short Time and set Input Mask
Length of Lesson	Number	Integer and set validation rule as Between 1 and 8
Collection Point	Text	Default value = 'Home Address' Field Size 30
Drop-Off Point	Text	Default value = 'Home Address' Field Size 30
Lesson Type	Text	Lookup table values (see below): Introductory, Standard, Pass Plus, Test Field Size 25

Figure 4.13

NB. When you run the Lookup Wizard choose to type the values in but you could look up the values from the table Lesson Type.

Save the table as **Lesson** and enter the data as shown in Figure 4.14.

Lesson No	Student ID	Instructor ID	Date	Start Time	Length of lesson	Collection Point	Drop-Off Point	Lesson Type
1	1	1	30/07/00	08:00	1	Home Address	City Centre	Standard
2	2	1	30/07/00	09:00	2	Derby Station	Home Address	Standard
3	2	2	31/07/00	12:00	1	Home Address	Home Address	Introductory
4	3	1	31/07/00	13:00	2	John Port School	Home Address	Standard
5	4	3	01/08/00	18:00	1	Home Address	Home Address	Test
6	5	1	31/07/00	08:00	1	Home Address	Home Address	Introductory
7	6	2	30/07/00	12:00	1	Home Address	Home Address	Standard
8	7	1	30/07/00	11:00	1	Home Address	Home Address	Standard
9	8	1	30/07/00	12:00	3	Home Address	Home Address	Standard
10	1	1	31/07/00	11:00	1	Home Address	Home Address	Standard
11	9	2	02/08/00	10:00	1	Home Address	Home Address	Standard

Figure 4.14

We do not need to store the name of the student or the name of the instructor in the Lesson table. These are already stored elsewhere.

The next chapter shows you how to link these tables together.

Further information on setting up tables

This section provides a little more detail on a number of the functions you met during setting up the student table. In particular:

- Data types

- Field properties

- Input masks

- Format field properties

- Default field properties

- Validation Rules

Data types

Access has different data types available to store different kinds of data. They are shown in Table 4.1.

Data type	Meaning
Text	This is the default setting. Used for shorter text entries. Can be a combination of text, numbers, spaces and symbols. Maximum length 255 characters but you can set it to less using the Field Size property
Memo	Used for longer text entries. Maximum length 65,535 characters!
Number	Used to store numeric data.
Date/Time	This stores a date or a time or a date and the time. There are several formats for a date/time field.
Currency	Monetary values. Normally in the UK this will be set to pounds and work to 2 decimal places.
AutoNumber	An AutoNumber field will number records automatically as you enter more data. The field acts as a counter. Duplicates are avoided and so AutoNumber fields are ideal as the key field. An AutoNumber cannot be edited and when an AutoNumber record is deleted Access does not allow you to go back and reuse this number.
Yes/No	Only allows logical values such as Yes/No,True/False
OLE Object	An object linked to or embedded in a Microsoft Access table. This might be an image or a sound or a file created in another package such as Microsoft Excel or Microsoft Word.

Data type	Meaning
Hyperlink	A hyperlink address. This can be linked to: 1. an object in your Access file, e.g. another table 2. another locally stored file 3. a web page 4. an e-mail address
Lookup Wizard	This data type creates a lookup table so that you can choose a value from a drop down box.

Table 4.1

Field properties

Table 4.2 describes the range of field properties.

Property	Description
Field Size	This is used to fix the maximum length of a text field. The default value is 50 characters. The maximum length is 255.
Format	This fixes how data can be displayed, for example dates can be displayed in many different forms such as 13/01/01 or 13 Jan 01 or 13 January 2001.
Input Mask	This sets a pattern for the data to be entered into this field.
Caption	This is the field label in a form or report.
Default Value	This is the value entered into the field when the record is created. It is usually left blank but can be very powerful.
Validation Rule	This defines the data entry rules.
Validation Text	This is the error message if data is invalid.
Required	This indicates whether an entry must be made or not. If an entry is required, it is best not to set this property until the database is fully working.
Indexed	This allows data to be stored in the order of this field which speeds up searches.
Allow Zero Length	This is used with text fields to decide whether records in that field are allowed to contain zero length or empty text strings.

Table 4.2

Setting input masks

Input masks make data entry easier. They display on screen a pattern for the data to be entered into a field.

For example you may be given the prompt --/--/-- to enter the date.

They are suitable for data that always has the same pattern such as dates, times, currency and also for codes like National Insurance numbers, stock numbers or postcodes.

Characters for input masks you are likely to use are as follows:

0   A number (0-9) must be entered

9   A number (0-9) may be entered

A number, + or – sign or space may be entered

L   A letter A-Z must be entered

?   A letter A-Z may be entered

A   A letter or digit must be entered

a   A letter or digit may be entered

C   Any character or space may be entered

&   Any character or space must be entered

<   All characters to the right are changed to lower case

>   All characters to the right are changed to upper case

Examples of input masks

A **National Insurance number** in the UK must be of the form **AB123456C** All letters are in capitals. Its input mask would be **>LL000000L** (it must be 2 letters followed by 6 numbers and 1 letter).

A **postcode** consists of one or two letters, then one or two numbers, then a space, a number and two letters. All the letters must be capital letters. Examples are **B1 1BB** or **DE13 0LL**. The input mask would be **>L?09 0LL**.

Car registration numbers such as W125 HGS could have **>L000 LLL** as an input mask.

A **driving licence no.** of the form BESWO150282 MB9BM could have **>LLLLL#000000#LL0LL** as an input mask.

Product codes of the format A2C-123-4567. A possible input mask might be **A0A-000-0000**.

Input masks are very powerful and need a lot of thought. It is possible to use the Input Mask Wizard to set up an input mask for a field. At this stage you may wish to ignore input masks unless you know the exact format of the input data.

The Format field property

The formats supplied with Access will suit practically all your needs. However it is possible to set a custom format of your own. Two commonly used examples follow:

>   will change text entered in the field to upper case

<   will change text entered in the field to lower case

> **Note** There is a significant difference between the Format and Input Mask field property. The Format property affects the data in the field after it is entered, e.g. if you enter 14/07/99 into a Long Date format field, it will appear as 14th July 1999.

The Input Mask property controls and restricts data entry. An Input Mask set to --/--/-- will only accept dates in the format 14/07/99

The default field property

Default values are added automatically when you add a new record. For example in a table of names and addresses you might set the County field to Derbyshire. Derbyshire then appears automatically each time a new record is added and the user can either leave it or change it to something else.

You can also use expressions in this field property. Typically =**Date**() will return the current date from your PC.

In a Library Book Loaning system, the default value for the **Date of Loan** field could be set to =**Date**() and similarly for the **Date of Return**, the default value could be set to =**Date()+14** (assuming a 14 day loan period).

Setting validation rules

Validation rules allow you to control the values that can be entered into a field.

By setting the validation text property you can choose the message that is displayed if the validation rule is broken.

You set up a validation rule by typing an expression into the field properties (see Figure 4.15).

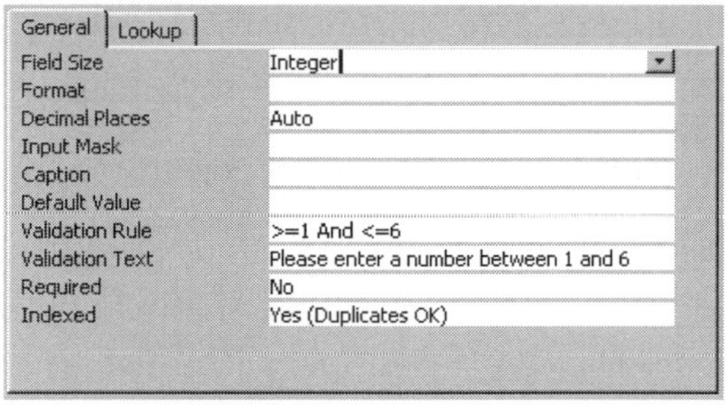

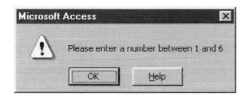

Figure 4.15

In the example in Figure 4.15 the user will be forced to only enter numbers between 1 and 6. If they do not the Validation Text message is displayed in Figure 4.16.

Figure 4.16

A number of comparison operators are available in Access:

Operator	Meaning
<	Less than
<=	Less than or equal to
>	Greater than
>=	Greater than or equal to
=	Equal to
<>	Not equal to
IN	Test for 'equal to' any item in a list
BETWEEN	Test for a range of values; the two values separated by the AND operator
LIKE	Tests a Text or Memo field to match a pattern string of characters

Table 4.3

Examples of validation rule settings	Possible validation text
>8000	Please enter a salary greater than £8000
<#01/01/01#	You must enter dates before January 1st 2001
>Date()	The date returned must be after today's date!
'S' or 'M' or 'L'	Sizes can only be S, M or L
Between 0 and 36	Goals scored cannot be greater than 36!
Like 'A???? '	Code must 5 characters beginning with A
<20	Age of student must be less than 20
IN('A','B','C')	Grades must be A, B or C

Table 4.4

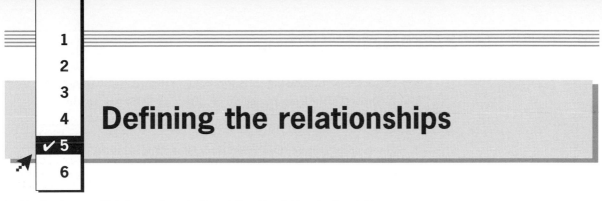

Defining the relationships

In this chapter we will define and create the relationships linking the four tables.

The links that need setting up are shown in Figure 5.1.

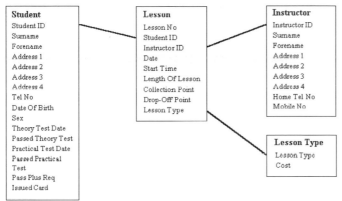

Student
Student ID
Surname
Forename
Address 1
Address 2
Address 3
Address 4
Tel No
Date Of Birth
Sex
Theory Test Date
Passed Theory Test
Practical Test Date
Passed Practical
Test
Pass Plus Req
Issued Card

Lesson
Lesson No
Student ID
Instructor ID
Date
Start Time
Length Of Lesson
Collection Point
Drop-Off Point
Lesson Type

Instructor
Instructor ID
Surname
Forename
Address 1
Address 2
Address 3
Address 4
Home Tel No
Mobile No

Lesson Type
Lesson Type
Cost

Figure 5.1

Adding the tables

1. In the Database Window open the **Relationships Window** by any of these three methods.

✔ Right click anywhere in the window and select **Relationships**

✔ Click on the **Relationships** icon on the Database toolbar if showing

✔ Click on **Tools, Relationships** from the menu bar

If it is the first time you've established a relationship then the Show Table dialogue box will appear as in Figure 5.2.

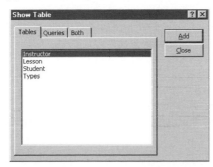

Show Table ? ✕

Tables | Queries | Both

Instructor
Lesson
Student
Types

Add
Close

Figure 5.2

NB. If the Show Table window is not present display it by clicking on **View, Show Table** from the menu or click on the **Show Table** icon.

2. Click on the **Instructor** table and click on **Add**.

3. Add the other three tables and then **Close** the window.

4. In the Relationships Window rearrange the position of the tables by dragging and resizing the Table windows (see Figure 5.3).

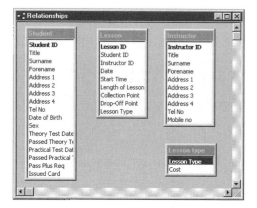

Figure 5.3

Setting the links

1. Click on **Instructor ID** in the **Instructor** table.

2. Drag it on top of **Instructor ID** in the **Lesson** table and let go. The Edit Relationships dialogue box appears (see Figure 5.4).

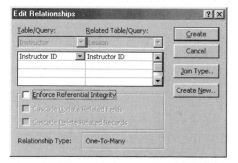

Figure 5.4

3. Check the **Enforce Referential Integrity** box and then check the **Cascade Delete Related Records** box. Click on **Create**.

A link called the **Relationship Line** is set up between the two tables.

4. Click on the **Student ID** field in the **Student** table and drag it on top of the **Student ID** field in the Lesson table.

5. Check the Enforce **Referential Integrity** box and then check the **Cascade Delete Related Records** box. Click on **Create**.

6. Repeat the process for the **Lesson Type** field, dragging it from the **Lesson Type** table to the **Lesson** table and check **Referential Integrity** and **Cascade Delete Related Records**.

The Relationship Window should now look like Figure 5.5.

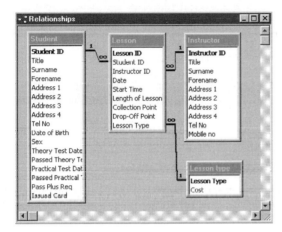

Figure 5.5

The number 1 and the infinity symbol mean that all three relationships are one-to-many. A Student ID can appear only **one** time in the Student table as it is a unique ID. However a Student ID can appear **many** times in the Lesson table as the student will need many lessons.

Similarly the Instructor ID can only appear once in the Instructor table but many times in the Lesson table. The Lesson Type can appear only once in the Lesson Type table but many times in the Lesson table.

7. Save your layout by clicking **File, Save** from the menu and confirming the option shown in Figure 5.6.

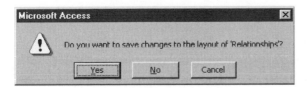

Figure 5.6

> **Note** As a rule the field you use to create a relationship must be of the same type. However, when you create a relation between tables using an AutoNumber field, the related field must be Numeric and set to Long Integer.

Referential integrity

Referential integrity is a system of rules that Microsoft Access uses to ensure that relationships between records in related tables are valid and that you don't accidentally delete or change related data.

For example with Referential Integrity set you would not be able to book a lesson for a Student ID 46 as no student with ID number 46 appears in the Student table. Similarly you could not book a lesson for an instructor who was not present in the Instructor table

Cascading Updates and Deletes

Cascading Updates and Deletes affect what Access does with the data when you update or delete a record in a table that is related to other records in other tables.

If cascade delete is set, then when you delete a record in the Primary table all related data in other tables is deleted. For example if a student is deleted from the Student table then all related records for that student in the Lesson table would also be deleted.

NB. We have checked Cascade Delete at this point in the development of the system, as we will need it later in the units.

Deleting relationships

If you wish to delete a relationship:

1. Open the Relationship Window as before.

2. Click on the Relationship Line of the relationship you wish to delete and press the DELETE key. Alternatively you can right click on it and choose delete.

If you wish to delete a field that contains a relationship, you will have to delete the relationship first.

Editing relationships

You can edit relationships by going to the Relationship Window and double clicking on the Relationship Line of the relationship you wish to edit.

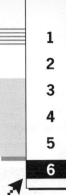

Select queries

In the previous chapters you set up tables to store information about the students, instructors and lesson bookings in the *Pass-It* Driving school.

In this section you will use queries to search and sort the data in your tables according to certain criteria. Queries provide an easy way of asking questions of your database and producing useful information.

For example we might want to:

- find details of lessons booked on a given date;
- find contact details for a student whose lesson needs to be cancelled;
- view details of instructors' names and addresses.

There are a number of different types of query available in Access:

- Select Query
- Parameter Query
- Multi-Table Query
- Action Query
- Crosstab Query

We will start by taking you through basic select and parameter queries, progressing to a query involving more than one table. You will meet the other query types as you work through the units.

As with many other parts of Microsoft Access, there is a wizard to help you design simple queries. We shall first look at setting up a query without the wizard.

Query 1 Finding details of lessons booked on a given day

There are usually five steps involved in planning a query:

- choosing which tables to use;
- choosing the fields needed in your query;
- setting the criteria to produce the output required;
- running the query;
- saving and/or printing the results.

1. Load the **Drivingschool** database.

2. In the Database Window click on **Queries** and select **New** (see Figure 6.1).

Figure 6.1

3. In the New Query window select **Design View** and click on **OK** (see Figure 6.2).

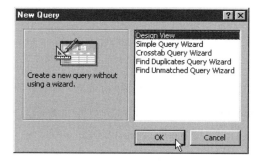

Figure 6.2

4. In the Show Table window select the table **Lesson**, click on **Add** and then **Close** the window (see Figure 6.3).

The Query Design View window is now shown.

The window is in two sections. The upper section contains the field list for the table used in the query and the lower section contains the QBE (Query by Example) grid where you design the query. It consists of primarily five headings (see Figure 6.4).

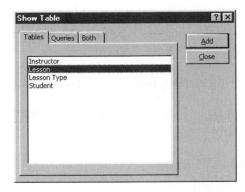

Figure 6.3

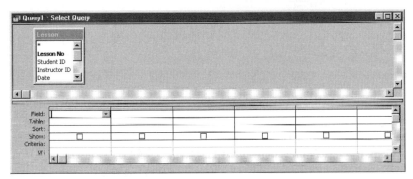

Figure 6.4

Field	Contains the names of the fields needed for your query
Table	Holds the name of the table containing the selected field
Sort	Offers ascending, descending sort options
Show	Allows you to hide fields from the output
Criteria	This is where you enter the criteria for your search

You can maximise the window and use the scroll bars in the usual way. You can resize the upper/lower panes by dragging the dividing line between them up or down.

5. If the Query Design toolbar is not showing, click on **View, Toolbars, Query Design** (see Figure 6.5).

Figure 6.5

The next stage is to select the fields needed in our query.

6. Double click on **Lesson No** in the **Lesson** table field list. Then double click on each of the next five fields in turn: Student ID, Instructor ID, Date, Start Time, Length of Lesson. The fieldnames will appear in the grid as shown in Figure 6.6.

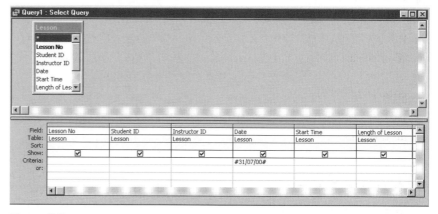

Figure 6.6

7. Now select the criteria by entering **31/07/00** in the criteria row of the fourth (Date) column of the QBE grid. Access surrounds the data with a #.

If you have added a field by mistake, click at the top of the column in the QBE grid to select the column and then press DELETE.

8. To run your query click on the **Datasheet View** icon, the **Run Query** icon or choose from the menu **Query, Run**. There should be four lessons (see Figure 6.7).

Lesson No	Student ID	Instructor ID	Date	Start Time	Length of Lesson
3	2	2	31/07/00	12:00	1
4	3	1	31/07/00	13:00	2
6	5	1	31/07/00	08:00	1
10	1	1	31/07/00	11:00	1

Record: 1 of 4

Figure 6.7

9. Once the Query has been run it can be printed using **File, Print**.

10. Save the query as **Lessons 31 July Query** by clicking on the save icon on the toolbar.

Selecting fields in Query Design View

There are a number of other ways of selecting a field from the Field list in the Query Design window. You need to select the one that suits you best.

- In each field cell on the grid is a drop down list from which fields can be chosen.

- Double click on the title bar in the Field List table. This highlights all the field names. Click on any one (not the *) and drag them to the field cell on the grid. On releasing the mouse button all fields will be entered into the grid.

- Highlight the field in the Field List table and drag it to the field cell on the grid.

Query 2 Finding the contact details for a student, e.g. student named Watson

1. In the Database Window click on **Queries** and select **New**.

2. In the New Query window select **Design View** and click on **OK**.

3. In the Show Table window select the table **Student**, click on **Add** and then **Close** the window.

The next stage is to select the fields needed in our query. We will add them to the QBE grid by dragging and dropping each field.

4. Select **Student ID** in the **Student table** and drag it to the field cell.

5. Drag and drop the fields **Surname**, **Forename** and **Tel No** in the same way. The fieldnames will appear in the grid as in Figure 6.8.

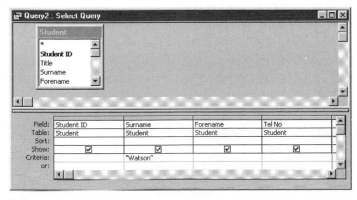

Figure 6.8

6. Now select the criteria by entering **Watson** in the criteria row of the Surname column in the QBE grid. Access puts in the quotation marks.

7. To run your query click on the **Datasheet View** icon, the **Run Query** icon or from the menu, select **Query, Run**. The details are shown in Figure 6.9.

Figure 6.9

8. Save your query as **Search for Student Query**.

Some further hints

Adding and removing tables

To remove a table from the Query Design grid, double click the title bar of the field list box and press DELETE.

To add a table to the Query Design grid click on the **Show Table** icon or select from the menu, **Query, Show Table** and add the tables required.

To clear the QBE grid from the menu select **Edit, Clear Grid**.

Renaming the field headings

You can give a different name to the column titles in the query grid.

In the field row, click the start of the field name, type in the new name followed by a colon, e.g. **Telephone number: Tel No**.

Changing the order of the fields chosen

Click the field selector at the top of the column.

Drag the field to the new location (see Figure 6.10).

Field:	Instructor ID	Surname	Forename	Address 1	Address 2	Address 3
Table:	Instructor	Instructor	Instructor	Instructor	Instructor	Instructor
Sort:						
Show:	☑	☑	☑	☑	☑	☑
Criteria:						
or:						

Figure 6.10

As you drag the field a solid bar appears showing where the relocated field will appear.

Deleting a query

Queries that are only used once are not really worth saving.

In the Database Window select the query to delete and press the DELETE key.

Query 3 Producing a list of Instructors' names and addresses

We will use the Query Wizard to design the next query.

1. In the Database Window click on **Queries** and select **New**.

2. In the New Query window select **Simple Query Wizard** and click on **OK**.

The Simple Query Wizard dialogue box is displayed.

3. Select the table **Instructor** from the Tables/Queries drop down list.

4. Select the field **Instructor ID** in the Available Fields and click the right arrow >.

5. Repeat this process for the fields **Surname**, **Forename**, **Address 1**, **Address 2**, **Address 3**, and **Address 4** as shown in Figure 6.11.

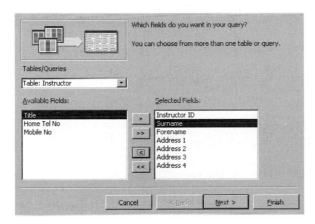

Figure 6.11

6. Click on **Next**, name the query **Instructor Addresses Query** and click on **Finish** (see Figure 6.12).

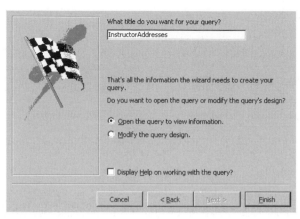

Figure 6.12

The resulting query opens in Datasheet view as shown in Figure 6.13, giving the details of the Instructors' names and addresses.

Instructor ID	Surname	Forename	Address 1	Address 2	Address 3	Address 4
1	Jones	Doug	57 Swanmore Road	Etwall	Derby	DE34 5FG
2	Batchelor	Arnold	13 Gairloch Close	Etwall	Derby	DE34 5FG
3	Smith	Andrew	5b Sunrise Road	Littleover	Derby	DE45 4ED
(AutoNumber)					Derby	

Figure 6.13

From the menu you can now select **View**, **Design View** to show the QBE grid (Figure 6.14) and refine your query if needed. For example click on the drop down list in the Sort cell of the Surname field to choose either ascending or descending sort order.

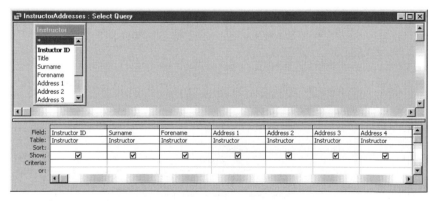

Figure 6.14

Further queries

Chapter 6 introduced you to simple **Select** queries and the Query Design window. In this chapter you will be shown how to take **Select** queries further and introduced to **Parameter** queries.

▶ Selecting records in ranges

Suppose we wish to view lessons between certain dates or print a list of lessons for the coming week.

You can select a range of records using the operators < , >, <= , >= , + , – , BETWEEN , AND , NOT .

Query 1 Finding lessons between 30 July and 2 August

1. In the Database Window click on **Queries** and select **New**.

2. In the New Query window select **Design View** and click on **OK**.

3. In the Show Table window select the table **Lesson**, click on **Add** and then **Close** the window.

4. Add the fields **Lesson No**, **Student ID**, **Instructor ID**, **Date** and **Collection Point**.

5. In the criteria row of the Date column enter >30/07/00 and <02/08/00 as shown in Figure 7.1.

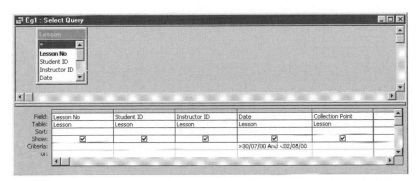

Figure 7.1

6. Run the query to view the records and then save the query as **Dates Query** (see Figure 7.2).

NB. This query could also have been designed by entering the expression Between >30/07/00 and 02/08/00 in the Date field cell.

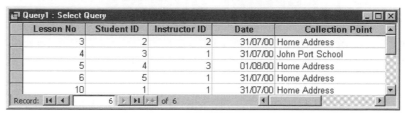

Figure 7.2

Using multiple criteria

It is possible to specify criteria in more than one field. For example you may want to see details of a specific instructor's lessons on a certain date. This is sometimes known as an AND search because it involves the Instructor ID field and the Date field.

Query 2 Finding lessons for Instructor 2 on 30 July

1. In the Database Window click on **Queries** and select **New**.

2. In the New Query window select **Design View** and click on **OK**.

3. In the Show Table window select the table **Lesson**, click on **Add** and then **Close** the window.

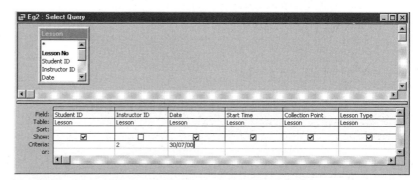

Figure 7.3

4. Add the fields **Student ID**, **Instructor ID**, **Date**, **Start Time**, **Collection Point** and **Lesson Type** (see Figure 7.3).

5. In the criteria row of the Instructor ID column enter **2** and enter **30/07/00** in the criteria cell for Date. Click on the check box so that it is unchecked to hide the Instructor ID from the output (see Figure 7.3).

6. Run the query to view the records shown in Figure 7.4. Save your query as **And Query**.

Student ID	Date	Start Time	Collection Point	Lesson Type
6	30/07/00	12:00	Home Address	Standard
0			Home Address	

Figure 7.4

You may wish to look for records which meet one criterion OR another. For example you may wish to view students who live in one area or another. This is sometimes known as an OR search.

1. In the Database Window click on **Queries** and select **New**.

2. In the New Query window select **Design View** and click on **OK**.

3. In the Show Table window select the table **Student**, click on **Add** and then **Close** the window.

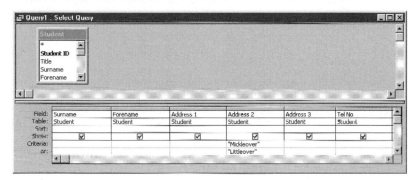

Figure 7.5

4. Add the fields **Surname**, **Forename**, **Address 1**, **Address 2**, **Address 3** and **Tel No** as shown (see Figure 7.5).

5. In the criteria row of the Address 2 column enter **Mickleover** and enter **Littleover** in the row below.

6. Run the query to view the records and then save as **Or Query** (see Figure 7.6).

Surname	Forename	Address 1	Address 2	Address 3	Tel No
Fowler	Sarah	19 Sea View Road	Mickleover	Derby	01332235751
Williams	Chalotte	21 Church Street	Littleover	Derby	01332293184
				Derby	

Record: 2 of 2

Figure 7.6

Using the Date() function

You will often want to search for records with the current date. For example you may want to view today's lessons at the driving school. You can do this using your computer's system clock and the Date function.

Query 3 Finding today's lessons

1. In the Database Window click on **Queries** and select **New**.

2. In the New Query window select **Design View** and click on **OK**.

3. In the Show Table window select the table **Lesson**, click on **Add** and then **Close** the window.

4. Add the fields **Lesson No, Student ID, Instructor ID, Date** and **Start Time** as shown in Figure 7.7.

5. In the criteria row of the date column enter ⁣ =Date() ⁣ (see Figure 7.7).

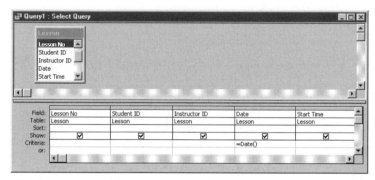

Figure 7.7

6. Run the query to view the records and save it as **Todays Lessons Query**.

NB. To run this query you will have to change some of the lessons in the lesson table to the current date.

The date function is a powerful tool in query work and will form the basis of a number of queries later in the units.

Parameter queries

All the queries so far have been **select queries**. Select queries are not very useful if you have to run the query frequently and use different criteria each time.

Parameter queries overcome this problem by allowing you to enter the criteria each time the query is run.

On running the query a dialogue box will appear asking you to enter the details (see Figure 7.8).

In the example shown you would enter the date and the records matching the criteria shown would be displayed.

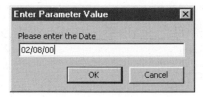

Figure 7.8

Query 4 Looking up a student's details

1. Load the **Drivingschool** database.

2. In the Database Window click on **Queries** and select **New**.

3. In the New Query window select **Design View** and click on **OK**.

4. In the Show Table window select the table **Student**, click on **Add** and then **Close** the window.

5. Select **Student ID** in the **Student** Table and drag it on to the QBE grid (see Figure 7.9).

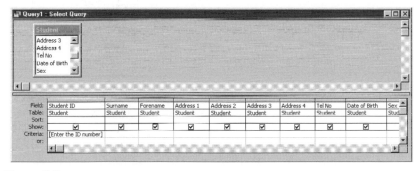

Figure 7.9

6. Drag and drop the fields **Surname**, **Forename**, **Address 1**, **Address 2**, **Address 3**, **Address 4**, **Tel No**, **Date of Birth** and **Sex** in the same way. The fieldnames will appear in the grid as in Figure 7.9.

7. In the criteria cell for the Student ID field type in **[Enter the ID number]**. The square brackets are required.

8. Run the query and enter **2** in the dialogue box as shown in Figure 7.10.

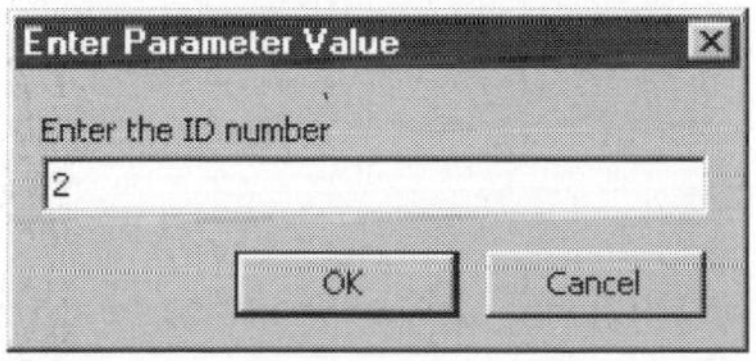

Figure 7.10

9. The query will display the details of Student number 2. Save your query as **Search by Student ID Query**.

Query 5 Looking up a student's lessons

1. In the Database Window click on **Queries** and select **New**.

2. In the New Query window select **Design View** and click on **OK**.

3. In the Show Table window select the table **Lesson**, click on **Add** and then **Close** the window.

4. Select **Student ID** in the **Lesson** Table and drag it on to the field cell (see Figure 7.11).

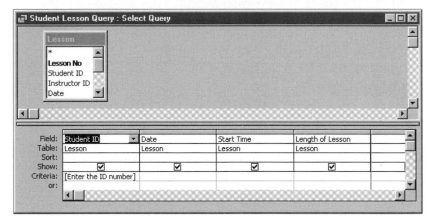

Figure 7.11

5. Drag and drop the fields **Date**, **Start Time** and **Length of Lesson** in the same way. The fieldnames will appear in the grid as above.

6. In the criteria cell for the Student ID field type in **[Enter the ID number]**. The square brackets are required.

7. Run the query and enter **2** in the dialogue box as shown in Figure 7.12.

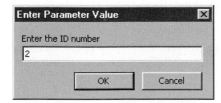

Figure 7.12

The query will display the lessons for Student number 2. Save your query as **Student Lesson Query**.

Query 6 Searching for lessons on any date

1. In the Database Window click on **Queries** and select **New**.

2. In the New Query window select **Design View** and click on **OK**.

3. In the Show Table window select the table **Lesson**, click on **Add** and then **Close** the window.

4. Add the fields to the QBE grid as shown in Figure 7.13.

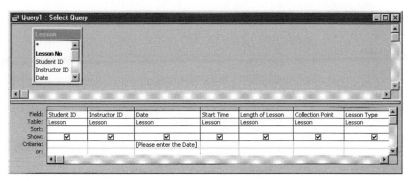

Figure 7.13

5. In the Criteria row of the Date column type in **[Please enter the Date]**. The square brackets here are vital.

6. Run the query and enter **02/08/00** in the dialogue box (see Figure 7.14).

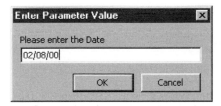

Figure 7.14

7. The result of the query is shown below. Save your query as **Search on Lesson Date Query** (see Figure 7.15).

Student ID	Instructor ID	Date	Start Time	Length of Lesson	Collection Point	Lesson Type
9	2	02/08/00	10:00	1	Home Address	Standard
0	0			0	Home Address	

Figure 7.15

Query 7 Searching for an instructor's lessons by date

1. In the Database Window click on **Queries** and select **New**.

2. In the New Query window select **Design View** and click on **OK**.

3. In the Show Table window select the table **Lesson**, click on **Add** and then **Close** the window.

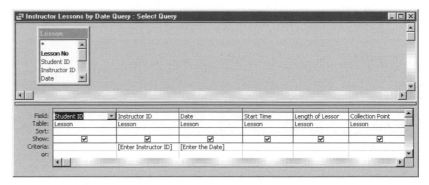

Figure 7.16

4. Add all the fields to the grid by double clicking the title bar in the Field List table and dragging the highlighted fields to the field cell (see Figure 7.16).

5. Remove fields **Lesson No**, **Drop-off Point** and **Lesson Type** by clicking the column selector and selecting from the menu **Edit**, **Delete Columns**.

6. In the criteria cell for the field Instructor ID type in **[Enter Instructor ID]**.

7. In the criteria cell for the field date type in **[Enter the Date]**.

8. Run the query and enter **1** for the **Instructor ID** (see Figure 7.17).

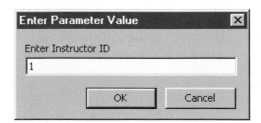

Figure 7.17

9. Enter **30/07/00** or the date (see Figure 7.18).

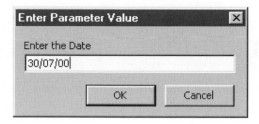

Figure 7.18

10. The result of the query is shown in Figure 7.19.

Instructor Lessons by Date Query : Select Query

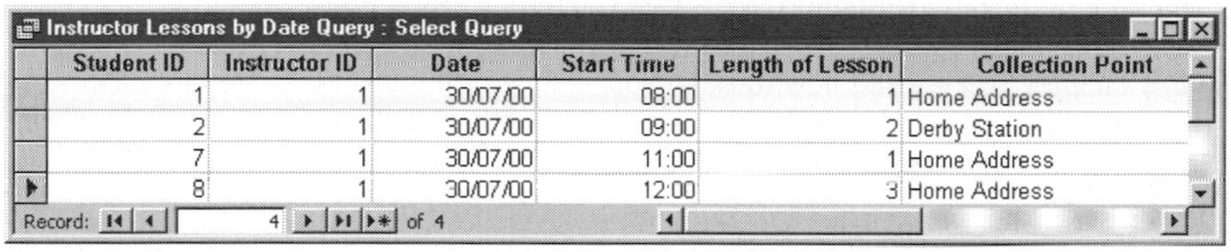

Student ID	Instructor ID	Date	Start Time	Length of Lesson	Collection Point
1	1	30/07/00	08:00	1	Home Address
2	1	30/07/00	09:00	2	Derby Station
7	1	30/07/00	11:00	1	Home Address
8	1	30/07/00	12:00	3	Home Address

Record: 4 of 4

Figure 7.19

11. Save your query as **Instructor Lessons by Date Query**.

The following queries set up in Units 6 and 7 were only for demonstration purposes. They are not needed as part of the Pass-It Driving School System. It is a good idea to go to the Database Window and delete them now.

- **Lessons 31 July Query**
- **Search for Student Query**
- **Instructor Addresses Query**
- **Dates Query**
- **And Query**
- **Or Query**

Setting up multi-table queries

In Chapters 3 and 4 you designed four tables: Student, Instructor, Lesson and Lesson Type. You later learned how to set up relationships between those tables.

For example when you book a lesson you do not want to have to key in the student's name and address every time when it is stored in the student table.

In this chapter you will see how to base your queries on more than one table and start to use the relationships you have set up. In addition you will see how you can use queries to do calculations.

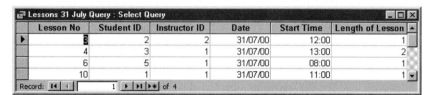

Figure 8.1

At the start of Chapter 6 you set up a query called **Lesson 31 July Query** to output the lessons booked on a given date.

The output is shown in Figure 8.1 based on the Lesson table. If we wanted the output to include the students' names we would have to base the query on the Lesson table (which stores the details of the lessons, dates and ID numbers) and the Student table (where the students' names are stored).

Query 1 To produce a list of lessons together with student names

1. Load the **Drivingschool** database.

2. In the Database Window click on **Queries** and select **New**.

3. In the New Query window select **Design View** and click on **OK** (see Figure 8.2).

4. In the Show Table window select the table **Lesson** and click on **Add** (see Figure 8.3).

5. Select the table **Student**, click on **Add** and then **Close** the window.

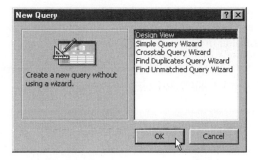

Figure 8.2

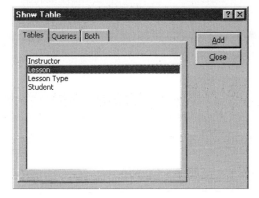

Figure 8.3

The Query Design View window is now shown with the two tables and their relationships (see **Figure 8.4**).

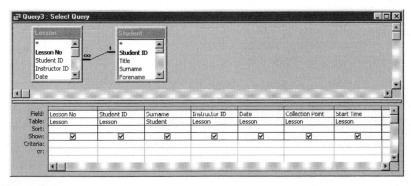

Figure 8.4

6. From the Lesson table drag and drop the fields **Lesson No, Student ID, Instructor ID, Date, Collection Point** and **Start Time** into the field cells.

7. From the Student table drag and drop the **Surname** field.

8. Move its position by clicking on the column header and dragging to a position after the Student ID column. Alternatively you could have entered the fields in the order shown.

9. Run the query and save it as **Lesson and Names Query**.
The results of your query are shown in Figure 8.5.

Lesson No	Student ID	Surname	Instructor ID	Date	Collection Point	Start Time
1	1	Brammer	1	30/07/00	Home Address	08:00
10	1	Brammer	1	31/07/00	Home Address	11:00
2	2	Jenkins	1	30/07/00	Derby Station	09:00
3	2	Jenkins	2	31/07/00	Home Address	12:00
4	3	Fowler	1	31/07/00	John Port School	13:00
5	4	Beswood	3	01/08/00	Home Address	18:00
6	5	Williams	1	31/07/00	Home Address	08:00
7	6	Windsor	2	30/07/00	Home Address	12:00
8	7	Trueman	1	30/07/00	Home Address	11:00
9	8	Spencer	1	30/07/00	Home Address	12:00
11	9	Watson	2	02/08/00	Home Address	10:00

Record: 11 of 11

Figure 8.5

Query 2 Searching for an instructor's lessons

This query will enable us to key in an instructor ID and find all their lessons.

1. In the Database Window click on **Queries** and select **New**.

2. In the New Query window select **Design View** and click on **OK**.

3. In the Show Table window select the table **Lesson** and click on **Add**.

4. Select the table **Instructor**, click on **Add** and then **Close** the window.

5. The Query Design grid is now shown with the two tables and their relationships (see Figure 8.6).

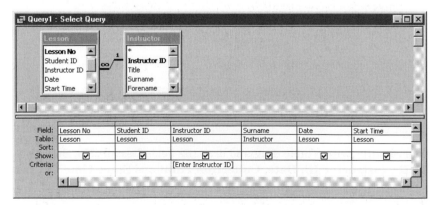

Figure 8.6

6. From the Lesson table drag and drop the fields **Lesson No, Student ID, Instructor ID, Date** and **Start Time**.

7. From the Instructor table drag and drop the **Surname** field.

8. Move its position by clicking on the column header and dragging to a position after the Instructor ID column.

9. In the criteria cell of the Instructor ID type **[Enter Instructor ID]**.

10. Run the query and enter **2** in the dialogue box shown in Figure 8.7.

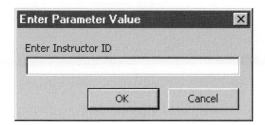

Figure 8.7

The query produces a list of lessons for instructor no 2 as shown in Figure 8.8.

Lesson No	Student ID	Instructor ID	Surname	Date	Start Time
3	2	2	Batchelor	31/07/00	12:00
7	6	2	Batchelor	30/07/00	12:00
11	9	2	Batchelor	02/08/00	10:00
(AutoNumber)					

Figure 8.8

11. Save the query as **Instructor Search Query**.

Query 3 Viewing all lessons with full details of instructor and student names

We will use the Query Wizard to design the next query.

1. In the Database Window click on **Queries** and select **New**.

2. In the New Query window select **Simple Query Wizard** and click on **OK**.

The Simple Query Wizard dialogue box is displayed (see Figure 8.9).

3. Select the **Lesson** table from the Tables/Queries drop down.

4. Click the double right arrow >> to put all the fields in the selected fields area.

5. Select the **Instructor** table from the Tables/Queries drop down.

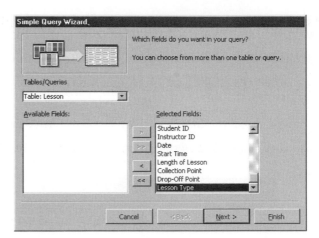

Figure 8.9

6. Select fields **Surname** and **Forename** and add to the selected fields by clicking the right arrow >.

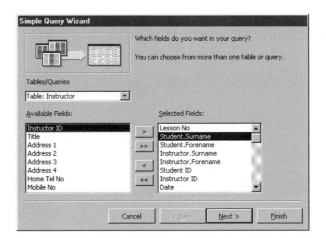

Figure 8.10

7. Select the **Student** table from the Tables/Queries drop down and add the fields **Surname** and **Forename** to the selected fields (see Figure 8.10).

8. Click on **Next**, choose **Detail**, click on **Next** again, call the query **Full Details Query** and click on **Finish**.

The resulting query opens in Datasheet View as shown in Figure 8.11, giving full details of the lessons, the students and instructors along with their names.

We are now going to develop two more queries which will be used later in these units.

Full Details Query : Select Query

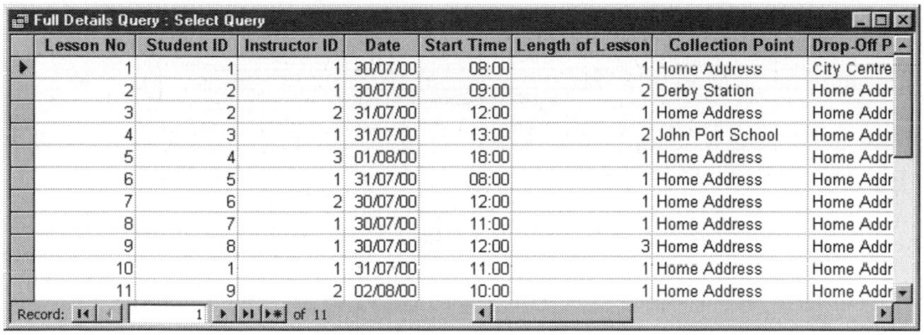

Lesson No	Student ID	Instructor ID	Date	Start Time	Length of Lesson	Collection Point	Drop-Off P
1	1	1	30/07/00	08:00	1	Home Address	City Centre
2	2	1	30/07/00	09:00	2	Derby Station	Home Addr
3	2	2	31/07/00	12:00	1	Home Address	Home Addr
4	3	1	31/07/00	13:00	2	John Port School	Home Addr
5	4	3	01/08/00	18:00	1	Home Address	Home Addr
6	5	1	31/07/00	08:00	1	Home Address	Home Addr
7	6	2	30/07/00	12:00	1	Home Address	Home Addr
8	7	1	30/07/00	11:00	1	Home Address	Home Addr
9	8	1	30/07/00	12:00	3	Home Address	Home Addr
10	1	1	31/07/00	11:00	1	Home Address	Home Addr
11	9	2	02/08/00	10:00	1	Home Address	Home Addr

Record: 1 of 11

Figure 8.11

Query 4 Viewing full details of lessons on a certain

1. Open the **Full Details Query** in Design View.
2. In the criteria row of the Date column, type **[Please enter the date]** (see Figure 8.12).

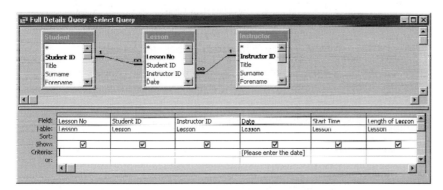

Figure 8.12

3. Use **File, Save As** to save the query as **Full Details by Date Query**.

When you run this query you will be prompted for a date. Access will display full details of the lessons on that date along with the names of the students and instructors.

Query 5 Viewing full details of lessons this week

1. Open the **Full Details by Date Query** in Design View again.
2. In the Criteria Row of the Date column enter `Between Date() and Date()+7`. This will return all lessons booked in the next 7 days

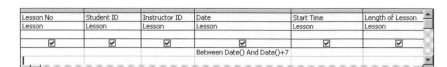

Lesson No	Student ID	Instructor ID	Date	Start Time	Length of Lesson
Lesson	Lesson	Lesson	Lesson	Lesson	Lesson
☑	☑	☑	☑	☑	☑
			Between Date() And Date()+7		

Figure 8.13

starting from the current date (see Figure 8.13).

3. Use **File, Save As** to save the query as **Next Weeks Lessons Query**.

4. To test the query adjust the dates in your table or adjust the time clock on your PC.

Query 6 Adding a calculated field to a query

A calculated field is an added field in a query that displays the results of a calculation. For example, if we multiply together the hourly rate for each lesson and the length of each lesson, we can use the query to work out the cost of each lesson.

1. In the Database Window click on **Queries** and select **New**.

2. Select the **Simple Query Wizard** and click on **OK**.

3. Click on the **Lesson** table and click on the double arrow >> to select every field.

4. Select the **Lesson Type** table and click on the field **Cost**. Click on the single arrow > to select just this field.

5. Select the **Instructor** table and click on the field **Forename**. Click on the single arrow to select just this field. Add the **Surname** field as well.

6. Select the **Student table** and click on the field **Forename**. Click on the single arrow to select just this field. Then add the **Surname, Address1 and Address2** fields as well.

7. Click on **Next**. Click on **Next** again and call the query **Lesson Cost Query**. Click on **Finish**.

8. Switch to **Design View**. You will need to rearrange the tables by dragging to more suitable positions (see Figure 8.14).

9. Using drag and drop rearrange the order of fields in the QBE grid so that Instructor ID comes after Lesson No, followed by Instructor Forename and Surname, then Student ID followed by Student Forename, Surname, Address1 and Address2.

10. Scroll to the right and find the first blank column of the QBE grid. If there is no blank column, select the last field and click on **Insert, Columns**.

11. In the field row of the blank column enter
TotalCost: [Length of lesson]*[Cost] (see Figure 8.15).

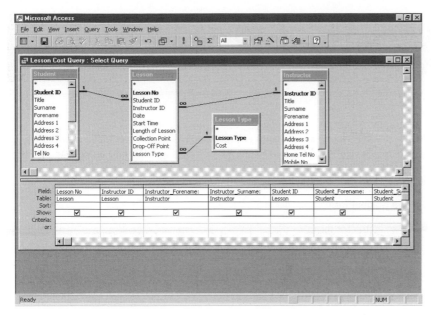

Figure 8.14

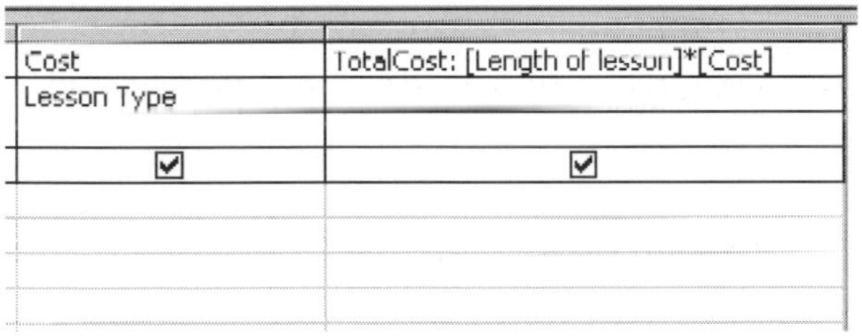

Cost	TotalCost: [Length of lesson]*[Cost]
Lesson Type	
☑	☑

Figure 8.15

12. Save the query again as **Lesson Cost Query**.

13. Click on the **Datasheet View** icon to test the calculations are correct (see Figure 8.16).

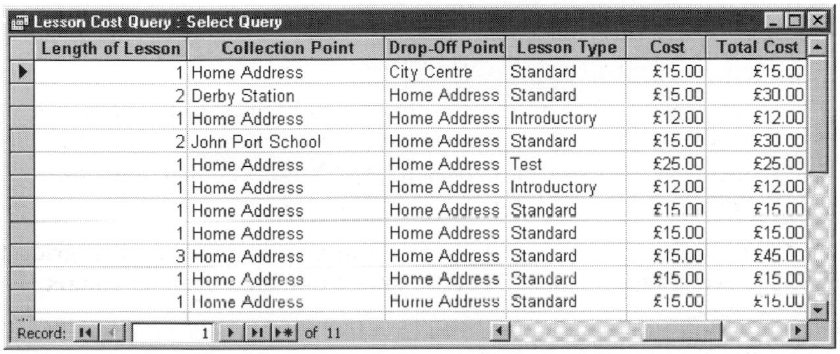

Length of Lesson	Collection Point	Drop-Off Point	Lesson Type	Cost	Total Cost
1	Home Address	City Centre	Standard	£15.00	£15.00
2	Derby Station	Home Address	Standard	£15.00	£30.00
1	Home Address	Home Address	Introductory	£12.00	£12.00
2	John Port School	Home Address	Standard	£15.00	£30.00
1	Home Address	Home Address	Test	£25.00	£25.00
1	Home Address	Home Address	Introductory	£12.00	£12.00
1	Home Address	Home Address	Standard	£15.00	£15.00
1	Home Address	Home Address	Standard	£15.00	£15.00
3	Home Address	Home Address	Standard	£15.00	£45.00
1	Home Address	Home Address	Standard	£15.00	£15.00
1	Home Address	Home Address	Standard	£15.00	£15.00

Record: 1 ▶ ▶I ▶* of 11

Figure 8.16

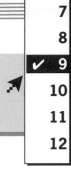

Setting up forms using the Form Wizard

In this chapter you will learn how to set up the forms to enter, edit and view data in the *Pass-It* Driving School database. Forms provide a user friendly on screen interface.

Initially we will set up three forms.

 a Student form;

 an Instructor form;

 a Lesson Type form.

Wizards can again be used to set up the forms. It is usually easier and common practice to use the wizard to set up a form but then to use Design View to customise the form to your requirements.

Setting up the Student Form using AutoForm

1. In the Database Window select **Forms** and click on **New**.

2. In the New Form window select **AutoForm: Columnar** (see Figure 9.1).

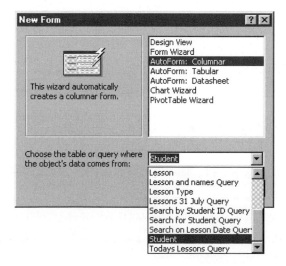

Figure 9.1

3. Select the **Student** table from the drop down list and click on **OK**.

4. The form is generated automatically. If the form is maximised and uses the full screen, click on the **Restore Window** icon (see Figure 9.2).

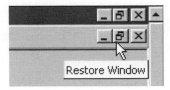

Figure 9.2

5. To ensure that the form is the correct size, click on **Window**, **Size** to **Fit Form**.

6. Save by closing the form and calling it **Student Form**

Size to Fit Form is not available if the window is maximised. When you next open the form it will open at its saved size.

The form is shown in Figure 9.3.

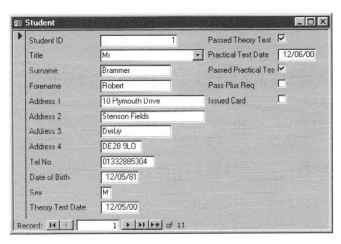

Figure 9.3

Setting up the Instructor Form using the Form Wizard

1. In the Database Window select **Forms** and click on **New**.

2. In the New Form window select **Form Wizard**, select the **Instructor** table from the Tables/Queries drop down and click on **OK** (see Figure 9.4).

3. Click the double arrow >> to put all available fields across to the selected fields and click on **Next**.

NB. The single arrow allows you to select one field at a time and the left arrows allow you to deselect fields. Use the single arrow to choose selected fields in a different order from that shown (Figure 9.5).

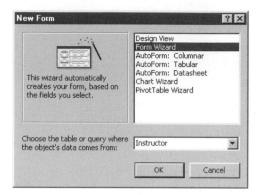

Figure 9.4

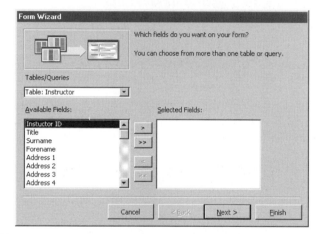

Figure 9.5

4. Select **Columnar** from the range of layouts shown and click on **Next** (see Figure 9.6).

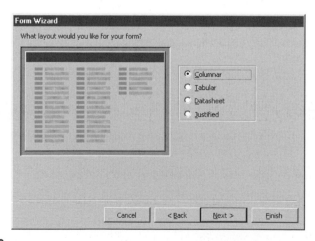

Figure 9.6

5. Select **Standard** style from the next Form Wizard window and click on **Next** (see Figure 9.7).

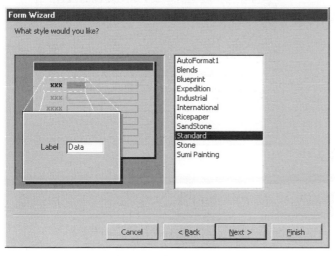

Figure 9.7

6. Save your form as **Instructor Form** and click on **Finish**. The form will open in **Form View** as shown in Figure 9.8.

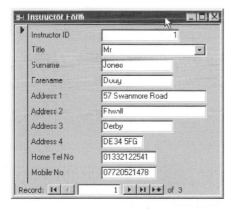

Figure 9.8

▶ Setting up the Lesson Type Form using AutoForm:Tabular

1. In the Database Window select **Forms** and click on **New**.

2. In the New Form window select **AutoForm:Tabular**.

3. Select the **Lesson Type** table from the drop down list and click on **OK**.

4. The form is generated automatically and opens in Form View as shown below. Save the form in the usual way calling it **Lesson Type Form** (see Figure 9.9).

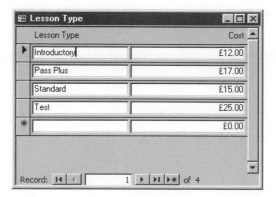

Figure 9.9

The different form views

There are three different views to a form

- Form View
- Datasheet View
- Design View

Form View

Form View allows you to view and edit records one at a time. Enter Form View from the Database Window by selecting the form and clicking on Open.

Datasheet View

Datasheet View allows you to view and edit the records all on one screen. The Lesson Type form is shown in Datasheet View (Figure 9.10).

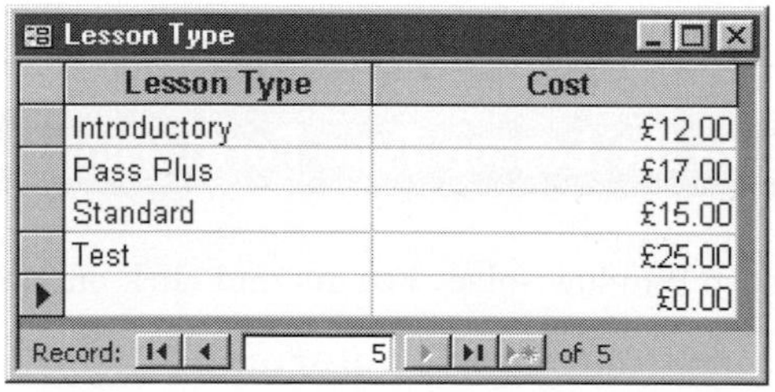

Figure 9.10

Design View

Design View allows you to edit the form and is described in Unit 10. Enter Design View from the Database Window by selecting the form and clicking on Design.

Switching between views

There are a number of ways of switching between the Form View, Design View and Datasheet View windows.

The easiest is to select from one of the first three options on the **View** menu (see Figure 9.11).

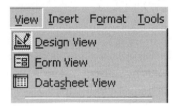

Figure 9.11

Entering data in Form View

1. Open the **Student Form** in Form View.

2. Use the Record navigation bar shown in Figure 9.12 to scroll through the records.

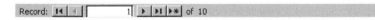

Figure 9.12

3. Click on the last icon to add a new record.

4. Add the details of some more students to practise entering data into a form.

Alternatively you can use the Page Up and Page Down keys to display Next and Previous records.

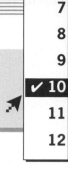

Working in Form Design View

The forms you have produced so far are all standard in layout. Form Design View allows you to customise your form to suit your requirements.

In this chapter you will learn how to:

- find your way around a form in Design View;
- move, align and edit objects on the form which are called controls;
- edit the appearance of your form.

▶ Form Design View

You will grasp the concepts more easily by practising and experimenting with the tasks in this section. We will start by working on a copy of a form so that it if you make a mistake it will not affect the final system.

1. In the Database Window click on **Forms** and select the **Student Form**. From the menu choose **Edit, Copy**.

2. Click in the Database Window and choose **Edit, Paste**. Call the form **Student Form Copy**.

3. Open the **Student Form Copy** in Design View as shown in Figure 10.1 by selecting **Student Form Copy** and clicking on **Design**.

The form opens with the following features showing:

- A **Form Header** section – this area can contain text, headings, titles and graphics. Toggle the **Form Header** off and back on by choosing from the menu **View, Form Header**.

- A **Detail** section – this contains the controls that display the data in your tables.

- A **Control** is made up of a **Label** containing the field name and a box which will contain the data in **Form View**.

- A **Toolbox** from which you can add text, lines, shapes, controls, buttons and other features. Toggle the **Toolbox** on and off by choosing from the menu **View, Toolbox**.

- A **Form Footer** section which can be used in the same way as the Header.

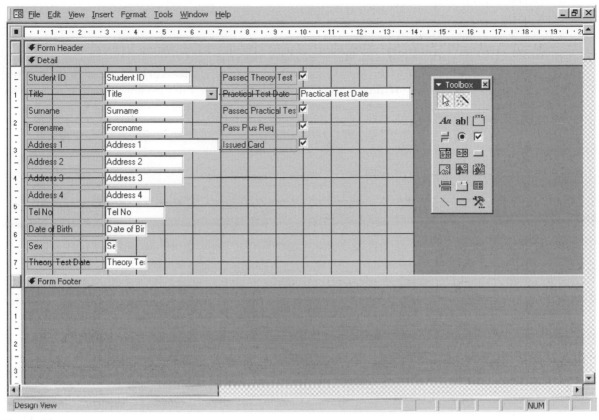

Figure 10.1

A **Right Margin** which can be dragged wider using the mouse.

A **Ruler** and **Grid** to help you with layout of your form. Toggle these features on and off by choosing from the menu **View**, **Ruler** or **View**, **Grid**.

You may also notice the **Page Header/Footer** options which can be added. They will print at the top and bottom of each page in any printout.

Getting a feel for your working area

With the **Student Form Copy** open in Design View as shown in Figure 10.1.

1. Move the mouse over the right margin until it turns into a cross and drag the margin wider by about 2 cm. You can use the ruler as a guide.

2. Move the mouse over the border between the Detail section and the Form Header and drag the Detail section down by about 1cm.

3. In the same way move the Form Footer section down toward the foot of the screen.

4. Switch to Form View by selecting **View**, **Form View** from the menu.

5. If the form is maximised, click on the **Restore Window** icon. Click on **Window**, **Size to Fit Form**. Access will give a best fit to your form as shown in Figure 10.2. It is **NOT** necessary to save this form.

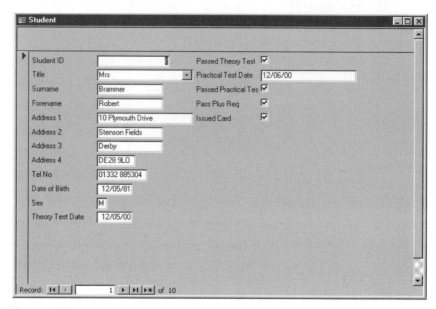

Figure 10.2

Working with controls

The Detail section is initially made up of controls which display the data from your tables. The controls are made up of text boxes and attached labels.

In the Database Window click on **Forms** and select the **Student Form Copy** again. Click on **Design** to open the form in Design View.

It is worth practising all the following steps on the currently opened **Student Form Copy** until you feel confident and competent with handling controls.

Selecting controls

To resize, move, delete, copy or change the properties of a control, first you must select it.

Simply click anywhere on the control and it will be highlighted with *sizing handles* as shown in Figure 10.3.

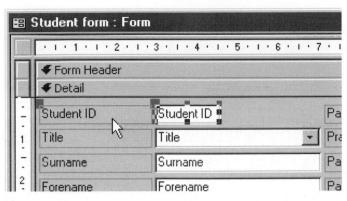

Figure 10.3

✈ To select more than one control, simply drag out a rectangle across the controls you wish to select or

✈ Select the first control and hold down SHIFT while selecting further controls.

Resizing controls

✈ Click on the control to select it and then drag the resizing handles in or out to resize it.

Moving controls

✈ Click on the control to select it. To move the control and its label, move the pointer to the border of the control. The pointer turns into an open hand as shown in Figure 10.4. Drag the control to a new position.

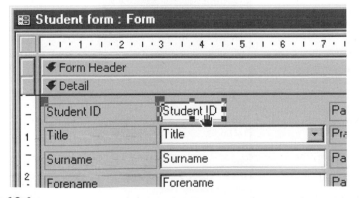

Figure 10.4

To move the control without its label, place the pointer over the *move handle* in the top left corner of the control. The pointer changes to pointing hand as shown in Figure 10.5. Drag the control to a new position.

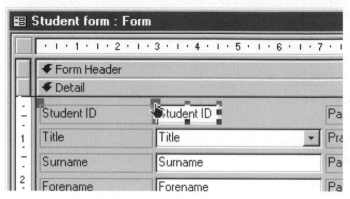

Figure 10.5

You can select more than one control as outlined earlier and move them at the same time.

Deleting controls

To delete a control simply select the control and press the DELETE key.

Adding a control

If you want to add a control for a field, for example because you have already deleted it. From the menu choose **View**, **Field List** (see Figure 10.6).

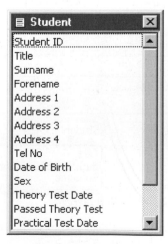

Figure 10.6

The Field list will appear on the screen and you can highlight the field and drag and drop it to the required position.

 Developing a form

1. Open the **Student Form Copy** in Design View.

2. Move each control in the left column down by about 2 cm to make room for a heading.

3. Select all the controls in the second column and move them down a little further.

4. Select the **Theory Test Date** control at the foot of the first column and move the control to the top of the second column.

Your controls should now be arranged something like that shown in Figure 10.7. Do not worry about accuracy, Access provides a number of formatting tools to help you.

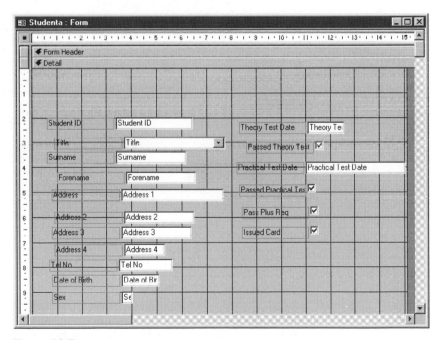

Figure 10.7

It is probable you will have to use the following steps to align all controls correctly. There is no set way but the following steps should ensure accuracy.

1. Highlight the labels in the first column of controls by dragging over them and select **Format, Align, Left**.

2. Highlight the text boxes on the first column of controls by dragging over them and select **Format, Align, Left**.

3. Repeat the same steps for the controls in the right hand column.

4. Align the control **Student ID** with **Theory Test Date** to establish the uppermost position for each column.

5. Highlight the first column of controls and select **Format, Vertical Spacing, Make Equal**.

6. Highlight the second column of controls and select **Format, Vertical Spacing, Make Equal**.

7. When you are happy with your design switch to **Form View** click on the **Restore Window** icon if the form is maximised and select **Window, Size to Fit Form**.

8. Save your form. It should appear as in Figure 10.8.

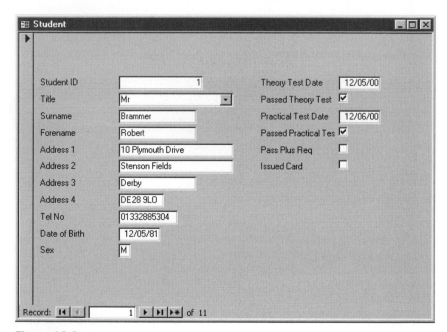

Figure 10.8

During the course of the next exercises you will be introduced to a number of ways of improving the appearance of your form. Throughout this section do not be afraid to practise and experiment – remember you can always delete it and start again or as a last resort get the wizards to do it again!

Fonts, colours and special effects

1. Open the **Student Form Copy** in Design View.

2. Ensure the Formatting toolbar is available by clicking on **View, Toolbars, Formatting (Form/Report)** (see Figure 10.9).

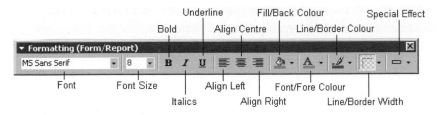

Figure 10.9

Most of the options here will be familiar to students who have a working knowledge of Windows Software.

3. Click on the **Detail** area and click the **Fill/Back Colour** drop down on the Formatting toolbar to show the colour palette as in Figure 10.10.

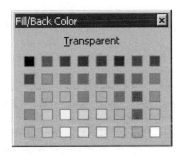

Figure 10.10

4. Select a suitable colour for the background to your form.

5. Select the labels of all the controls and set the font to **Arial Black** (or one of your choice) by clicking the Font Drop down on the Formatting toolbar and then clicking on **Bold**.

You will probably have to spend some time resizing the labels or click **Edit**, **Undo** to try another font.

6. Select all the labels again and click the **Fill/Back Colour** drop down on the Formatting toolbar.

7. Choose a colour to make your labels stand out from the background colour of the form.

8. With labels still selected click the **Special Effect** drop down and choose **Raised** from the Special Effect window shown in Figure 10.11.

Figure 10.11

NB. If you right click in the Detail area or on any control you will get a menu from which a number of toolbar options are offered.

Using the Toolbox to add a text box, rectangle and lines

The toolbox offers a number of features many of which you will meet later in this book (see Figure 10.12).

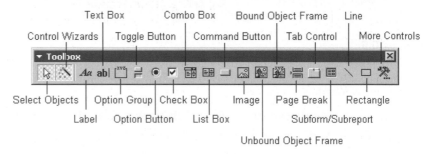

Figure 10.12

1. Click on the Label icon and drag out a rectangle near the top of your form.

2. Type in a suitable heading and press return.

3. Set the font, background colour and special effect as required.

4. Select the Rectangle tool and drag out a box around the controls.

5. Select the box and choose a style from the **Line/Border Width** drop down on the Formatting toolbar (see Figure 10.13).

Figure 10.13

Making a start on the Student Form

We now need to go back to our original Student Form and develop it for later use.

1. Open the **Student Form** in Design View.

2. Move the controls down to make room for a title and move the **Passed Theory Test** control to the top of the right column as you did earlier in this unit (see Figure 10.14).

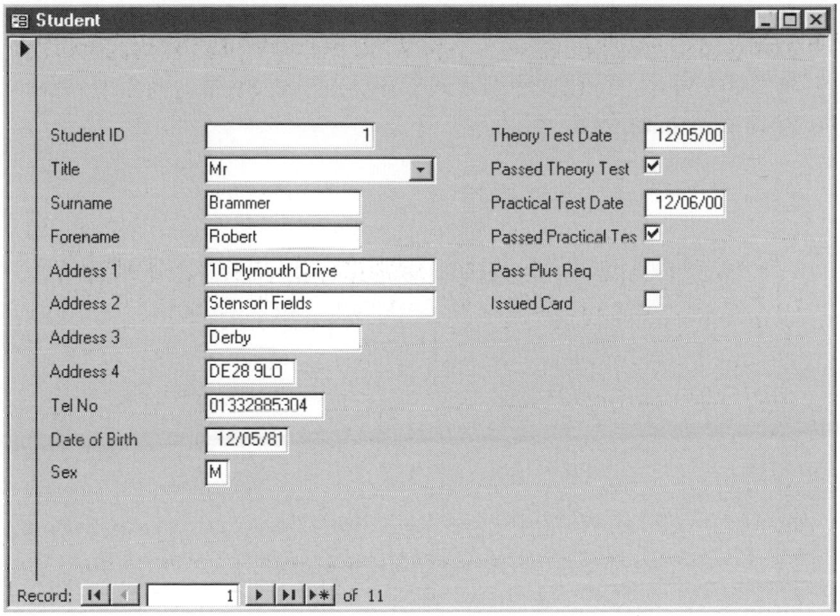

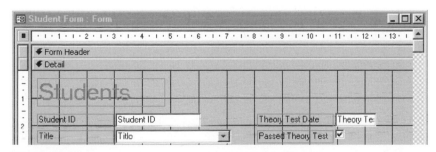

Figure 10.14

3. Click on the **Label** icon in the Toolbox (see Figure 10.15).

Figure 10.15

4. Drag out a rectangle near the top of the form, type in the text **Students** and press return (see Figure 10.16).

Figure 10.16

5. With the new control selected set the font, font size, foreground colour and border colour as required using the **Formatting** toolbar. We have chosen only to set the font colour to green and font size to 24 point.

6. Save your form.

Taking form design further

This section describes some of the additional features that you can add to your forms to create a professional feel to your system.

You will learn how to:

- add graphics;
- add command buttons;
- add combo boxes;
- set form properties;
- create forms to display data from more than one table.

The Toolbox

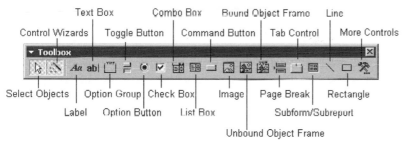

Figure 11.1

The Toolbox (see Figure 11.1) should appear when you are in Design mode. It allows you to add control objects to your forms. If it is not visible click **View, Toolbox** from the menu.

NB. Some of the functions available can be set up using wizards. If you wish to use the wizards you must ensure the Control Wizards icon is selected.

Adding graphics to the form

Graphics can easily be added to your form using copy and paste. The graphic appears in an unbound object frame enabling you to move or size the frame as needed

Alternatively follow these steps:

1. Ensure the image is already saved in a format that Access can recognise, e.g. **jpg**, **gif** or **bmp**. Our image is the *Pass-It* logo (see Figure 11.2).

Figure 11.2

2. Open the **Student** form in **Design View**.

3. Select the Image icon in the Toolbox (see Figure 11.3).

Figure 11.3

4. Drag out a rectangle near the bottom right of the form.

5. Select the image you wish to add to the form from the Insert Picture Dialogue Box. If the image does not fit the frame then right click on the image, select **Properties** and set the **Size Mode** to **Zoom**.

6. Save your form as **Student Form**. It should appear as in Figure 11.4.

Figure 11.4

The Instructor Form

In the exactly the same way as you developed the Student Form, you now need to set up the Instructor Form to look as shown in Figure 11.5.

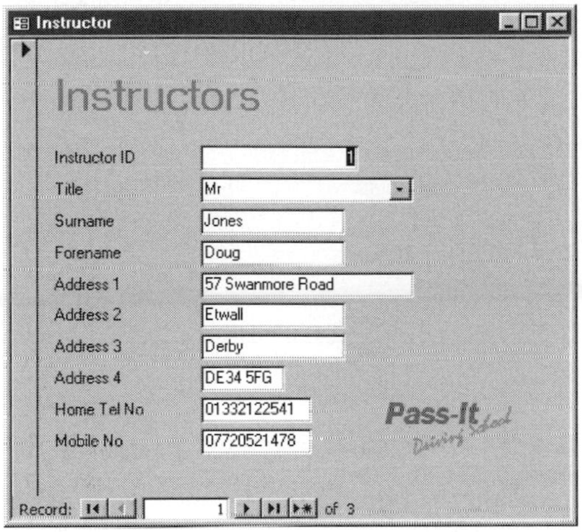

Figure 11.5

Adding command buttons

Access allows you to automate tasks by creating command buttons and placing them on your form.

Command buttons can be added to deal with a number of operations including:

- record navigation;
- opening forms and reports;
- printing;
- other commonly used operations.

You can set up a command button in one of two ways:

- Use the Command Button wizard to set up the button and attach the operation.
- Create the button without the Wizard and attach it to a macro or code.

We will be dealing with macros later. We will start by using the Wizards to set buttons to move between the records, add a new record and quit the application for our Student Form (see Figure 11.6).

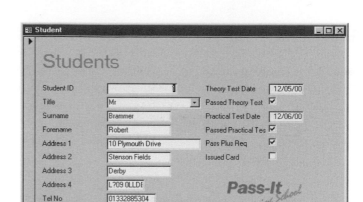

Figure 11.6

1. Open the **Student Form** in Design View.

2. We are going to add the buttons to the lower right of the form. You may have to drag out the detail area to create a little room.

3. Make sure the Toolbox is showing and the **Control Wizards** tool is selected (see Figure 11.7).

Figure 11.7

4. Select the **Command Button** tool and drag out a button on your form.

This displays the Command Button Wizard dialogue box (see Figure 11.8).

5. In the Categories list select **Record Operations**.

6. In the Actions list select **Add New Record** and click on **Next**.

The next window offers you a choice of putting pictures or text on the button. If you choose text you can type in the text you want to go on the button.

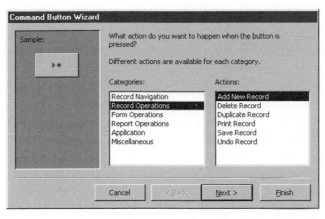

Figure 11.8

If you choose Picture you can select from a list or browse the file area to find one of your own (see Figure 11.9).

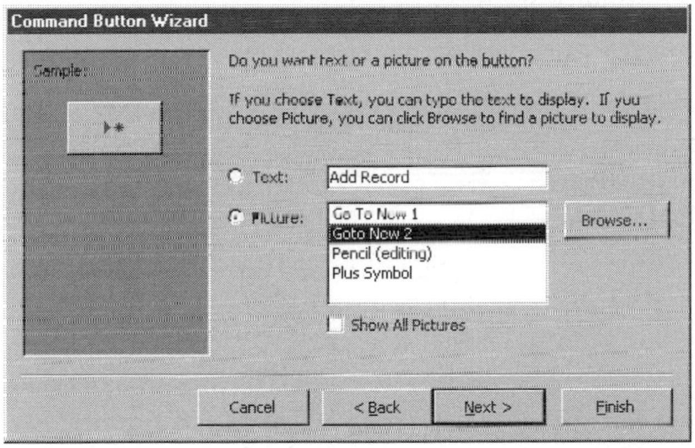

Figure 11.9

7. We are going to use pictures so choose **Go To New 2** and click on **Next** (see Figure 11.10).

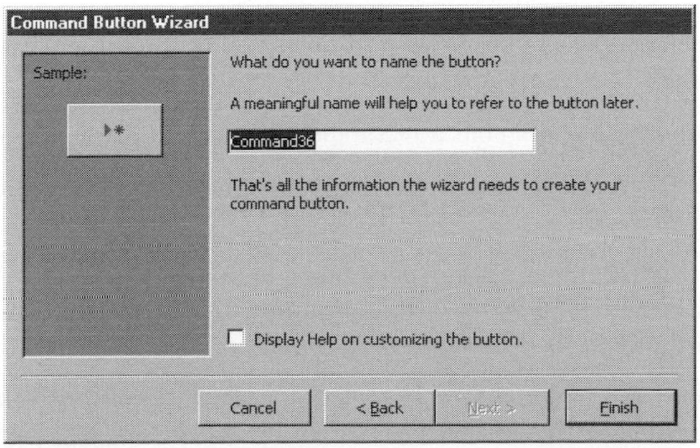

Figure 11.10

8. Give your button a sensible name and click on **Finish**.

The lower half of your form should look something like Figure 11.11 with the **Add New Record** button positioned as shown.

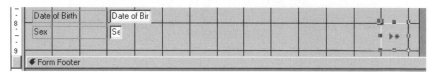

Figure 11.11

9. Add extra buttons from the **Record Navigation Category** using the actions **Goto First Record**, **Goto Previous Record**, **Goto Next Record** and **Goto Last Record**. Don't worry about aligning the buttons yet.

10. Add the **Close Form** button from the **Form Operations** category.

You need to arrange the buttons in the order shown in Figure 11.12.

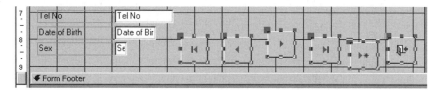

Figure 11.12

11. Group all the buttons and align with **Format**, **Align**, **Top**.

12. Distribute the buttons evenly by again selecting all and choosing from the menu **Format**, **Horizontal Spacing**, **Make Equal**.

13. You may wish to make the buttons smaller and use the **Format**, **Size** option to make all buttons the same size.

▶ Adding a control panel

It is common practice to keep user buttons away from data entry areas. We are going to add a background to give a control panel effect.

1. From the toolbox drag out a rectangle big enough to cover the buttons.

2. Select the rectangle and set its colour to light blue. Set its **Special Effect** to **Sunken**.

3. Select the rectangle and use copy paste to make a copy of it. Use the resizing handles to make it slightly larger than the first and set its **Special Effect** to **Raised**.

4. Position the smaller rectangle over the larger and centre the buttons on the panel. If the buttons are hidden by the rectangles you may need to use **Format**, **Bring to Front** (see Figure 11.13).

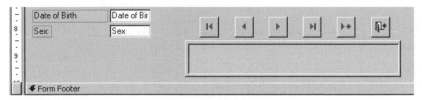

Figure 11.13

Your form should now appear as in Figure 11.14.

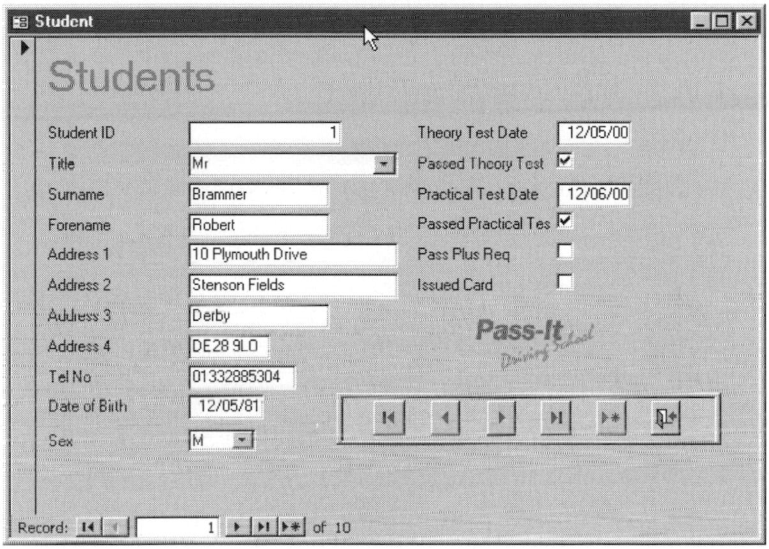

Figure 11.14

You now need to set up buttons in exactly the same way on the **Instructor Form**.

Combo boxes

Combo boxes are drop down boxes which allow the user to enter data from a list of choices. We will set up a combo box on the Student Form so that users can simply enter M or F in the Sex field from a drop down box.

Adding a combo box to enter student details

1. Open the **Student Form** in Design View.
2. Select the **Sex** control and press the DELETE key.
3. Click on the Combo Box tool in the Toolbox (see Figure 11.15).
4. Drag out a small rectangle where the Sex control was.

Figure 11.15

5. The Command Button Wizard dialogue box is displayed. Check '**I will type in the values I want**' and click on **Next** (see Figure 11.16).

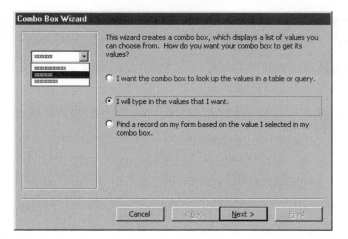

Figure 11.16

6. Enter **M** and the **F** pressing TAB in between entries and click on **Next**.

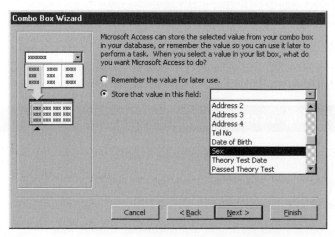

Figure 11.17

7. Check the **'Store that value in this field'** option and select **Sex** from the drop down box. Click **Next** (see Figure 11.17).

8. Set the label to **Sex** and click on **Finish**. You will need to align the control with the others.

9. Save your form as **Student Form**. The combo box should appear as in Figure 11.18.

| Date of Birth | 12/05/81 | |
| Sex | M ▾ | ◀ |

Figure 11.18

▶ Adding a combo box to look up student details

We are going to set up a combo box to display the names of all our students.

When a student is selected in the combo box, their details will appear on the form.

1. Open the Student Form in Design View.

2. Click on the Combo Box tool in the Toolbox.

3. Drag out a rectangle near the title at the top of the form to start the **Combo Box Wizard**. You will have to group the controls and move them down to create room for the new control (see Figure 11.19).

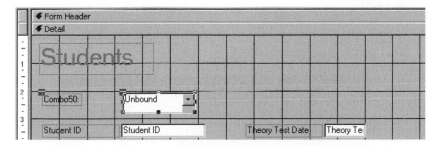

Figure 11.19

4. Click on **Find a record on my form based on a value I selected in my combo box** Click on **Next** (see Figure 11.20).

5. Click on the **Surname** field and select it with the > icon. Click on **Next** (see Figure 11.21).

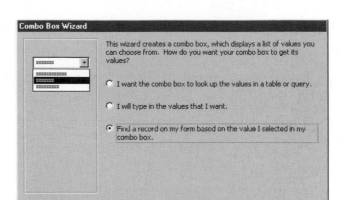

Figure 11.20

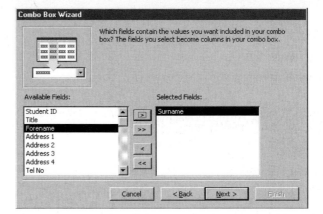

Figure 11.21

6. The Combo Box Wizard dialogue box then displays the names. Click on **Next** again (see Figure 11.22).

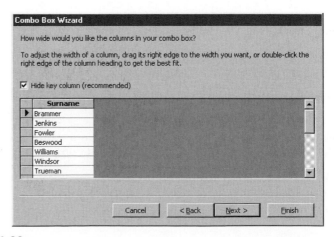

Figure 11.22

7. Give the combo box the name **Find Record** and click on **Finish**

8. Switch to Form View, the Student Form should appear as in Figure 11.23.

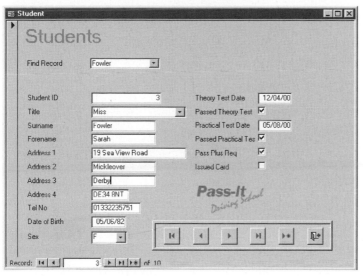

Figure 11.23

Displaying the names in the combo box in alphabetical order

The names in the drop-down list from the combo box on the Student form are in student ID order and not alphabetical order. To sort these names into alphabetical order:

1. Open the Student form in Design View and select the **Find Record** Combo box.

2. Click on the **Properties** icon or right click the combo box and click on Properties. Click on the **Data** tab.

3. Click on **Row Source** and click on the three dots icon as shown in Figure 11.24.

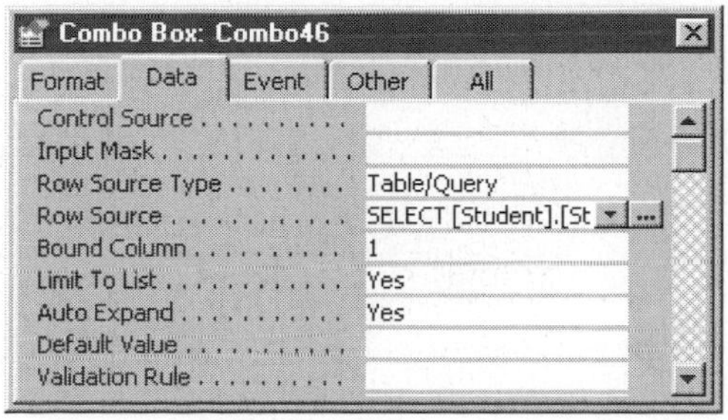

Figure 11.24

4. The SQL Statement Query Builder window opens. It looks similar to Query Design View. In the **Student Surname** column of the QBE grid, select **Ascending** in the Sort row (see Figure 11.25).

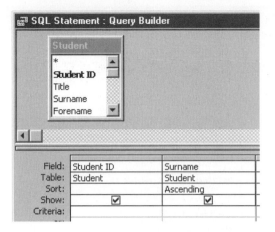

Figure 11.25

5. Close the Query Builder window and save the changes.

6. Go into Form View and test that the names are in alphabetical order.

Setting form properties

You can control the behaviour and appearance of your form by setting the form's properties.

In the Student Form you have just completed it may look better without a number of features. It still has the Record Selector, the Record Navigation Controls, maximize, minimize and close buttons. These can be removed using the Form Properties window.

1. In Design View, double click on the **Form Selector** at the top left of the form in Design View or click on **View**, **Properties** (see Figure 11.26).

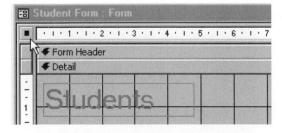

Figure 11.26

2. This displays the **Form Properties** window.

There are far too many properties to cover all the available options here.

You will meet some later in the Units but Microsoft Help will give details of all the available options.

The properties are grouped for easier access. Clicking on the **Format** tab will give a range of options covering the appearance of your form.

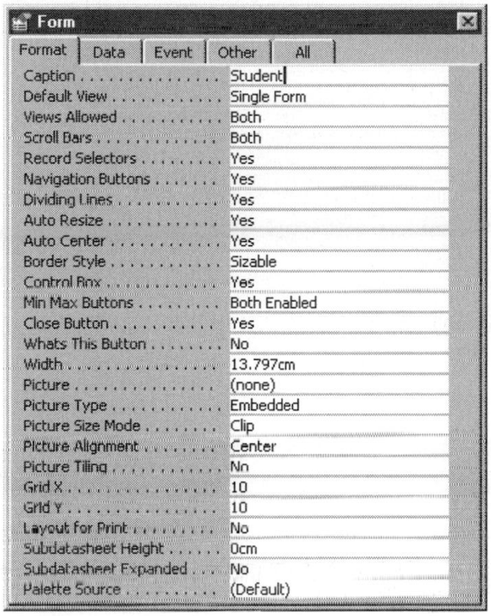

Figure 11.27

3. Change the form caption using the **Caption** property to **Student Details**.

4. Remove the scroll bars at the bottom and right hand side of the form by setting the **Scroll Bars** property to **Neither**.

5. Remove the record selector on the form by setting the **Record Selectors** property to **No**.

6. Remove the navigation buttons at the bottom of the form by setting the **Navigation Buttons** property to **No**.

7. Remove the dividing lines at the bottom of the form by setting the **Dividing Lines** property to **No**.

8. Make the form appear in the middle of the screen by setting the **Auto Center** property to **Yes**.

9. Remove the maximise and minimise buttons from a form by setting the **Max Min Buttons** property to **None**.

NB. The record selector is a column on the left hand side of a form used to select a whole record in a form, for example to delete a record rather than just delete one field.

Your finished form should appear as in Figure 11.28.

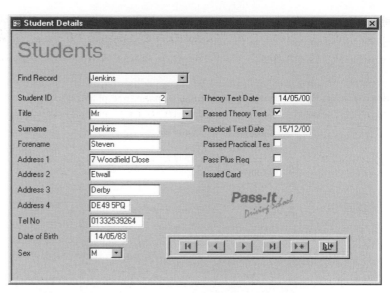

Figure 11.28

Create a form to display data from more than one table

In Chapter 9 we used the wizards to design simple Student and Instructor forms. We could also have designed a form to book lessons as shown in Figure 11.29. The form is based on the table Lesson.

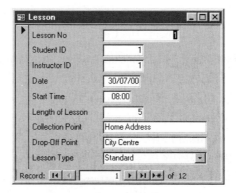

Figure 11.29

In the real system it is probable the student would not know their ID number or the operator booking their lesson would like to confirm an ID by seeing the student name on screen.

In this section we will set up the Lesson Booking Form. You will find out how to base a form on a query. This will enable us to key in the Student ID on the Booking Form and Access will find the student's name in the student table.

Creating the Lesson Booking Form

1. In the **Database Window** click on **Queries**, select the **Lesson Cost Query** and click **Open** to run the Query.

The output in Figure 11.30 shows the query bringing in the information from all the tables. This is the information that will be displayed in your form.

Lesson No	Instructor ID	Instructor	Instructor	Student ID	Student_Forer	Student_Surn;	Address 2	Cost
1	1	Doug	Jones	1	Robert	Brammer	Stenson Fields	£15.00
2	1	Doug	Jones	2	Steven	Jenkins	Etwall	£15.00
3	2	Arnold	Batchelor	2	Steven	Jenkins	Etwall	£12.00
4	1	Doug	Jones	3	Sarah	Fowler	Mickleover	£15.00
5	3	Andrew	Smith	4	Michael	Beswood	Allestree	£25.00
6	1	Doug	Jones	5	Charlotte	Williams	Littleover	£12.00
7	2	Arnold	Batchelor	6	David	Windsor	Allenton	£15.00
8	1	Doug	Jones	7	Mary	Trueman	Allestree	£15.00
9	1	Doug	Jones	8	Victoria	Spencer	Stenson Fields	£15.00
10	1	Doug	Jones	1	Robert	Brammer	Stenson Fields	£15.00
11	2	Arnold	Batchelor	9	Greg	Watson	Etwall	£15.00
(AutoNumber)								

Figure 11.30

2. Close the Query, select **Forms** and click on **New**.

3. In the **New Form** window select the **Form Wizard** and choose the **Lesson Cost Query** from the drop down list. Click on **OK**.

4. Click the double arrow >> to select all fields as shown in Figure 11.31 and click on **Next**.

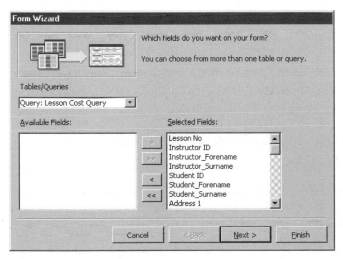

Figure 11.31

5. Select **Columnar** and click on **Next**.

6. Select **Standard** and click on **Next**.

7. Call the form **Lesson Booking Form** and click on **Finish**.

8. Open the form and **Size to Fit**. It should appear as in Figure 11.32.

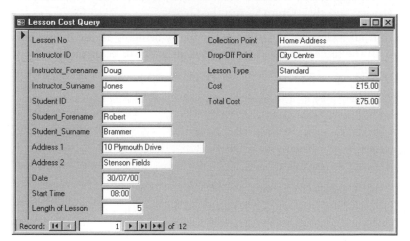

Figure 11.32

We now need to customize the form to give it the same look and feel as the Student and Instructor Forms.

In Form Design View make the following changes :

⟋ Move the fields down to make room for a heading.

⟋ Add a title Lessons in the same font, font size and colour.

⟋ Edit the labels for the Instructor and Student name control by removing the text and underscore.

⟋ Add the Pass-It logo.

⟋ Add the control panel (not the buttons) by using copy paste from one of the other forms.

⟋ Add the buttons using the Wizards as before.

⟋ Set the form properties to the same as the other forms.

Your finished **Lesson Booking** form should appear as in Figure 11.33.

When you go to a new record and enter an instructor ID number, when you click on another control or press the TAB key, the instructor's forename and surname will appear.

Similarly after you enter the student ID, when you click on another control or press the TAB key, the student's forename, surname and address will appear.

1. At the Database Window click on **Reports** and click on **New**.

2. Click on **AutoReport: Tabular** and in the drop down list click on **Instructor**. Click on **OK** (see Figure 12.2).

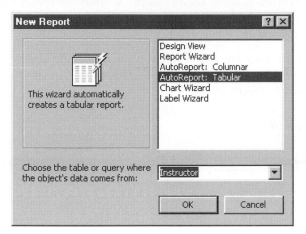

Figure 12.2

The wizard generates the report which is shown in Figure 12.3.

Instructor

Instructor ID	Title	Surname	Forename	Address 1	Address 2	Address 3	Address 4
1	Mr	Jones	Doug	57 Swanmore Road	Etwall	Derby	DE34 5FG
2	Mr	Batchelor	Arnold	13 Gairloch Close	Etwall	Derby	DE34 5FG
3	Mr	Smith	Andrew	5b Sunrise Road	Littleover	Derby	DE45 4ED

Figure 12.3

If you scroll down to the bottom of the report, you will see that the wizard automatically inserts the date and the page number (see Figure 12.4).

07 January 2001   *Page 1 of 1*

Figure 12.4

Close the report and save it as **Instructor Report**.

The different report views

There are three different views to a report:

🖋 Print Preview

🖋 Design View

🖋 Layout Preview

■ Print Preview

The Print Preview window allows you to see what the report will look like when you print it out. Figure 12.6 is part of the Print Preview window of the Instructor report.

As the cursor moves over the report it turns into a magnifying glass. Click once to zoom out to see the whole page. Click again to zoom in to actual size as shown in Figure 12.5.

Instructor

Instructor ID	Title		Surname	Forename	Address 1
1	Mr		Jones	Doug	57 Swanmore Road
2	Mr	🔍	Batchelor	Arnold	13 Gairloch Close
3	Mr		Smith	Andrew	5b Sunrise Road

Figure 12.5

When you zoom out the Instructor Report will appear as in Figure 12.6.

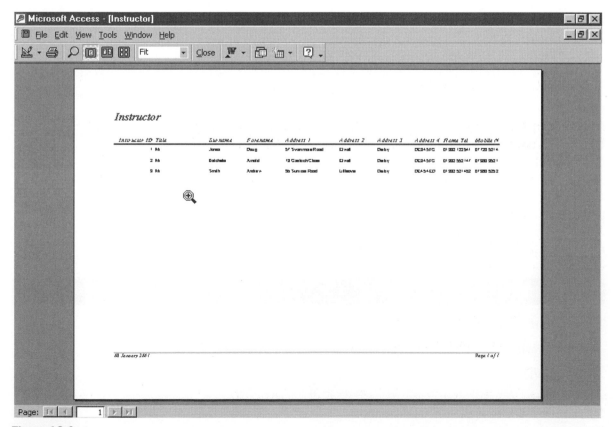

Figure 12.6

There is a Print Preview toolbar as shown in Figure 12.7.

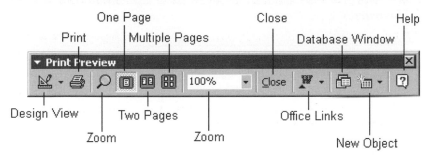

Figure 12.7

If this toolbar is not displayed, click on **View**, **Toolbars**, **Print Preview**.

If there is more than one page in the report you can use the page navigation bar shown in Figure 12.8 to scroll through the pages.

Figure 12.8

Printing a report

To print a report, simply open the report at the Database Window in Print Preview and click on the Print icon.

Design View

The Design View window allows you to customise your report to suit your requirements. Reports are edited in the same way as editing forms. As with forms it is possible to:

- add, edit and remove fields;
- add text and titles;
- change the style and layout;
- change the font format and colours;
- add controls and command buttons;
- add images

Click on **View**, **Design View** to see the Instructor Report in Design View as shown in Figure 12.9.

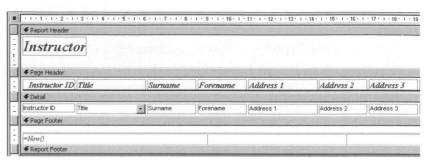

Figure 12.9

The top part of the report is the **Report Header**. Controls in the Report Header appear only once at the beginning of the report. It is suitable for titles.

The second part of the report is the **Page Header**. Controls in the Page Header appear at the top of every page. It is suitable for column headings.

The third part of the report is the **Detail**. This is used for the data in the report.

The fourth part of the report is the **Page Footer**. Controls in the Page Footer appear at the bottom of every page. It is here the wizard has inserted the page number and the date.

The final part of the report is the **Report Footer**. Controls in the Report Footer appear only once at the end of the report.

We will use Design View to customise the appearance of the Instructor Report.

■ Toolbars

There are two toolbars used in designing reports, the Report Design toolbar (Figure 12.9) and the Formatting (Form/Report) toolbar (Figure 12.10). Always ensure these toolbars are displayed when in Report Design View by clicking on **View**, **Toolbars**, **Report Design** and **View**, **Toolbars**, **Formatting (Form/Report)**.

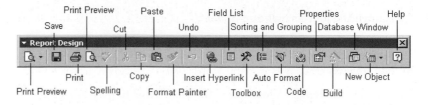

Figure 12.10 The Report Design Toolbar

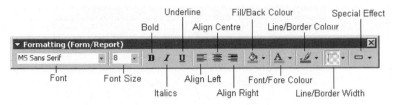

Figure 12.11 The Formatting (Form/Report) Toolbar

Two other useful features of Report Design View are the Field List and the Toolbox. If they are not showing they can be found on the **View** menu.

Right click menu

If you right click on an object in Report Design View, you get a short-cut menu. Different options are available depending on the object chosen. From this menu you can control the properties of objects on your report (see Figure 12.12).

Figure 12.12

Orientation of a report

In Design View you can also set a report to either portrait or landscape format. Landscape format is often better when the report has many fields in columns. Click on **File, Page Setup** and click on the **Page** tab to set the orientation of a report to portrait or landscape (see Figure 12.13).

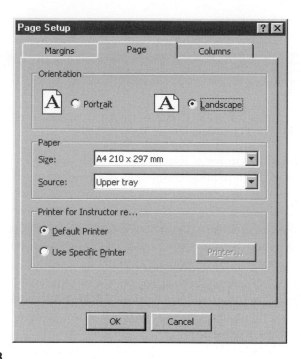

Figure 12.13

■ Layout Preview

The Layout Preview window provides a quick way of seeing the layout of a report when you are in Design View to check that it appears how you want it to. However if your report is based on a query, layout preview may not include all the data in the report.

■ Switching between views

There are a number of ways of switching between the Print Preview, Design View and Layout Preview windows.

The easiest is to select from one of the first three options on the **View** menu.

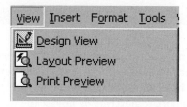

Figure 12.14

> **Note**
>
> You cannot switch from Layout Preview to Print Preview or from Print Preview to Layout Preview. To go between these windows, you must first switch to Design View.

Customising the Instructor Report

We are going to edit the Instructor Report, some of the columns (e.g. Title) are too wide and some (e.g. Mobile No) are too narrow.

1. Open the report in Design View.

2. Click on the title in the Report Header, then drag the resizing handles out to increase the size of the control and change the text in the control to **Instructor Report** (see Figure 12.15).

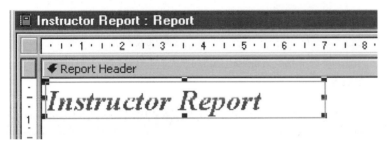

Figure 12.15

3. Select the **Title** control in the Detail section and holding the SHIFT key down select the Title control in the Page Header section (see Figure 12.16).

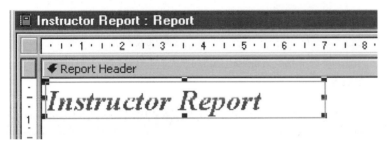

Figure 12.16

4. Drag the resizing handles in to make one of the controls smaller. The other control will also be resized (see Figure 12.17).

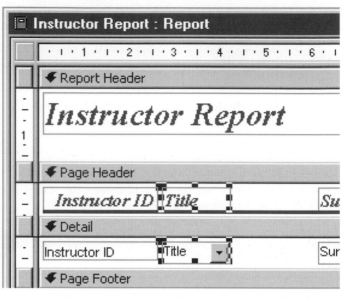

Figure 12.17

5. Select all the other controls to the right of Title in the Page Header and the Detail sections. (Click on one, then hold down the SHIFT key and click on each of the others in turn.) With care you may find it easier to drag out a rectangle across the controls.

NB. All the controls on a report can be selected with CTRL+A, then it is sometimes quicker to deselect by simply clicking on the controls not required.

6. Using the 'open hand,' slide all these controls to the left (see Figure 12.18).

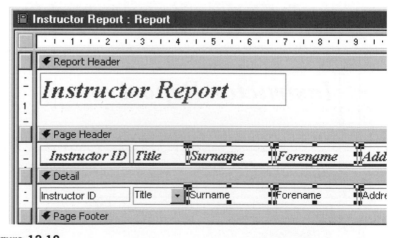

Figure 12.18

7. Select the control for the Mobile No. and use the resizing handles to enlarge it.

8. Select the Instructor Report control in the Report Header and move it five centimetres to the right.

9. Click on the **Image** icon in the Toolbox and drag out a rectangle on the Report Header. Find the image you wish to insert as the logo and click on OK.

If your image is too big for the rectangle you have drawn, either:

*   Resize the rectangle or

*   Right click on the image. Click on **Properties**. Click on the **Format** tab and in the **Size Mode** box click on **Zoom**.

Alternatively you can use copy and paste to import an image from another application.

10. Click on **View**, **Layout Preview** to view your report in Layout Preview mode (see Figure 12.19).

Pass-It *Driving School* *Instructor Report*

Instructor ID	Title	Surname	Forename	Address 1	Address 2
1	Mr	Jones	Doug	57 Swanmore Road	Etwall
2	Mr	Batchelor	Arnold	13 Gairloch Close	Etwall
3	Mr	Smith	Andrew	5b Sunrise Road	Littleover

Figure 12.19

Further customisation

We can further improve our report as follows:

1. Switch back to Design View and expand the detail area as shown in Figure 12.20.

2. Increase the font size of the data (currently size 8) to size 10 by selecting all the controls in the detail section and choosing size 10 in the formatting toolbar.

3. Delete the labels in the Page Header for Surname, Forename, Address 2, Address 3, Address 4 and Mobile No. (Select each label and press delete in turn.)

4. Edit the remaining labels to read Instructor ID, Name, Address and Phone (see Figure 12.21).

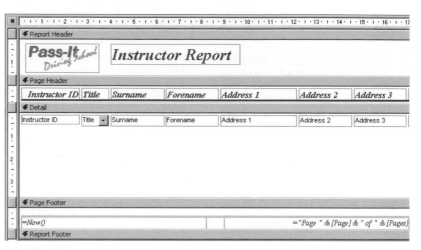

Figure 12.20

Figure 12.21

5. Move the controls in the details section into roughly the position shown. Select all the address controls and then click on **Format**, **Align**, **Left** to get the controls in a straight line. Click on **Format**, **Vertical Spacing**, **Make Equal** to space the controls equally (see Figure 12.22).

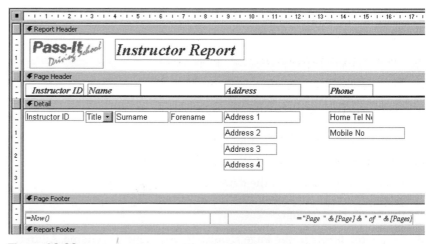

Figure 12.22

6. Switch to **Layout Preview** to see the finished report (see Figure 12.23).

Pass-It *Driving School* *Instructor Report*

Instructor ID Name			Address	Phone
1 Mr	Jones	Doug	57 Swanmore Road	01332 122541
			Etwall	07720 521478
			Derby	
			DE34 5F	
2 Mr	Batchelor	Arnold	13 Gairloch Close	01332 552147
			Etwall	07980 352145
			Derby	
			DE34 5F	
3 Mr	Smith	Andrew	5b Sunrise Road	01332 521452

Figure 12.23

▶ Report 2: Student Report using the Report Wizard

We want to set up a report to show a list of all the students. This report will be based on the Student table.

1. At the **Database Window** click on **Reports** and click on **New**.

2. Click on **Report Wizard** and in the drop down list click on **Student**. Click on **OK**

3. Click on the double arrow to choose all the fields for your report and click on **Next**.

4. Click on **Next** to ignore any grouping levels.

5. Click on **Next** to ignore sort options.

6. Select **Tabular and Landscape** and click on **Next**.

7. Select **Corporate** and click on **Next**.

8. Call the report **Student Report** and click on **Finish**.

The report will open in Report View. Switch to Design View as in Figure 12.24. You will need to edit the report. There is no set way to do this.

Carefully select all the controls in the Detail area by dragging across them and use **Format**, **Horizontal Spacing**, **Increase** to create room for editing the controls. You will then need to resize and reposition the labels in the Page Header.

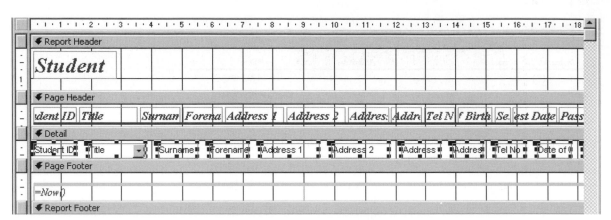

Figure 12.24

Further reports

In this chapter we are going to design two further reports, both will be based on Queries:

🖎 A report to produce a membership card for one student;

🖎 A report to produce all the instructors' timetables for a particular date.

▶ Report 1: Membership Card Report

We will set up a report to produce a membership card for a single student. When this report is opened, it will ask for the Student ID number and produce a membership card for that student.

The report will be based on the Query called **Search by Student ID Query** that we set up in Chapter 7. We will use **AutoReport: Columnar** to set the report up.

1. At the Database Window click on **Reports** and click on **New**.

2. Click on **AutoReport: Columnar** and select **Search by Student ID Query** from the list. Click on **OK** (see Figure 13.1).

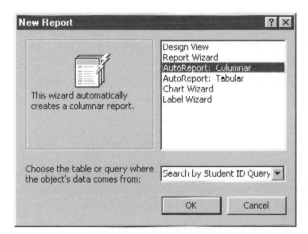

Figure 13.1

3. The report will load. As the report is based on a parameter query, this dialogue box will be displayed (see Figure 13.2).

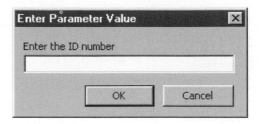

Figure 13.2

4. Enter a Student ID, e.g. 6 and you will see the membership card for student number 6 (see Figure 13.3).

Student ID Query

Student ID	6
Forename	David
Surname	Windsor
Address 1	86 Milford Road
Address 2	Allenton
Address 3	Derby
Address 4	DE57 4PT
Tel No	01332 389144
Date of Birth	18/08/82
Sex	M

Figure 13.3

5. Close the window and save the report as **Membership Card Report**.

However the report needs to be customised. The wizard puts all the data in boxes with a border which we don't want.

6. Switch to Design View.

7. Select all the controls in the detail section by dragging a rectangle over all of them or by pressing CTRL+A and deselecting the header and footer controls (click the control with SHIFT held down) (see Figure 13.4).

8. Click on the toolbar **Properties** icon or click on **View, Properties**.

9. Click on the **Format** tab and click in the **Border Style** box and select **Transparent** (see Figure 13.5).

Figure 13.4

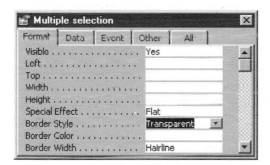

Figure 13.5

10. Switch to Print Preview to check that the boxes have been removed as shown in Figure 13.6.

As you can see two controls, Student ID and Date of Birth are not left aligned.

11. Switch back to Design View. Select each of these controls in turn and click on the **Align Left** icon. (You can also align the text by clicking on **View, Properties**, clicking on the **Format** tab and set the **Text Align** property to left.)

12. Click on the **Image** icon from the Toolbox and drag out a box in the report header to add the company logo image as before.

13. Change the title in the report header to **Membership Card**.

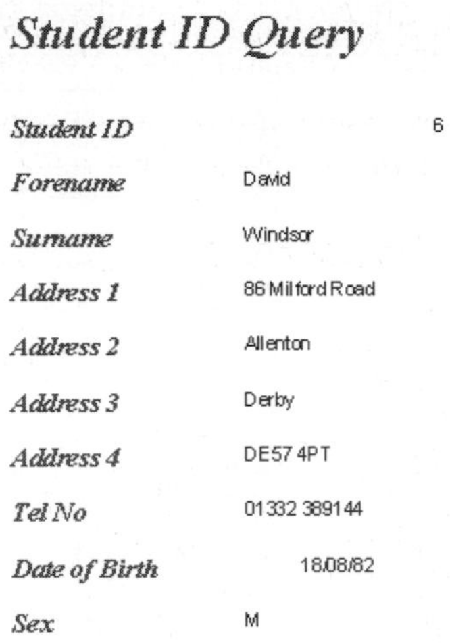

Student ID Query

Student ID	6
Forename	David
Surname	Windsor
Address 1	86 Milford Road
Address 2	Allenton
Address 3	Derby
Address 4	DE57 4PT
Tel No	01332 389144
Date of Birth	18/08/82
Sex	M

Figure 13.6

14. Expand the Page Footer by dragging the border down. Delete the date and page number controls. Click on the Label icon in the Toolbox. Drag out a rectangle in the Page Footer. Enter the text as shown (Use SHIFT+ENTER to force a return) (see Figure 13.7).

Pass-It Driving School *Membership Card*

Student ID	5
Forename	Charlotte
Surname	Williams
Address	21 Church Street
	Littleover
	Derby
	DE33 8RD
Tel No	01332 2931
Date of Birth	30/03/81
Sex	F

Please keep this membership card safe and bring it with you to lessons.

Please inform us if any information is incorrect.

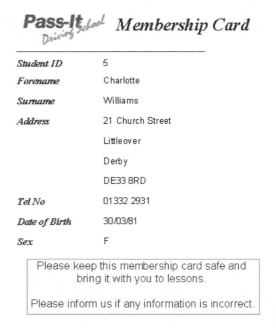

Figure 13.7

15. Save the report as **Membership Card Report**. Test the report for different Student IDs.

▶ Report 2: Instructors' Timetable Report

We are going to set up a report showing all the instructors' timetables for a particular date. We will base this report on the query called **Full Details by Date Query** set up in Chapter 8.

This report introduces you to grouping data in reports. We need to group together all the lessons for instructor number 1, then instructor number 2 and so on. If you want to group data, it is easier to use the Report Wizard rather than AutoReport.

1. At the Database Window, click on **Reports** and click on **New**.

2. Click on **Report Wizard** and select **Full Details by Date Query** from the list. Click on **OK** (see Figure 13.8).

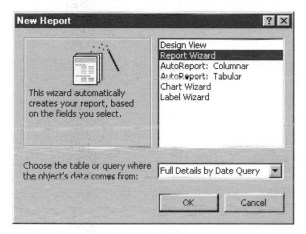

Figure 13.8

3. Click on each of these fields in turn then click on the **single arrow** (>) to add the fields. **Student_Forename, Student_Surname, Instructor ID, Start Time, Length of Lesson**. Click on **Next**.

4. The next dialogue box asks how you want to view your data. Click on **by Lesson**. Click on **Next** (see Figure 13.9).

5. When asked do you want to add any grouping levels, click on **Instructor ID** to group by instructor and click on the arrow icon (>). Click on **Next** (see Figure 13.10).

6. Sort by **Start Time**. Click on **Next**

7. Click on **Align Left 1** and click on **Next**.

8. Click on **Corporate** and click on **Next**.

9. Call it **Instructors' Timetable Report** and click on **Finish**.

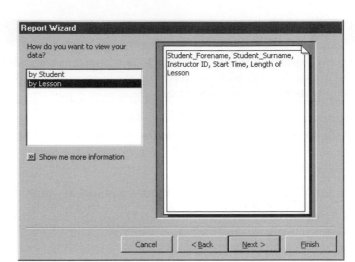

Figure 13.9

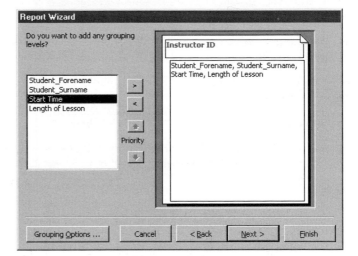

Figure 13.10

10. Enter the date 30/07/00 when prompted.

The report should look like the one in Figure 13.11.

We can see that the output is grouped by instructor, but it is rather unsatisfactory because:

⚹ the instructors' names are not on the report;

⚹ the date is not on the report;

⚹ the column headings are Student_Forename and Student_Surname.

Instructors' Timetable Report

Instructor ID			1	

Start Time	Student_Forename	Student_Surname	Length of Lesson
08:00	Robert	Brammer	1
09:00	Steven	Jenkins	2
11:00	Mary	Trueman	1
12:00	Victoria	Spencer	3

Instructor ID			2	

Start Time	Student_Forename	Student_Surname	Length of Lesson
12:00	David	Windsor	1

Figure 13.11

Switch to Design View and:

1. Alter the Student Forename column heading in the Instructor ID Header to read **Name**;

2. Delete the Student_Surname column heading by selecting it and pressing the DELETE key;

3. If the Field List is not displayed, click on the **Field List** icon or click on **View, Field List**;

4. Drag **Date** from the Field List on to the Report Header;

5. Select the new Date control. Click on the **Properties** icon and click on the **Format** tab. Set the first (**Format**) property to **Long Date** (see Figure 13.12).

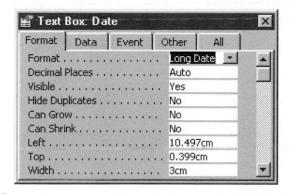

Figure 13.12

6. Select the label for the **Date** field and delete it by pressing the DELETE key.

7. Drag both the **Instructor_Forename** and **Instructor_Surname** from the Field List on to the Instructor ID Header.

8. Select the labels for these fields and delete them.

9. Move the title and add a company logo as before.

The report looks like that in Figure 13.13 in Design View.

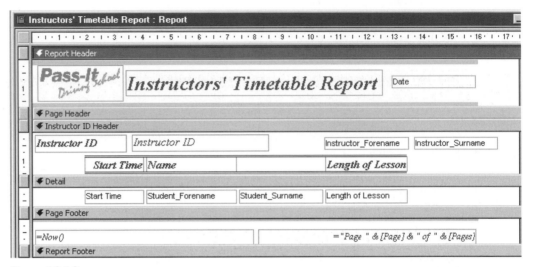

Figure 13.13

10. Switch to Print Preview mode. Enter the date   30/07/00 . The report should look like the one in Figure 13.14.

Pass-It *Driving School* *Instructor's Timetable Report*   30 July 2000

Instructor ID		*1*	Doug	Jones

Start Time Name			*Length of Lesson*
08:00 Robert	Brammer		1
09:00 Steven	Jenkins		2
11:00 Mary	Trueman		1
12:00 Victoria	Spencer		3

Instructor ID		*2*	Arnold	Batchelor

Start Time Name			*Length of Lesson*
12:00 David	Windsor		1

Figure 13.14

Putting each instructor on a new page

Sometimes you might want each section of a report on a new page. For example in the above report, you may want the timetable for each instructor printed on a separate page, one to give to each instructor.

To force a new page in a report:

1. Load the report in **Design View**. We need an **Instructor ID Footer**. Click on the **Sorting and Grouping Icon** or click on **View, Sorting and Grouping** (see Figure 13.15).

Figure 13.15

2. In the dialogue box that appears, click on **Instructor ID** and change **Group Footer** to **Yes** (see Figure 13.16).

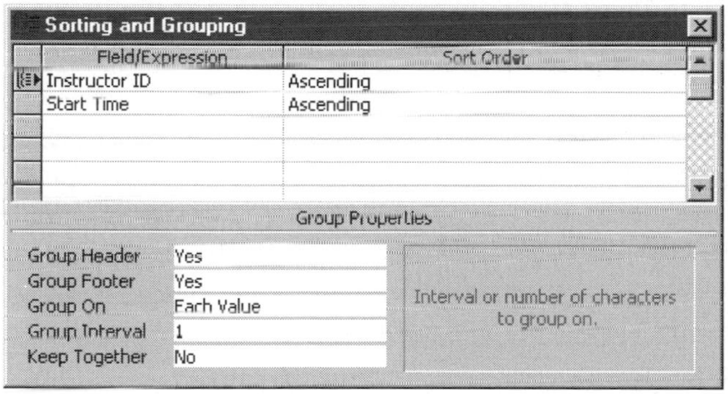

Figure 13.16

A blank **Instructor ID Footer** has now appeared below the Detail section (see Figure 13.17).

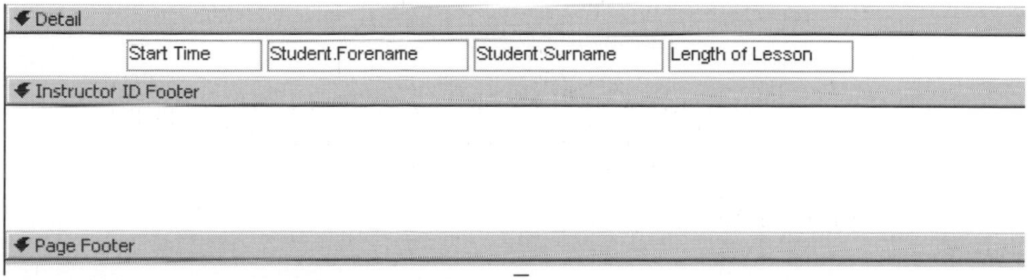

Figure 13.17

3. Click in the Instructor ID Footer.

4. Click on the **Properties** icon or click on **View, Properties**.

5. Click on the **Format** tab and set the **Force New Page** row to **After Section** (see Figure 13.18).

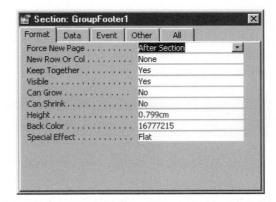

Figure 13.18

6. Switch to **Print Preview** mode to check that each instructor is on a new page.

> **Note**
>
> The driving school logo and details should be in the Page Header and not the Report Header so that they appear on every page. Enlarge the Page Header, then select the contents of the Report Header and drag them into the Page Header.

Macros

A **macro** contains a series of Access instructions linked together as a single command. Macros are used to make it easier to perform common tasks. Macros can be run by clicking a button, e.g. on a form or a switchboard or can be triggered by some event, such as closing a form.

The Pass It system consists so far of the three forms to manage information about the Students, Instructors and Lessons Bookings and a number of reports.

In this chapter you will learn how to use a few simple macros to begin to automate the system. Macros will be dealt with in more detail later.

▶ Macro 1: A macro to open the Student Form

1. At the database window click on **Macros** and click on **New**.

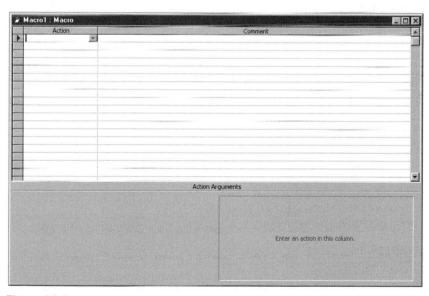

Figure 14.1

The Macro window opens as shown in Figure 14.1. It consists of an Action column from which you choose the actions and a Comments column where you can add comments to remind you of each function.

2. Click on the drop down arrow in the **Action** column and click on **OpenForm** (see Figure 14.2).

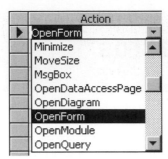

Figure 14.2

You now need to choose which form to open in the Action Arguments section (see Figure 14.3).

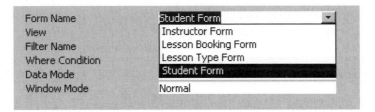

Figure 14.3

3. Click on the **Form Name** box in the Action Arguments and click on **Student Form** from the drop down list as shown in Figure 14.3.

The **View** box will be set by default to **Form** and **Window Mode** to **Normal** as shown in Figure 14.4.

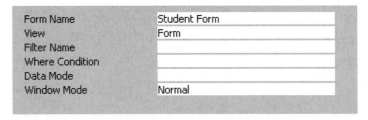

Figure 14.4

4. Close the Macro Window and save as **Student macro**.

5. At the Database Window, test the macro by clicking on the Run icon.

Macros can have more than one action. When you open a form, you may want to add a new student. We can edit the macro to open the form with a new blank record.

6. Open the **Student** macro in Design View. In the second row of the Actions column select **GotoRecord** from the drop down list (see Figure 14.5).

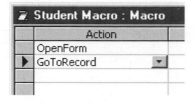

Figure 14.5

7. In the arguments section set **Record** to **New** (see Figure 14.6).

Object Type	
Object Name	
Record	New
Offset	

Figure 14.6

8. Save the macro. Go back to the Database Window and test that it works.

Macro 2: Set up another macro called **Instructor Macro** to open the **Instructor Form** in the same way.

Macro 3: Set up another macro called **Lesson Macro** to open the **Lesson Booking Form** in the same way.

 Macro 4: Setting up a message box

Most software packages have an About message box giving details of the company or developer. This can be set up using a macro.

1. At the database window click on **Macros** and click on **New**.

2. Select **MsgBox** in the Action column.

3. In the Action Arguments, click on the **Message** box and type Created by C.A. Robins © 2001 .

4. In the **Beep** box select **Yes**.

5. In the **Type** box select **Information**.

6. In the **Title** box type Pass-It Driving School (see Figure 14.7).

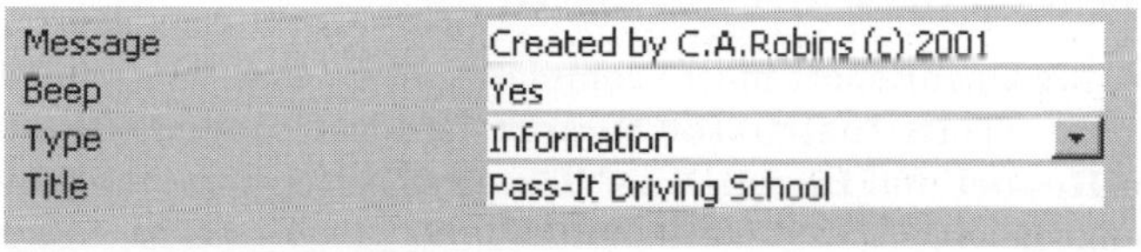

Message	Created by C.A.Robins (c) 2001
Beep	Yes
Type	Information
Title	Pass-It Driving School

Figure 14.7

7. Save the macro as **About** and test it (see Figure 14.8).

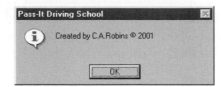

Figure 14.8

Macros are developed further in Chapter 17.

Using macros to customise a Front End

You can use macros to pull your system together an produce an automated front end. You may use this as an alternative to the switchboard shown in Chapter 15.

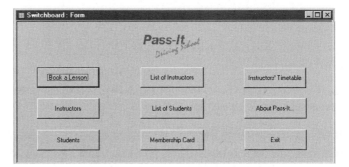

Figure 14.9

1. To set up a front end, at the database window, click on **Forms**. Click on **New**. Click on **Design View**. Click on **OK**. This produces a blank grey form. you will need to enlarge it.

2. Use the **CommandButton** icon in the Toolbox and add command buttons to run the macros to open the **Student**, **Instructor** and **Lesson Booking** forms. You will have to click on **Miscellaneous** and select **Run Macro**. Set the text for the buttons as shown.

3. Add another button to run the **About** Macro. Set the text to **About Pass-It...**

4. Set up another command button. Click on **Application**. Click on **Quit Application** and set the text to **Exit**.

5. Using the OpenReport macro command set up macros to run the following reports **Instructor Report**, **Student Report**, **Membership Card Report** and **Instructors' Timetable Report**. Complete the form as shown.

6. Refer to the tricks and tips section, tip number 42, to set up a macro called **autoexec** to load this form automatically when the file is opened.

Adding a switchboard

In the previous chapters you have designed the tables, queries, forms and reports that go to make up the Pass-It system.

All these options need to be available from a menu that loads when you start up your system. This is sometimes known as the front end or in Access the switchboard (see Figure 15.1).

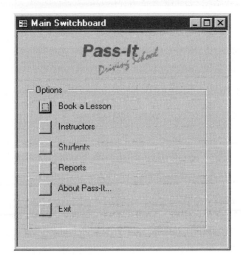

Figure 15.1

In this chapter we look at creating the switchboard shown above.

The switchboard will need to be able to:

- open the Lesson Booking Form to find out lesson details or to book a lesson;

- open the Student Form to find out student details;

- open the Instructor Form to find out instructor details;

- produce a list of instructors (Instructor Report);

- produce a list of students (Student Report);

- produce a membership card (Membership Card Report);

- produce a timetable for an instructor (Instructors' Timetable Report);

- run the About (message box) macro;

- exit from the system.

To fit on all these options, it is best to use two switchboards. One switchboard will link to the reports; the main switchboard will link to the other options. The switchboards will link as shown in Figure 15.2.

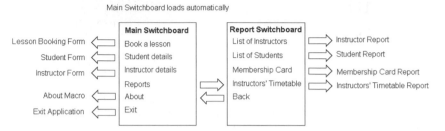

Figure 15.2

There is a switchboard manager wizard to help you set up a switchboard.

Creating a switchboard with the Switchboard Manager

To set up a switchboard go to the Database Window.

1. In Access 2000, click on **Tools**, **Database Utilities**, **Switchboard Manager**.

    In Access 97, click on **Tools**, **Add-Ins**, **Switchboard Manager**. It will ask if you want to create a switchboard. Click on **Yes** (see Figure 15.3).

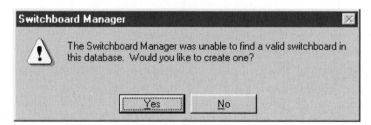

Figure 15.3

This sets up a default switchboard called the Main Switchboard. From here we need to set up another for the reports.

2. At the **Switchboard Manager** dialogue box click on **New**. Enter the name of the second switchboard, **Report Switchboard** and click on **OK** (see Figure 15.4).

3. Select the **Main Switchboard** and click on **Edit**.

4. At the **Edit Switchboard Page,** click on **New** (see Figure 15.5).

5. Edit the Text in the Edit Switchboard Item dialogue box so that it reads **Book a Lesson**.

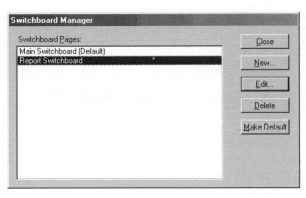

Figure 15.4

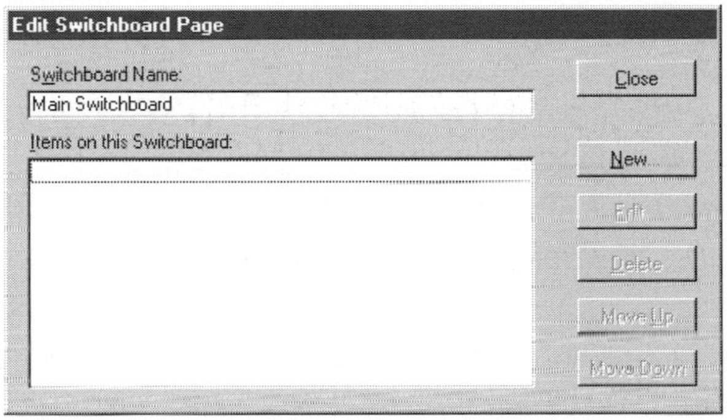

Figure 15.5

6. Click on **Open Form in Edit Mode** from the drop down in the **Command** box.

7. Click on **Lesson Booking Form** in the **Form** box. Click on **OK** (see Figure 15.6).

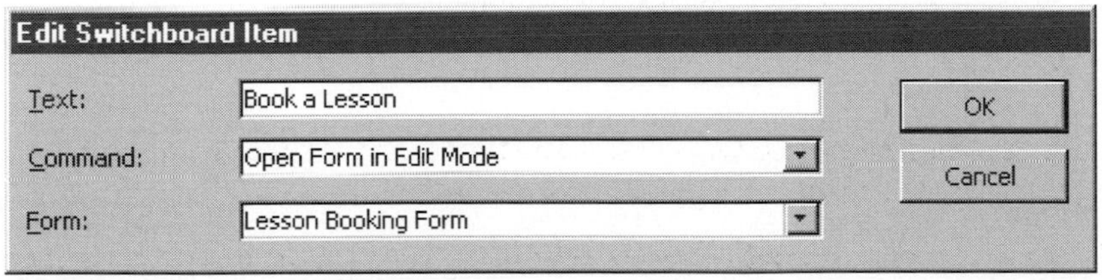

Figure 15.6

These steps set up the first button on our switchboard with the text Book A Lesson. When you click the button it will open the Lesson Booking Form.

There are many options at this stage. It is worth exploring the different options (see Figure 15.7).

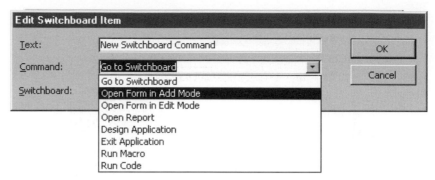

Figure 15.7

We will now continue to set up the other buttons on the switchboard.

8. Click on **New** to set up another Switchboard item. The text should be **Instructors** Click on **Open Form in Edit Mode** in the **Command** box. Select **Instructor Form**. Click on **OK**.

9. Click on **New** to set up another Switchboard item. The text should be **Students** Click on **Open Form in Edit Mode** in the **Command** box. Select **Student Form.** Click on **OK**.

10. Click on **New** to set up another Switchboard item. The text should be **Reports**. Click on **Go to Switchboard** in the **Command** box. Select **Report Switchboard**. Click on **OK**.

11. Click on **New** to set up another Switchboard item. The text should be **About Pass-It...** Click on **Run Macro** in the **Command** box. Select **About**.

12. Click on **New** to set up another Switchboard item. The text should be **Exit**. Click on **Exit Application** in the **Command** box (see Figure 15.8).

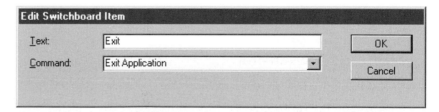

Figure 15.8

13. The **Edit Switchboard Page** will now appear. You can use this page to edit the switchboard, delete or add new items. You can also move items up and down the switchboard list (see Figure 15.9).

14. You have now set up a switchboard with six options. Click on **Close** twice to go back to the Database Window.

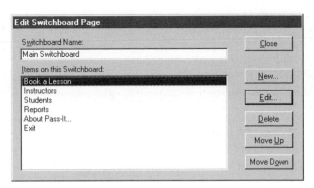

Figure 15.9

There will now be a new form listed called **Switchboard** (see Figure 15.10).

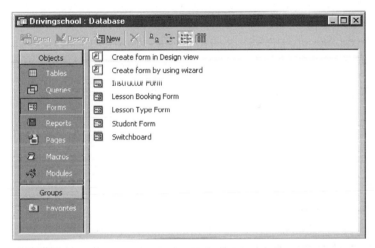

Figure 15.10

15. Open the **Switchboard** form. It will look something like that shown in Figure 15.11.

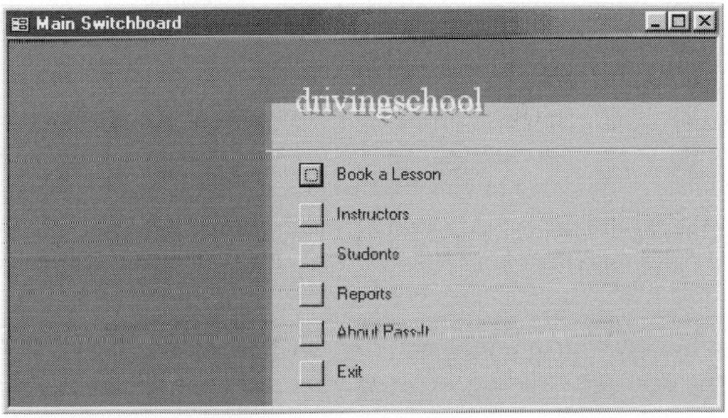

Figure 15.11

Test that each of the buttons works. The Report Switchboard will not yet be available.

 Customising the switchboard

1. Open the switchboard in Design View so that it can be edited like any other form. You will notice that there are eight buttons even though we only set up six of them. (Do not delete the bottom two buttons.) You will also notice that the label for each button is not shown.

2. Select the title and delete it.

3. There are two green rectangles, one dark grey rectangle and a sunken line. Select them and delete them.

4. Insert your logo near the top of the form in the usual way (see Figure 15.12).

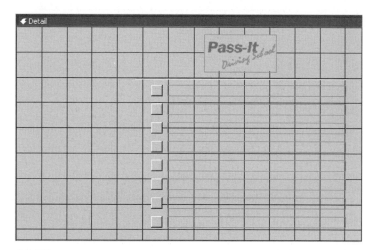

Figure 15.12

5. Highlight all the controls by pressing CTRL and A. Move all the controls to the left of the form and then make the form narrower. It will help to reduce the size of the button labels (see Figure 15.13).

6. From the Toolbox click on the Rectangle icon and draw a rectangle around the six options. Add a label **Options**, you will need to set its **Back Style** property to **Normal** and its background colour to grey.

The completed switchboard is shown in Figure 15.14.

Figure 15.13

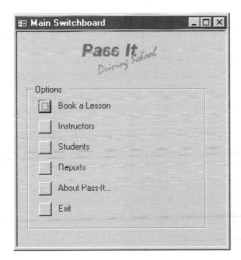

Figure 15.14

Adding the Report Switchboard

1. At the database window, load the **Switchboard Manager** again. Click on **Report Switchboard** and click on **Edit**.

2. Click on **New** to set up another Switchboard item. The text should be **List of Instructors**. Select **Open Report** in the **Command** box. Select **Instructor Report**. Click on **OK** (see Figure 15.15).

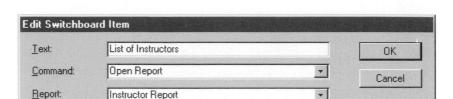

Figure 15.15

3. Click on **New** to set up another Switchboard item. The text should be **List of Students**. Select **Open Report** in the **Command** box. Select **Student Report**. Click on **OK**.

4. Click on **New** to set up another Switchboard item. The text should be **Membership Card**. Select **Open Report** in the **Command** box. Select **Membership Card Report**. Click on **OK**.

5. Click on **New** to set up another Switchboard item. The text should be **Instructors' Timetable**. Select **Open Report** in the **Command** box. Select **Instructors' Timetable Report**. Click on **OK**.

6. Click on **New** to set up the final Switchboard item. The text should be **Back**. Click on **Go to Switchboard** in the **Command** box. Select **Main Switchboard**.

The Edit Switchboard Page now appears as in Figure 15.16.

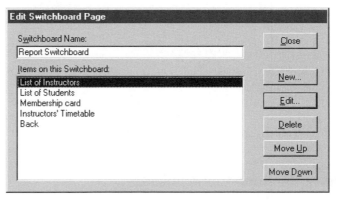

Figure 15.16

7. Click **Close** twice to exit from the Switchboard Manager.

8. At the Database Window, click on Forms to open the Switchboard and test that all the buttons on both switchboards work. The Report Switchboard will look the one shown (see Figure 15.17).

If you go back to the Database Window and click on **Tables**, you will see that an additional table called **Switchboard Items** has been set up. If you open the table, you can see that it controls the switchboard (see Figure 15.18).

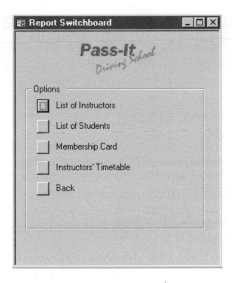

Figure 15.17

SwitchboardID	ItemNumber	ItemText	Command	Argument
1	0	Main Switchboard	0	Default
1	1	Book a Lesson	2	Lesson Form
1	2	Instructors	3	Instructor Form
1	3	Students	3	Student Form
1	4	Reports	1	2
1	5	About Pass-It...	7	Message
1	6	Exit	6	
2	0	Report Switchboard	0	
2	1	List of Instructors	4	Instructor Report
2	2	List of Students	4	Student Report
2	3	Membership Card	4	Membership Card Rep
2	4	Instructors' Timetable	4	Instructors' Timetable
2	5	Income Report	4	Income Report
2	6	Back	1	1
0	0		0	

Record: I◄ ◄ | 1 | ► ►I ►* | of 14

Figure 15.18

This table can be used to edit the switchboard text.

Setting the Startup options

We want the switchboard to load automatically when the file is opened.
One way of doing this is to use **Tools, Startup** from the menu.

Set it up as follows:

1. At the Database Window, click on **Tools, Startup** to load the **Startup**
   dialogue box (see Figure 15.19).

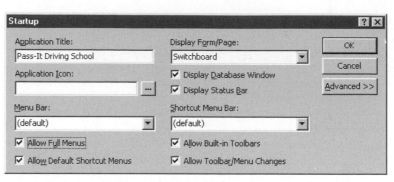

Figure 15.19

2. Click on the **Display Form/Page** drop down arrow and select **Switchboard**. This is the name of the form you want to load on start-up.

3. In the **Application Title** box enter Pass-It Driving School . This is the text that appears at the top of the Access screen.

This dialogue box can also be used to disable the right click, hide the database window and customise the menu bars. **Be careful**. While developing your system you need access to most of these options.

4. Close your system and reload it. Test that the switchboard opens when the system loads and that the application title is displayed.

Using SubForms

In this chapter you will learn how to use SubForms.

In Access systems there will be many instances when it is necessary to see data from related tables on one screen. Using a SubForm is one of a number of ways of doing this.

For example:

In a video loans system you may wish to have membership details on screen alongside details of videos loaned by that member.

In a customer ordering system when a customer phones up with an order enquiry it would be useful to have the customer details and details of their orders on screen.

In the Pass-It Driving School you may wish to view instructor details alongside their lessons as shown in Figure 16.1. The Instructor form is set just to show details of name and ID. A SubForm is added showing details of the lessons for that instructor.

Figure 16.1

Typically in this sort of scenario a main form is set up based on the primary table Instructor with a SubForm based on the Lesson table. This is the simplest way forward but you will see later how to have greater control over the SubForm by basing it on a query.

The following three examples take you through setting up similar uses of SubForms but in slightly different ways. It is worth while practising the different methods to grasp the concepts involved here.

► **Example 1**

The following steps show you how to set up the SubForm as shown above. We will use the wizard to make a start.

1. At the Database Window select **Forms** and click on **New** to bring up the New Form dialogue box.

2. Choose **Form Wizard** and select the **Instructor** table from the drop down. Click **OK** (see Figure 16.2).

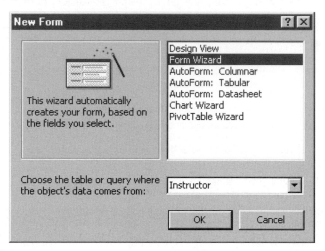

Figure 16.2

3. Select the **Instructor** table and choose the fields **Instructor ID, Surname** and **Forename** from the available fields. Remember you can select the fields one by one by clicking the single arrow. Do not click **Next** yet.

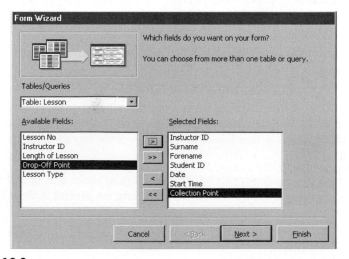

Figure 16.3

4. We now want to select the fields for the SubForm. Select the **Lesson** table from the drop down and add **Student ID, Date, Start Time** and **Collection Point** from the available fields. Click on **Next** (see Figure 16.3).

5. The Form Wizard then asks you 'How do you want to view your data?' Make sure by **Instructor** is selected and **Form with SubForms(s)** is checked and click on **Next**.

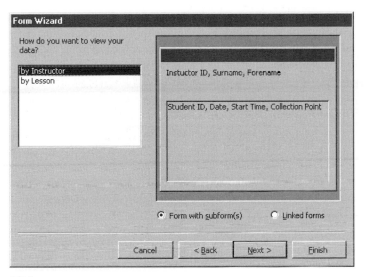

Figure 16.4

6. Select a **Tabular** layout and click on **Next**. Select a **Standard** style and click on **Next**.

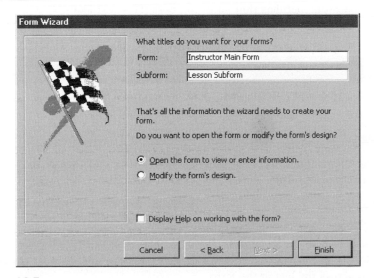

Figure 16.5

7. Name the form **Instructor Main Form** and the SubForm **Lesson Subform**. Click on **Finish** (see Figure 16.5).

Your Main form/SubForm should appear as at the start of the unit. Its appearance will need a little fine-tuning.

8. Go into Design View and double click on the **Form Selector** on the main form to bring up the Properties. Remove the **Scroll Bars, Record Selectors** and **Dividing Lines**.

9. At the Database Window open the **Lesson Subform** in Design View as shown below. From here you can edit the labels, adjust the size of the form and call up the properties of each control by right clicking on the control and selecting properties.

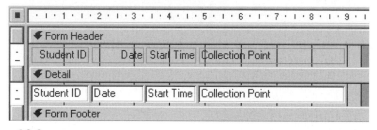

Figure 16.6

10. Format, resize and reposition the form as required and double click on the **Form Selector** and remove the **Navigation buttons**. Save your work.

11. Scroll through the instructor details to view the details of their lessons in the SubForm.

There are a number of ways of setting up SubForms in Access. As ever you choose the methods that suits you best. The next example will take you through setting up a SubForm in a slightly different way.

Example 2

We are going to set up a SubForm on the Student form giving details of each student's lessons.

1. At the Database Window select **Forms** and click on **New**.

2. Set up a student form by choosing **AutoForm: Columnar** and selecting the **Student** table from the drop down.

3. Go into Design View to remove the fields just leaving the student ID, name and address fields. Rearrange as shown in Figure 16.7.

4. Go into Design View and from the toolbox click on the **Subform/Subreport** icon and drag out a rectangle about 13 cm by 2 cm across the foot of the form.

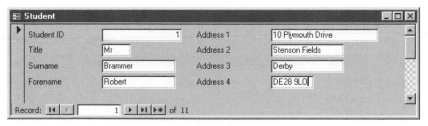

Figure 16.7

5. The SubForm Wizard is displayed. Check **Use existing tables** and click on **Next** (see Figure 16.8).

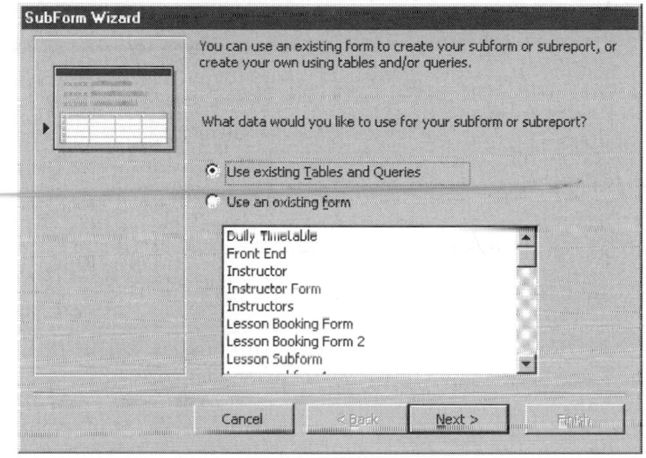

Figure 16.8

6. From the next SubForm Wizard dialogue box, select the **Lesson** table from the drop down and select the fields as shown below. Click on **Next** (see Figure 16.9).

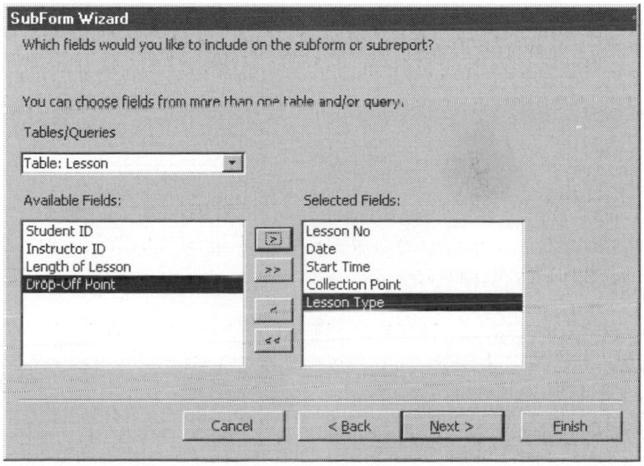

Figure 16.9

7. In the next SubForm Wizard dialogue box the wizard detects the linking fields for you so just click on **Next** (see Figure 16.10).

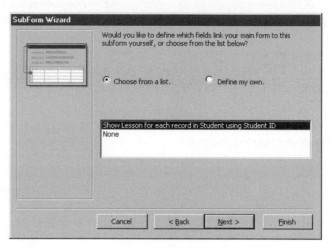

Figure 16.10

8. Call your SubForm **Lesson Details** and click on **Finish**.

9. Save your form as **Student Lesson Details**.

10. Open **Student Lesson Details** form in Form View. You will see that it needs some editing to improve its appearance.

11. Select Design View, double click on the Form Selector of the main form and remove the **Record Selector, Scroll Bars** and **Dividing Lines**.

12. Switch back to Form View. The SubForm appears by default in Datasheet View from which you can easily change the widths of the columns by dragging in/out the columns as required.

13. At the Database Window open the **Lesson Details** SubForm in Design View. Edit the labels and align the text as required.

Your form should look something like Figure 16.11.

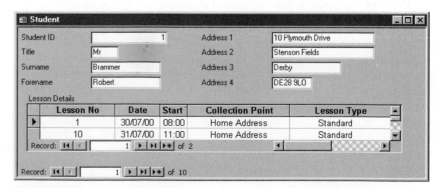

Figure 16.11

NB None of the forms developed in this section so far is part of the Pass-It system. To avoid confusion it is recommended you go into the Database Window and delete the forms **Instructor Main Form, Lesson Details, Lesson Subform** and **Student Lesson Details** by selecting each in turn and pressing DELETE.

▶ Example 3

In the next example we will set up our forms without using the wizards. Very simply the main form and the SubForm are set up separately and then the SubForm is dragged and dropped on to the main form.

1. At the Database Window select **Forms** and click on **New**.

2. Set up a Student form by choosing **AutoForm: Columnar** and selecting the Student table from the drop down.

3. Go into Design View to remove the fields just leaving the name and address. Rearrange as shown in Figure 16.12.

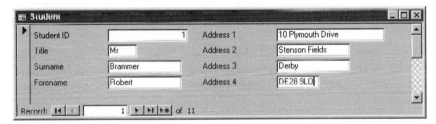

Figure 16.12

4. Save the form as **Student Main Form**.

5. Use the Form Wizard to set up a form based on the **Lesson** table. Select the fields **Lesson No, Date, Start Time, Collection Point** and **Lesson Type**.

6. Select a **Tabular** layout, **Standard** style and call the form **Lesson Details** (you may decide to call it by a different name if you don't want to delete your previous work) (see Figure 16.13).

7. Open the **Student Main Form** in Design View.

8. Press F11 to view the Database Window and drag and drop the icon for the **Lesson Details** form onto the lower area of the Students form (see Figure 16.14).

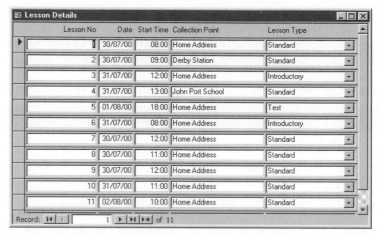

Figure 16.13

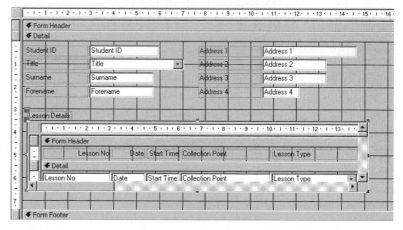

Figure 16.14

If you view the properties for the SubForm by double clicking the form selector you will notice that Access has identified the linking fields in the tables as the Student ID.

The LinkChildFields property contains the name of the linking fields in the Subform and the LinkMasterFields property contains the name of the linking fields in the Main form (see Figure 16.15).

Figure 16.15

9. Click on Form Properties for the **Student Main Form** and remove the Scroll Bars, Record Selectors and Dividing Lines.

10. Position and resize the form as shown in Figure 16.16.

Student			
Student ID	1	Address 1	10 Plymouth Drive
Title	Mr	Address 2	Stenson Fields
Surname	Brammer	Address 3	Derby
Forename	Robert	Address 4	DE28 9LO

Lesson Details

	Lesson No	Date	Start Time	Collection Point	Lesson Type	
▶	1	30/07/00	08:00	Home Address	Standard	
	10	31/07/00	11:00	Home Address	Standard	
*	(AutoNumber)			Home Address		

Record: |◄| ◄| 1 |►|►|►*| of 2

Record: |◄| ◄| 1 |►|►|►*| of 10

Figure 16.16

NB Neither of these forms are needed in the Pass-It system and you may decide to delete them.

Setting up the SubForms in the Pass-It Driving School system

We are going to set up two SubForms in the Pass-It system. Both will be based on queries and both will be accessed and displayed from the main Lesson Booking form at the heart of the system.

When a student rings up to book a lesson the driving school will want to be able to view quickly lesson availability for that day and perhaps for the week for their attached instructor.

This section will also introduce you to using Tab Controls. The Tab Control is selected from the Toolbox as shown in Figure 16.17.

Figure 16.17

These are particularly useful when the information you wish to view is too much for one form.

1. Load the **Lesson Booking** form in Design View.

2. Drag out the right margin and Form Footer to fill the screen.

3. Select the left hand controls and drag them toward the top of the screen.

4. Select the right hand controls and drag to a position below the left hand controls as shown in Figure 16.18. This creates room for our Tab Controls.

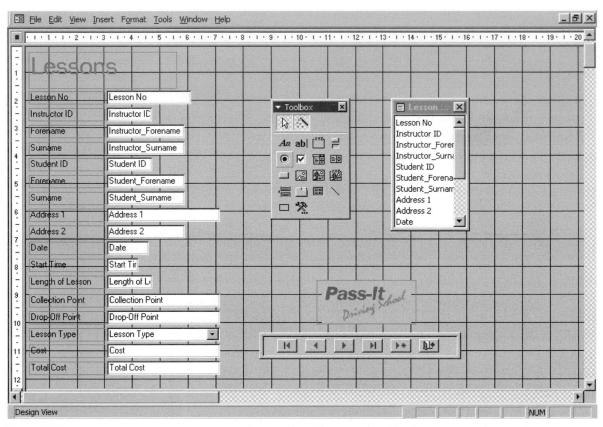

Figure 16.18

5. From the toolbox choose the **Tab Control** and drag out a rectangle across the screen about 12 cm by 7 cm (see Figure 16.19).

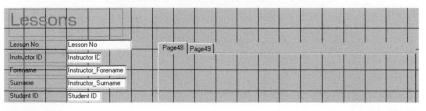

Figure 16.19

The Tab Control will be headed by some page numbers as shown. Double click on the left one and set its caption property to **Daily Timetable** (see Figure 16.20).

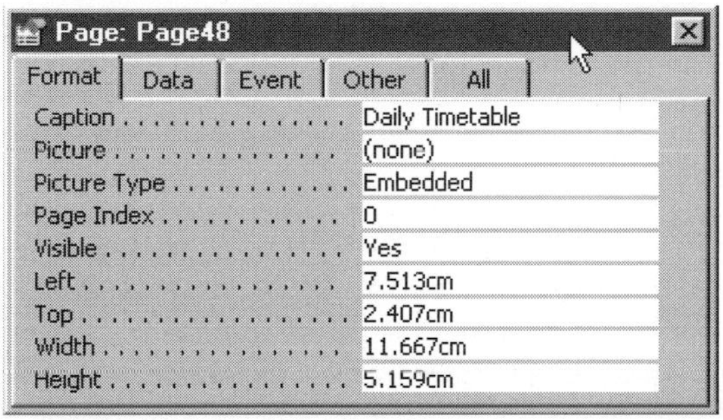

Figure 16.20

6. Double click on the other one and set its caption property to **Weekly Timetable**.

7. We are now going to try and create a little more space. Delete the labels for Instructor Surname and Student Surname.

8. Move the Text boxes for Instructor Surname and Student Surname as shown in Figure 16.21.

9. You will need to align the controls, format the vertical spacing and edit the labels but your form should appear as in Figure 16.21 after a little tinkering.

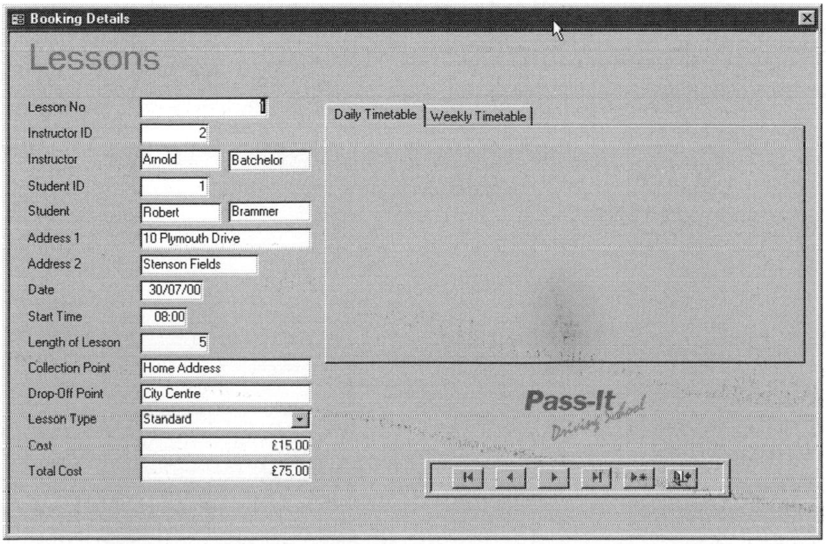

Figure 16.21

Adding the SubForm

1. Load the above form in Design View.

2. From the toolbox click on the **SubForm/SubReport** icon and drag out a rectangle in the Tab control area.

3. The SubForm Wizard opens. Click on **Use existing Tables and Queries** and click on **Next**.

4. In the next window choose the **Full Details Query** and select the available fields as shown in Figure 16.22. Click on **Next**.

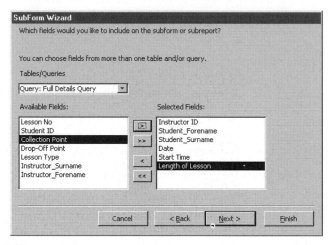

Figure 16.22

5. You then have to define your linking fields. Check **Define my own** and select **Instructor ID** and **Date** from the drop downs as shown in Figure 16.23. Click on **Next**.

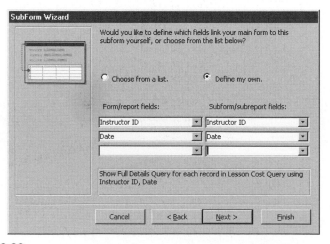

Figure 16.23

6. Call your SubForm **Daily Timetable** (see Figure 16.24).

Figure 16.24

If you now open the Lesson Booking form in Form View you will see it needs resizing and positioning. This can be tricky and take a lot of patience.

There are a number of general steps you can take (see Figure 16.25).

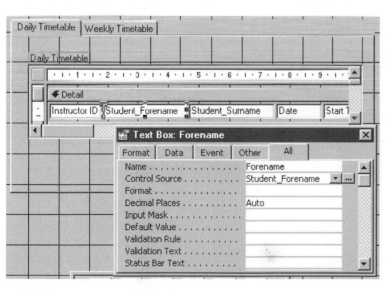

Figure 16.25

1. To change the column headings: In Design View select in turn each text box in the **Detail** area of the SubForm. Right click and choose **Properties**. Click on the **Other** tab and edit the **Name**. Change Student_Forename, Student_Surname, Start Time and Length of Lesson to **Forename, Surname, Start** and **Length**.

2. Using the same technique set the **Text Align** property for **Student_Forename** and **Student_Surname** to **Left**. Set the **Text Align** property for **Length of Lesson** to **Center**.

3. Delete the SubForm label **Daily Timetable**.

4. In Design View, use the ruler to ensure the Tab Control does not go more than 19 cm from the left margin of the form.

5. Go into Form View and adjust the column widths by dragging out or in the column dividers. Right click on the Instructor ID column and select **Hide Columns**.

It will take a little time but your form should eventually appear as in Figure 16.26!

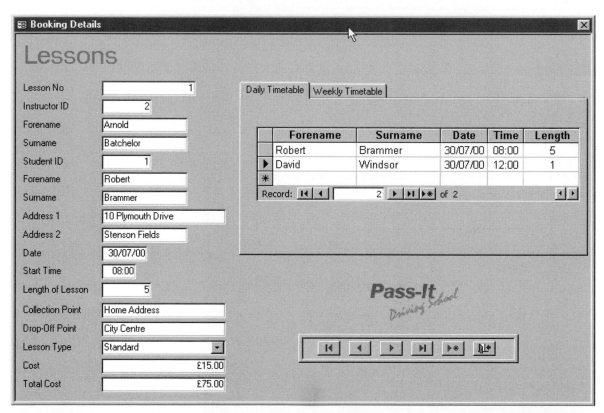

Figure 16.26

Adding the SubForm to display the Weekly Timetable

The process is nearly exactly the same as for the Daily Timetable but you need to base the form on a different query.

You will need to work on the second Tab Control called Weekly Timetable. Drag out a SubForm as before and base it on the **Next Weeks Lessons Query** set up in Chapter 8.

Use the fields **Instructor ID, Student_Forename, Student_Surname, Date, Start Time** and **Length of Lesson** as before.

When you link the fields in the SubForm, only link the **Instructor ID** and *not* the Date.

Again you will need to format, resize and reposition the SubForm (see Figure 16.27).

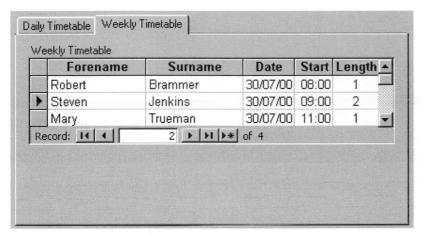

Figure 16.27

To test the new SubForm you will need to adjust the dates in your table or adjust the time clock on your PC.

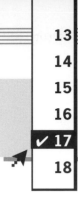

Setting up search and sort options

The user of the Pass-It Driving School will often need to quickly search and sort through records of Bookings, Students and Instructors.

In this chapter we will add user options to search and sort data. A further option will be added to cancel a lesson. The chapter also includes an option to deal with the scenario when a student phones to book a lesson and cannot remember their ID.

To add these options we will need to add a further Tab Control.

Setting up a new Tab Control

1. Open the **Lesson Booking Form** in Design View.

2. Select the **Tab Control Page** and from the menu choose **Insert, Tab Control Page**. Access adds another Tab Control with a Page Number.

3. Double click on the new Tab Control and in the Property sheet set the **Name** property to **Search Options**. Save your new **Lesson Booking** form. It should appear as in Figure 17.1.

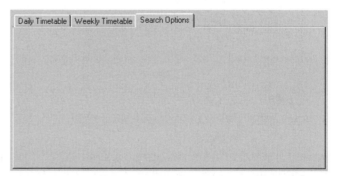

Figure 17.1

Adding filters

It is possible to filter data displayed in a form to display only the lessons with a particular student or only the lessons on a certain date.

We will set up a Command Button on the new Tab Control Page to run a macro to run a filter.

1. Create a new query based on the Lesson Table. Add all the fields from the table.

2. Type [Enter the ID number] into the Criteria row of the Student ID column of the QBE grid.

3. Save the query as **Student Lesson Query**.

4. Create a new macro. In the action column select **ApplyFilter**. In the Action Arguments set the **Filter Name** to **Student Lesson Query**.

5. Save the macro as **Search by Student** (Do not run the macro at this stage.)

6. Open the **Lesson Booking Form** in **Design View**. Click on the **Search Options** Tab. From the Toolbox add a Command Button to the Tab.

7. In the Command Button Wizard window choose the **Miscellaneous** category, select **Run Macro** and click on **Next**.

8. In the next window choose the **Search by Student** macro and click on **Next**.

9. Select the Text option in the next window and set it to read **Filter by Student**. Click on **Next** and click **Finish** (see Figure 17.2).

Figure 17.2

10. Go into **Form View** and test the button. You will be asked the Student ID. Scroll through the records to view this student's lessons.

11. Set up another Command Button to add a **Filter by Date** option. You will first need to set up a macro as before using the **Apply Filter** action based on the **Search on Lesson Date Query**. Call the macro **Search by Date**.

When you use the option to filter data into a sub group of records it is important to restore all records before the next search. We will add a button to the Tab Control to remove the filter.

1. Create a new macro called **Show All Records**. It has just one action **ShowAllRecords**.

2. Add a Command Button to the Tab Control Page to run this macro. The text on the button should read **Show all Records**. Your Tab Control Page should appear as below. You will need to use the **Format, Align** and **Format, Size** menu options to position and size the buttons (see Figure 17.3)

Figure 17.3

Adding sort options

You can sort the data displayed in a form into different orders. For example, you may want to cycle through the records in order of Student Id, Lesson Number or by Date.

We will set up a macro to sort the records and then use a Command Button to run the macro. The following steps take you through setting up the **Sort by Lesson** option.

1. Create a new macro. In the Action column select **GoToControl**. In the Action Arguments set the **Control Name** to **Lesson No**.

2. In the Action column select **Run Command**. In the Action arguments select **Sort Ascending** from the drop down arrow.

3. Save the macro as **Sort Lesson**.

4. Open **Lesson Booking Form** in **Design View**. Click on the **Search Options** tab. Use the Command Button wizard to add a button to run the macro **Sort Lesson** and add the text **Sort by Lesson**.

5. Add further buttons to **Sort by Instructor** and **Sort by Student** (see Figure 17.4).

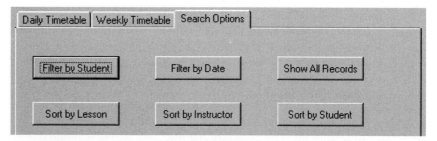

Figure 17.4

6. Go into Form View and test that the buttons work.

Adding further options

When a student phones the Pass-It Driving School to book a lesson they quite often forget their Student ID.

The procedure is:

- A student phones the school to book a lesson, the operator clicks on **Book a Lesson** to open the **Lesson Booking Form**.

- The student cannot remember their ID so the operator opens the student form and uses the drop down to find the student's surname and hence their ID.

- The operator will then be able to click a button and Access will place the ID number into the Booking Form.

1. Open the **Lesson Booking Form** in Design View. Click on the **Search Options** Tab and use the Command Button Wizard to add a button to open the **Student Form**. Set the text on the button to **Find Student**.

2. Save the form and test the button opens the **Student Form**.

3. The Student form is already set up with a combo box to select the student. We need to create a macro to paste these details into the **Lesson Booking Form**.

4. Create a new macro. The Actions are as follows:

GoToControl	Control Name **Student ID**	
RunCommand	Command **Copy**	
Close	Object Type **Form**	Object Name **Student Form**
Open Form	Form **Lesson Booking Form**	View **Form**
GoToControl	Control Name **Student ID**	
RunCommand	Command **Paste**	

5. Save the macro as **Select Student**.

6. Load the Student Form in Design View and add a button to run this macro. Label the button **Select Student** (see Figure 17.5).

When you test this procedure you will find that the system places the ID into the Booking Form but you then have to press return to activate the form. This can be avoided by these simple steps.

1. Create a new macro called **Update** with the single action **Run Command** and argument **Refresh Page**.

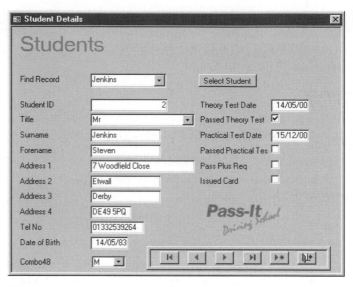

Figure 17.5

2. Open the Lesson Booking Form in Design View and right click on the Student ID field to display its properties.

3. Click on the Event Tab and set its On Change property to run the macro called Update.

The Cancel Booking option

Often students will phone up to cancel a lesson. We need to add an option for the user to be able to cancel bookings.

Use the Command Button Wizard to set up a button based on the Category: **Record Operations** and the Action: **Delete Record**. Set the text on the button to **Cancel Booking**.

Save the **Lesson Booking** form. Your finished Tab Control for the Search Options should appear as in Figure 17.6.

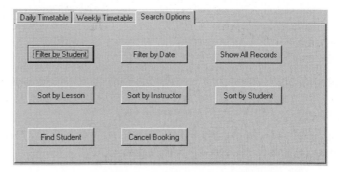

Figure 17.6

Calculations in reports

▶ Adding data in a report

The **Lesson Cost Query** in Chapter 8 set up a calculated field to
work out the cost of each lesson.

We want to set up a report to add up the total income for each instructor.

1. Create a new report based on the **Lesson Cost Query** using the
   Report Wizard.

2. Use the arrow icon (>) to select these fields in this order: **Instructor
   ID, Instructor_Forename, Instructor_Surname,
   Student_Forename, Student_Surname, Date and TotalCost.**
   Click on **Next** (see Figure 18.1).

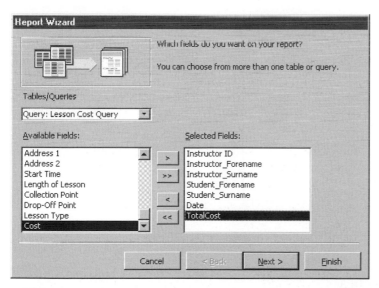

Figure 18.1

3. If the records are not grouped by **Instructor ID** by default, click on
   Instructor ID and click on the right arrow. (>) Then click on **Next** (see
   Figure 18.2).

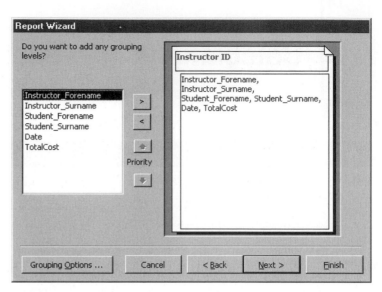

Figure 18.2

4. Sort by Date and click on **Next** (see Figure 18.3).

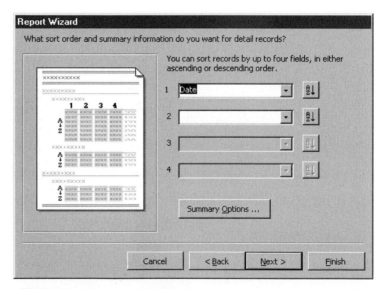

Figure 18.3

5. Click on **Align Left** 1 and click on **Next** (see Figure 18.4).

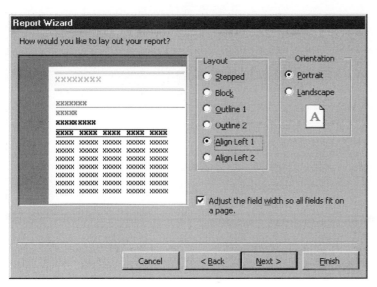

Figure 18.4

6. Click on **Corporate** and click on **Next** (see Figure 18.5).

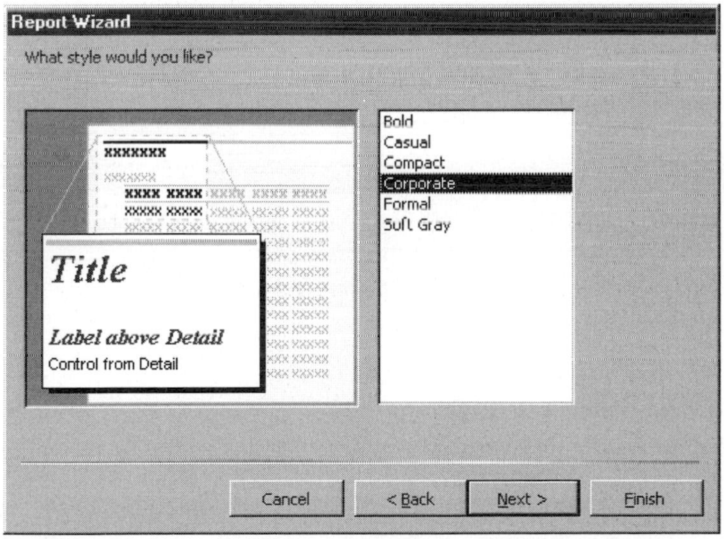

Figure 18.5

7. Call it **Income Report** and click on **Finish**.

The report opens and is shown in Figure 18.6.

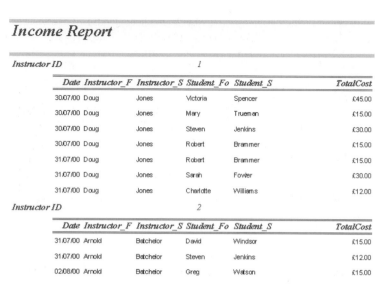

Income Report

	Date	Instructor_F	Instructor_S	Student_Fo	Student_S	TotalCost
Instructor ID			1			
	30.07/00	Doug	Jones	Victoria	Spencer	£45.00
	30.07/00	Doug	Jones	Mary	Trueman	£15.00
	30.07/00	Doug	Jones	Steven	Jenkins	£30.00
	30.07/00	Doug	Jones	Robert	Brammer	£15.00
	31.07/00	Doug	Jones	Robert	Brammer	£15.00
	31.07/00	Doug	Jones	Sarah	Fowler	£30.00
	31.07/00	Doug	Jones	Charlotte	Williams	£12.00
Instructor ID			2			
	31.07/00	Arnold	Batchelor	David	Windsor	£15.00
	31.07/00	Arnold	Batchelor	Steven	Jenkins	£12.00
	02/08/00	Arnold	Batchelor	Greg	Watson	£15.00

Figure 18.6

We want to add up the total cost for each instructor.

8. Click on the **Design View** icon or click on **View, Design View** to switch to **Design View**.

9. Click on the **Sorting and Grouping** icon or click on **View, Sorting and Grouping** (see Figure 18.7).

Figure 18.7

10. Add an **Instructor ID Group Footer** by selecting **Instructor ID** and setting **Group Footer** to **Yes**. Close the dialogue box (see Figure 18.8).

Figure 18.8

11. Click on the **Text Box icon** in the Toolbox and drag out a Text Box in the Instructor ID Group Footer. It will say something like **Text27** and **Unbound** (see Figure 18.9).

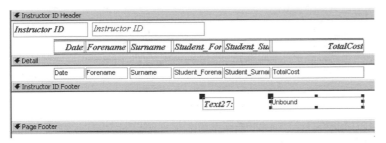

Figure 18.9

12. With the new text box selected, click on the **Properties** icon. Click on the **Data** tab. In the **Control Source** row type in =Sum([TotalCost]) .

NB The fieldname in the square brackets must be exactly the same as the calculated field name set up in Unit 8. There is no space between Total and Cost (see Figure 18.10).

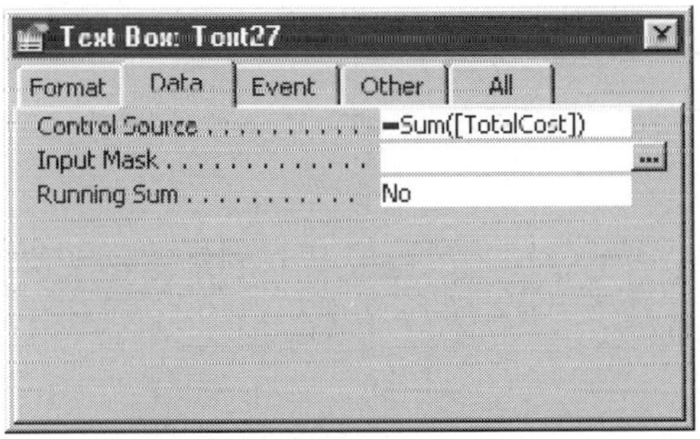

Figure 18.10

13. Still in the Properties window, click on the **Format** tab. In the Format row choose **Currency**. Set the **Font Weight** Property to **Bold** (see Figure 18.11).

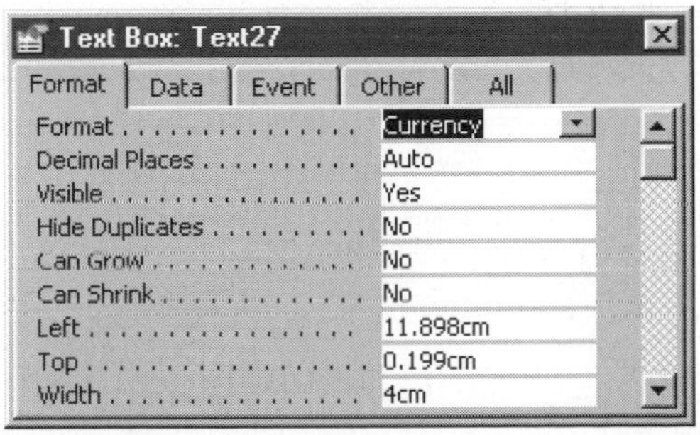

Figure 18.11

14. Close the Properties window.

15. Edit the text in the label of the new text box (Text27) to read **Total** (see Figure 18.12).

▼ Instructor ID Footer

		Total:		=Sum([TotalCost])

Figure 18.12

16. Drag **Instructor Forename** and **Instructor Surname** from the Detail into the Instructor ID Header.

17. Delete the **Instructor Forename** and **Instructor Surname** column headings.

18. Change the Student_Forename column heading to Student. Delete the Student_Surname column heading.

19. Add the company logo as before.

20. Go into Print Preview mode and test the report (see Figure 18.13).

Pass-It Driving School *Income Report*

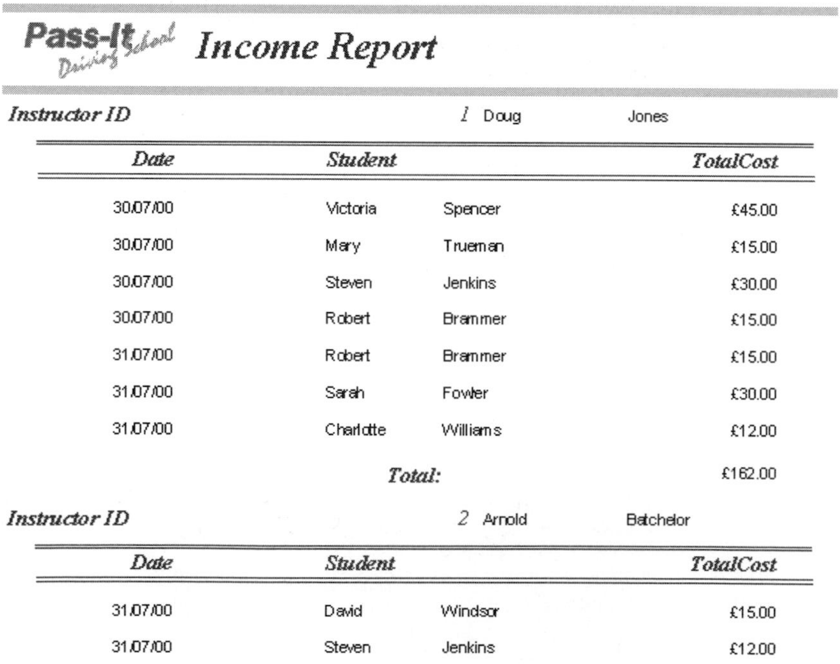

Instructor ID		*1* Doug	Jones	
Date	*Student*			*TotalCost*
30.07/00	Victoria	Spencer		£45.00
30.07/00	Mary	Trueman		£15.00
30.07/00	Steven	Jenkins		£30.00
30.07/00	Robert	Brammer		£15.00
31.07/00	Robert	Brammer		£15.00
31.07/00	Sarah	Fowler		£30.00
31.07/00	Charlotte	Williams		£12.00
		Total:		£162.00

Instructor ID		*2* Arnold	Batchelor	
Date	*Student*			*TotalCost*
31.07/00	David	Windsor		£15.00
31.07/00	Steven	Jenkins		£12.00

Figure 18.13

How to count records in a report

Sometimes you might want to count the number of records in a report. For example in the above report, you may want to know the number of lessons for each instructor.

1. Open the report in Design View.

2. Click on the Text Box icon and add a small text box to the Instructor ID Footer section (see Figure 18.14).

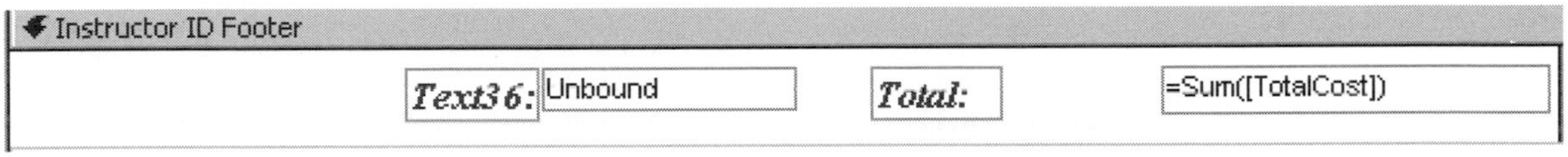

⬥ Instructor ID Footer

Text36: Unbound   *Total:*   =Sum([TotalCost])

Figure 18.14

3. Select the new text box and click on the Properties icon.

4. Click on the **Data** tab and set the Control Source to =Count([TotalCost]) (see Figure 18.15).

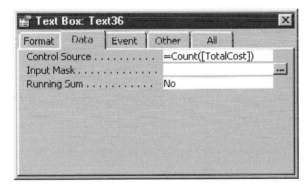

Figure 18.15

5. Edit the text box label so that it says **Count** (see Figure 18.16).

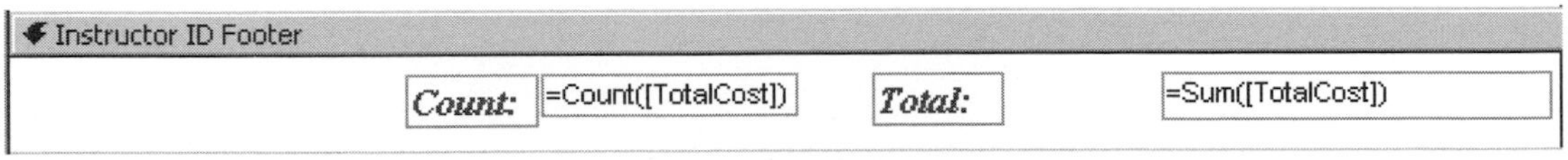

⬥ Instructor ID Footer

Count: =Count([TotalCost])   *Total:*   =Sum([TotalCost])

Figure 18.16

6. Switch the Print Preview to check that the count is correct (see Figure 18.17).

Instructor ID				*1* Doug	Jones	

Date	*Student*		*TotalCost*
30/07/00	Victoria	Spencer	£45.00
30/07/00	Mary	Trueman	£15.00
30/07/00	Steven	Jenkins	£30.00
30/07/00	Robert	Brammer	£15.00
31/07/00	Robert	Brammer	£15.00
31/07/00	Sarah	Fowler	£30.00
31/07/00	Charlotte	Williams	£12.00
Count:	7	*Total:*	£162.00

Figure 18.17

How to get a running total in a report

Sometimes you might want a running total in a report. For example in the above report, you may want the Total to be a running total and give the income for all instructors.

To set the total to be a running total:

1. Load the Report in **Design View**.

2. Select the **Total** control.

3. Click on the **Properties** icon or click on **View, Properties**.

4. Click on the **Data** tab and set the **Running Sum** row to **Over All** (see Figure 18.18).

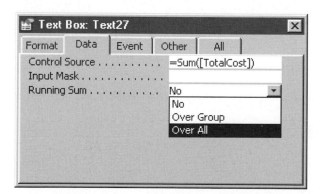

Figure 18.18

5. Close the Properties window and change the label Total to **Running Total**.

6. Switch to Print Preview mode and check that the running total is correct (see Figure 18.19).

Instructor ID			2 Arnold	Batchelor	
Date	*Student*				*TotalCost*
31/07/00	David	Windsor			£15.00
31/07/00	Steven	Jenkins			£12.00
02/08/00	Greg	Watson			£15.00
Count: 3			*Running Total:*		£204.00
Instructor ID			3 Andrew	Smith	
Date	*Student*				*TotalCost*
01/08/00	Michael	Beswood			£25.00
Count: 1			*Running Total:*		£229.00

Figure 18.19

Reports with no records

Some reports have no data in them. For example you might be searching for lessons on a day when none has been booked. It is possible to check if there is no data in a report and give a warning to the user.

1. Set up a macro called **No Data** that displays this message box (see Figure 18.20).

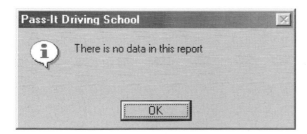

Figure 18.20

The action is **MsgBox** (see Figure 18.21).

Figure 18.21

The arguments are as shown below (see Figure 18.22).

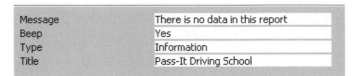

Message	There is no data in this report
Beep	Yes
Type	Information
Title	Pass-It Driving School

Figure 18.22

2. Save the macro and test it.

Attaching a macro to a form or a report

We want to run this macro when we open the Instructors' Timetable Report. We can set this up using the report properties.

3. At the Database Window, click on **Reports**.

4. Select the **Instructors' Timetable Report** and click on **Design**.

5. Click on the **Properties** icon or click on **View, Properties**

The Report properties will be displayed.

6. Click on the **Event** tab (see Figure 18.23).

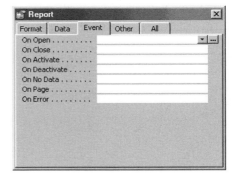

Figure 18.23

You can now select macros to run when the report:

On Open	When the report opens
On Close	When the report closes
On Activate	When the report becomes the active window.
On Deactivate	When the report stops being the active window
On No Data	When the report has no data
On Page	When a page of a report is formatted for printing.
On Error	When there is an error

7. We want the **No data** macro to run when there is no data in the
report so set the **On No Data** property to No data using the drop
down list as shown in Figure 18.24.

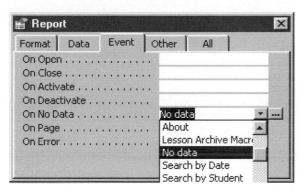

Figure 18.24

8. Save the report and test that the macro works when there is no data
by opening the report and entering a date when you know that there
are no lessons. (The message box actually will appear twice before the
blank report loads.)

9. Attach the No Data macro to the Membership Card report in the
same way.

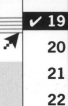
Using action queries

In Chapters 6, 7 and 8 you learned how to use a range of queries to view your data.

In this chapter you will learn how to use action queries. Action queries actually do something to the data in your system by moving it, changing it or deleting it.

At the end of the unit we will update the switchboard to include these features.

There are four types of action query.

- Append query
- Delete query
- Update query
- Make Table Query (not used in the Pass-It Driving School)

Append queries

An append query will take data from one table and add it to another.

In a club membership system you may decide to keep details of members who have not renewed their subscriptions rather than delete their records immediately. An append query will enable you to remove their details from the main membership table and transfer them to a table of, for example, expired memberships.

Similarly in a school or college, at the end of each year you could delete all leavers from the system but it is likely you will need to keep records for a period of time. An append query could be set up to transfer leaver details to a table of leavers.

Delete queries

A delete query will remove records from one or more tables according to set criteria.

In the school or college system above you may decide to keep records of ex-students for three years. At the end of each college year you would remove details of all students who left three or more years ago.

Similarly in a video hire/library loans system details of loans will build up. After a period of time you will need to clear old details from the system.

A delete query can be used to carry out these operations.

Update queries

An update query will make changes to data in one or more tables.

In an ordering system you may decide to reduce the prices of all products by 7.5%. At the end of each year in our school system all students will move up a year from Year 7 to Year 8 and so on.

Update queries allow you to make these changes to the data in your tables automatically.

 Managing lesson details

In the Pass-It Driving School we need our system to handle information about old lessons.

⚹ After a lesson has taken place, we want to move details to a table of old lessons. (**Append query**).

⚹ The details also need removing from the Lesson table. (**Delete query**).

⚹ After a period of a year we will remove them from the Old Lesson table altogether. (**Delete query**).

When working with action queries it is a good idea to make a copy of your lesson table because you are going to be moving and changing the data. Making a copy will save you re-entering data at a later stage.

1. At the Database Window, click on **Tables.** Click on the **Lesson** table and click on **Edit, Copy** or click on the **Copy** icon.

2. At the Database Window, click on **Edit, Paste** or click on the **Paste icon.**

3. Call the new table **Lesson Copy** and click on **Structure and Data.** Click on OK (see Figure 19.1).

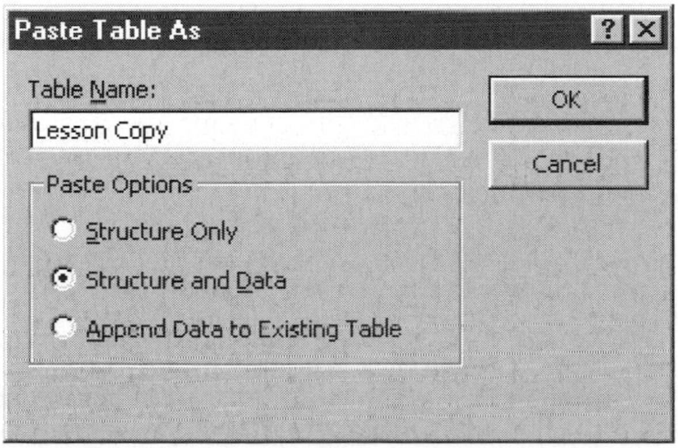

Paste Table As	? X
Table Name:	OK
Lesson Copy	
Paste Options	Cancel
○ Structure Only	
● Structure and Data	
○ Append Data to Existing Table	

Figure 19.1

As action queries are often based on dates that clearly change you will have to edit the lesson dates before you start.

4. Open the **Lesson** table and change the dates as follows.

Hint:

■ Use **Edit, Replace** to change all the lessons for one day at once.

Change all the 01/08/00 lessons to today's date.

Change all the 02/08/00 lessons to tomorrow's date.

Change all the 31/07/00 lessons to yesterday's date.

Change all the 30/07/00 lessons to the date exactly one year ago today.

Append Query to transfer lesson details

We are going to move details of all old lessons from the Lesson table to a table called Old Lesson.

1. At the Database Window, click on **Tables**. Click on the **Lesson** table and click on **Edit, Copy** or click on the **Copy** icon.

2. At the Database Window, click on **Edit, Paste** or click on the **Paste icon.**

3. Call the new table **Old Lesson** and click on **Structure Only.** Click on **OK.**

4. This has created a new empty table called **Old Lesson.** Open this table in **Design View.**

5. Set the Data Type of the **Lesson No** to **Number.** (This is vital. It will not work if you don't do this.)

6. Save the table and close it.

7. At the Database Window, click on **Queries.** Click on **New.** Click on **Simple Query Wizard** Click on **OK.**

8. Select the **Table: Lesson** from the drop down. Click on the double arrow to choose all the fields and then click on **Next.**

9. In the Simple Query Wizard window click on **Next** again.

10. Call the query **Old Lesson Append Query** and click on **Finish.**

11. Open the query in **Design View** and set the Criteria row in the **Date** column to **<Date**().

12. If the Query design toolbar is showing click on the **Query Type** icon and click on **Append Query** or click on **Query, Append Query** (see Figure 19.2).

Figure 19.2

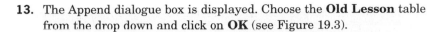

13. The Append dialogue box is displayed. Choose the **Old Lesson** table from the drop down and click on **OK** (see Figure 19.3).

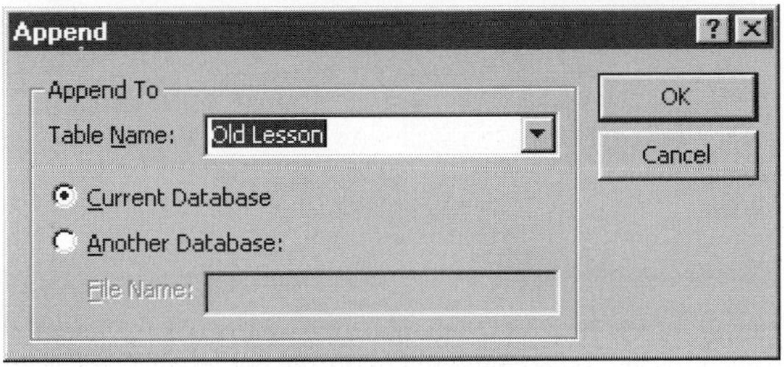

Figure 19.3

Details of the query are then displayed as shown in Figure 19.4.

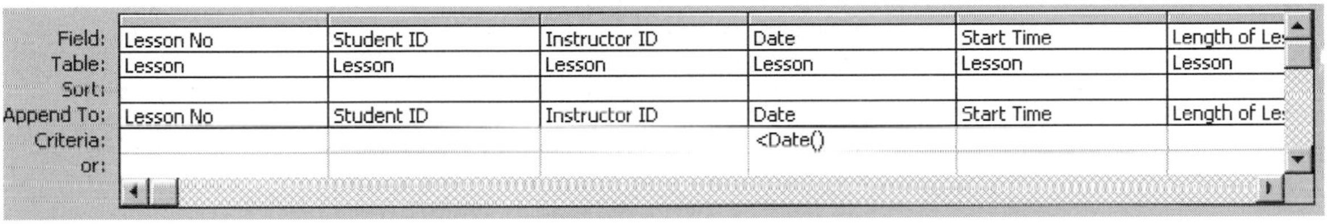

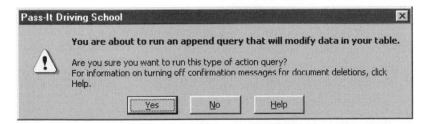

Field:	Lesson No	Student ID	Instructor ID	Date	Start Time	Length of Le
Table:	Lesson	Lesson	Lesson	Lesson	Lesson	Lesson
Sort:						
Append To:	Lesson No	Student ID	Instructor ID	Date	Start Time	Length of Le
Criteria:				<Date()		
or:						

Figure 19.4

14. Save the query and close it.

15. At the Database Window, click on **Open** to run the query.

16. You will be prompted with two warning messages. Click on **Yes** (see Figure 19.5).

Pass-It Driving School

You are about to run an append query that will modify data in your table.

Are you sure you want to run this type of action query?
For information on turning off confirmation messages for document deletions, click Help.

Yes   No   Help

Figure 19.5

17. Click on **Yes** at the second (see Figure 19.6).

18. At the Database Window, open the Old Lesson table. Nine records should have been added.

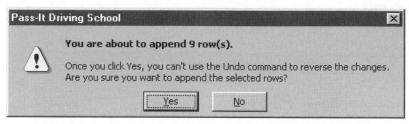

Figure 19.6

Delete Query to remove lesson details from the Lesson table

We now need to clear out the details of all the old lessons which are still stored in the Lesson table. These should be the same nine records.

1. At the Database Window, click on **Queries.** Click on **New.** Click on **Simple Query Wizard** Click on **OK.**

2. Select the **Table: Lesson** from the drop down. Click on the double arrow to choose all the fields and then click on **Next.**

3. In the Simple Query Wizard window click on **Next** again.

4. Call the query **Old Lesson Delete Query.**

5. Open the query in **Design View.** If the Query design toolbar is showing click on the **Query Type** icon and click on **Delete Query** or click on **Query, Delete Query.**

6. Set the Criteria row in the **Date** column to **<Date**() (see Figure 19.7).

Field:	Lesson No	Student ID	Instructor ID	Date	Start Time	Length of Le
Table:	Lesson	Lesson	Lesson	Lesson	Lesson	Lesson
Delete:	Where	Where	Where	Where	Where	Where
Criteria:				<Date()		
or:						

Figure 19.7

7. Save the query and close it.

8. At the database window, click on **Open** to run the query.

9. On running the query you will get the following warning prompts. Just click on **Yes** (see Figures 19.8 and 19.9).

10. At the Database Window, click on **Tables**. Open the **Lesson** table and see that all but two lessons have been deleted.

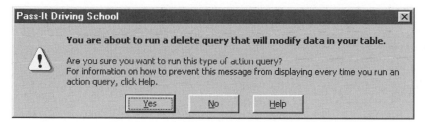

Figure 19.8

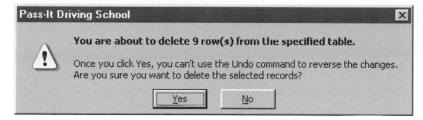

Figure 19.9

Delete Query to clear out lesson details after a year

We wish to delete details of all lessons over a year old.

1. At the Database Window, click on **Queries.** Click on **New.** Click on **Simple Query Wizard** Click on **OK.**

2. Select the **Table: Old Lesson** from the drop down. Click on the double arrow to choose all the fields and then click on **Next.**

3. In the Simple Query Wizard window click on **Next** again.

4. Call the query **Over One Year Delete Query**.

5. Open the query in **Design View**. If the Query design toolbar is showing click on the **Query Type** icon and click on **Delete Query** or click on **Query, Delete Query.**

6. Set the Criteria row in the **Date** column to `<=Date()-365` (see Figure 19.10).

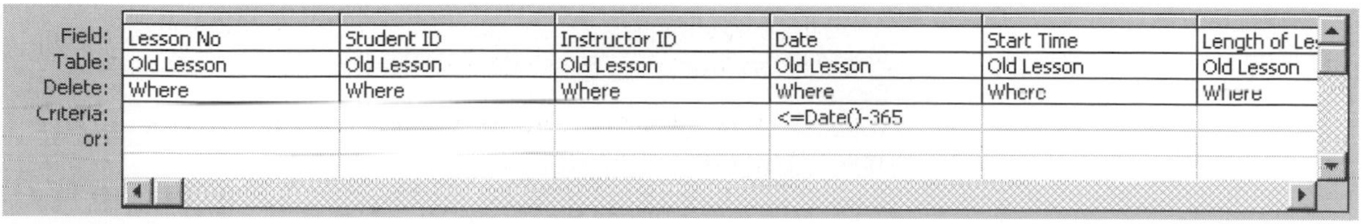

Field:	Lesson No	Student ID	Instructor ID	Date	Start Time	Length of Le
Table:	Old Lesson	Old Lesson	Old Lesson	Old Lesson	Old Lesson	Old Lesson
Delete:	Where	Where	Where	Where	Where	Where
Criteria:				<=Date()-365		
or:						

Figure 19.10

7. Save the query and close it.

8. At the Database Window, click on **Open** to run the query.

9. Click on **Yes** to accept the warning prompts.

10. Open the Old Lesson table to check that the year old lessons have been deleted.

Setting a macro to automate this task

To have to do this every day or every week is an awkward job. We want the user to be able to it at the click of a button. We will design a macro to do this task and later attach it to a button on the menu.

1. In the Database Window click on **Macros** and select **New.**

2. Click on the drop down arrow in the Action column and click on **SetWarnings.** When you do this the Action Arguments section appears in the lower half of the screen. Set the argument to **No** (this will turn off the warning prompts when running the macro).

3. In the Action Column select **OpenQuery** and in the arguments section choose **Old Lesson Append Query** from the drop down.

4. In the Action Column select **OpenQuery** and in the arguments section choose **Old Lesson Delete Query** from the drop down.

5. In the Action Column select **OpenQuery** and in the arguments section choose **Over One Year Delete Query** from the drop down (the queries must be run in this order) (see Figure 19.11).

Action
SetWarnings
OpenQuery
OpenQuery
OpenQuery
▶ MsgBox

Figure 19.11

6. In the Action Column select **MsgBox** and in the arguments section enter the details as shown.

Message	Function completed successfully
Beep	Yes
Type	None
Title	

Figure 19.12

7. Save the macro as **Lesson Archive Macro.**

8. Set your data back to the original state and test the macro moves all the data correctly.

▶ Managing lesson prices

The driving school might occasionally want to increase or decrease its prices. We will use an update query to automate this process.

1. At the database window, click on **Queries.** Click on **New.** Click on **Simple Query Wizard** and then **OK.**

2. Select **Table: Lesson Type** from the drop down. Choose **Cost** from the available fields by clicking on the single arrow and clicking on **Next.**

3. In the next Simple Query Wizard window, ensure that **Detail** is checked and click on **Next** again.

4. Call the query **Price Update Query** and click **Finish.**

5. In **Design View,** click on the **Query Type** icon and then click on **Update Query** or click on **Query, Update Query** (see Figure 19.13).

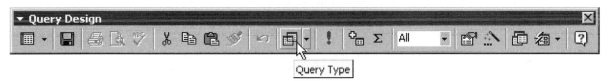

Figure 19.13

6. In the **Update To** row of the **Cost** column of the QBE grid, enter [Cost]*1.05 .

This increases the value by 5 per cent.

To increase by 25 per cent, use the formula [Cost]*1.25 (see Figure 19.14).

To increase by £1, use the formula [Cost]+1 ., etc.

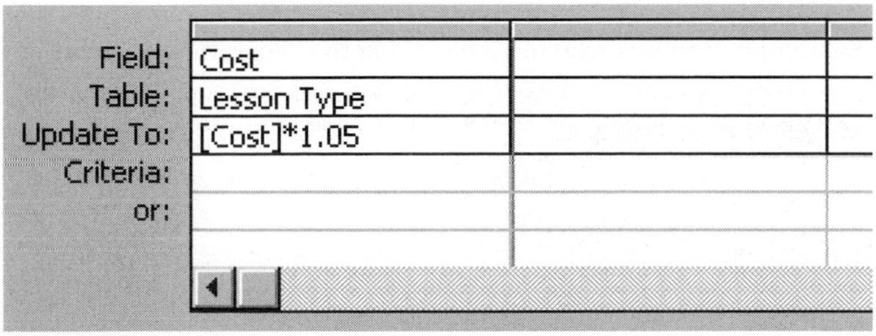

Field:	Cost		
Table:	Lesson Type		
Update To:	[Cost]*1.05		
Criteria:			
or:			

Figure 19.14

7. Click on the **Run** icon on the Query Design toolbar or from the menu select **Query, Run** to update the records (see Figure 19.15).

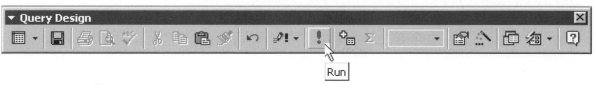

Run

Figure 19.15

8. You will get a warning message. Click on **Yes** (see Figure 19.16).

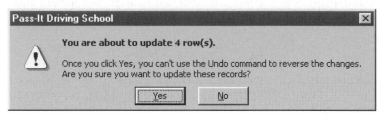

Figure 19.16

9. The original prices were £12.00, £17.00, £15.00 and £25.00. Click on the View icon to check that the prices have been updated to £12.60, £17.85, £15.75 and £26.25.

10. Set up a macro called **Adjust Prices** to remove the warnings and run this query.

> **Note**
> To stop a query after you start it, press ⟨CTRL⟩ + ⟨BREAK⟩.

Further development

Using an append query and two delete queries, set up a macro called **Student Archive Macro** that will:

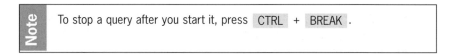 Search for students who have passed both theory and practical tests and do not require the Pass Plus Course and transfer their details to an Old Student table.

Delete students from the Old Student table if at least 30 days have elapsed since they passed their tests.

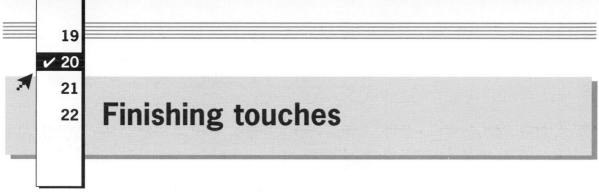

Finishing touches

In this section we will put on the finishing touches to our system including updating the switchboard, tidying up our forms, adding a splashscreen, adding a clock to the switchboard and customising the menu.

▶ Updating the switchboard

After completing the additions to the system in Units 16 to 19, it is necessary to edit the switchboard to include the new options.

1. Open the **Switchboard Manager** and click on **New**. Enter the name of the third switchboard, **System Switchboard** and click on **OK** (see Figure 20.1).

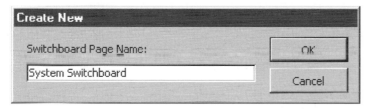

Figure 20.1

2. Select the Main Switchboard and click on **Edit**. Click on **New**. Enter the text **System Functions**. Select the command **Go to Switchboard**. Select the **System Switchboard** (see Figure 20.2).

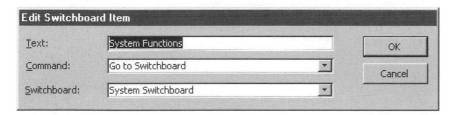

Figure 20.2

3. Use the **Move Up** button so that this option is below the Reports option.

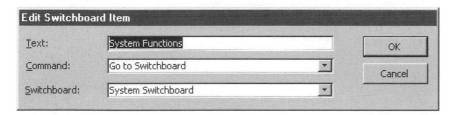

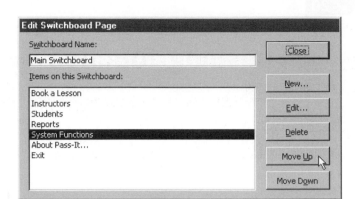

Figure 20.3

4. Click on **Close** and then select the **Report Switchboard**. Click on **Edit**.

5. Add a new option to open the **Income Report** (see Figure 20.4).

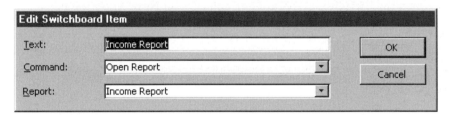

Figure 20.4

6. Use the **Move Up** button so that the Income Report option is above the Back option.

7. Click on **Close** and then select the **System Switchboard**. Click on **Edit**.

8. Add a new option to run the **Lesson Archive Macro** (see Figure 20.5).

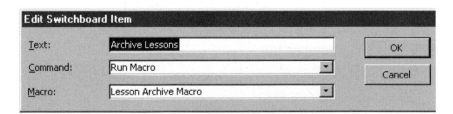

Figure 20.5

9. If you set up the **Student Archive Macro** at the end of Chapter 19, add an option to run it.

10. Add a new option run the **Adjust Prices** macro (see Figure 20.6).

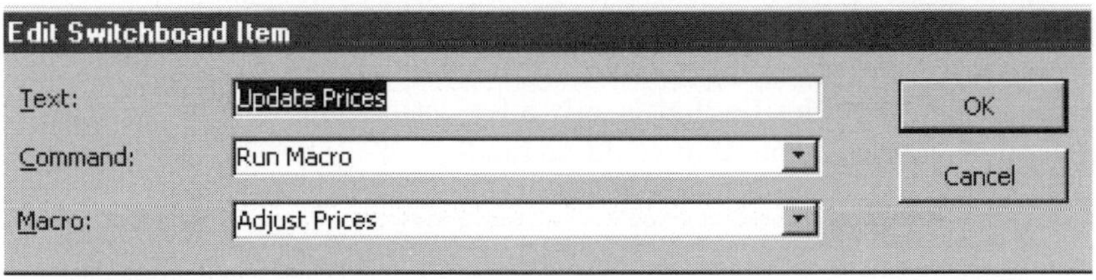

Edit Switchboard Item

Text:	Update Prices	OK
Command:	Run Macro	Cancel
Macro:	Adjust Prices	

Figure 20.6

11. Add a new option named Back to return to the Main Switchboard (see Figure 20.7).

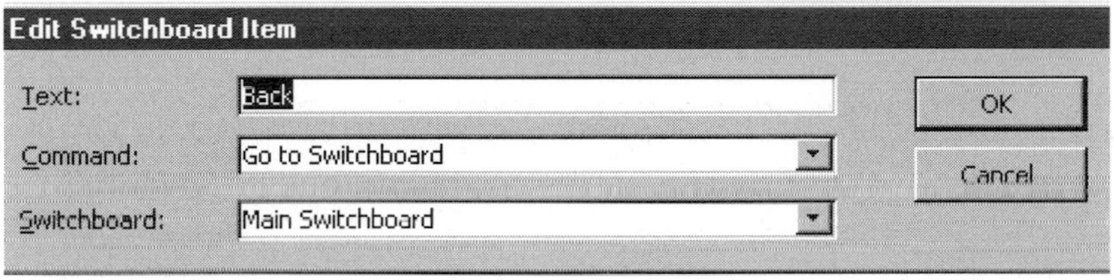

Edit Switchboard Item

Text:	Back	OK
Command:	Go to Switchboard	Cancel
Switchboard:	Main Switchboard	

Figure 20.7

12. Close the Switchboard Manager.

13. At the database Window click on **Forms** and open the **Switchboard**. The new Main Switchboard should now look like that shown on Figure 20.8. Test all the buttons to see that they work.

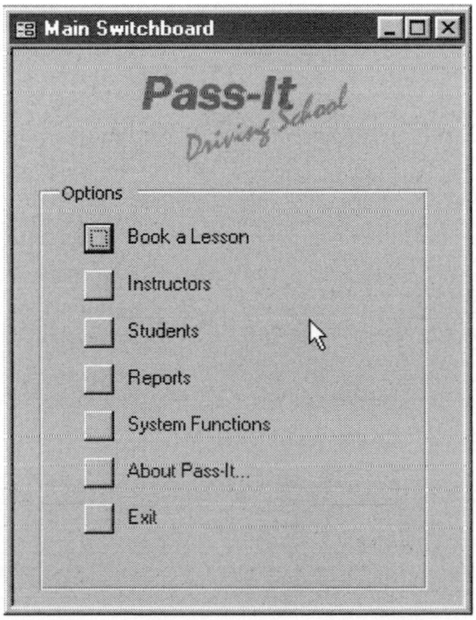

Main Switchboard

Pass-It Driving School

Options

- Book a Lesson
- Instructors
- Students
- Reports
- System Functions
- About Pass-It...
- Exit

Figure 20.8

Tidying up forms

The form in Figure 20.9 works as expected but is a little untidy. The Student ID control is much too long for a small number. The title control is much too big for a title that is only a few letters long. You can probably see other improvements that could be made.

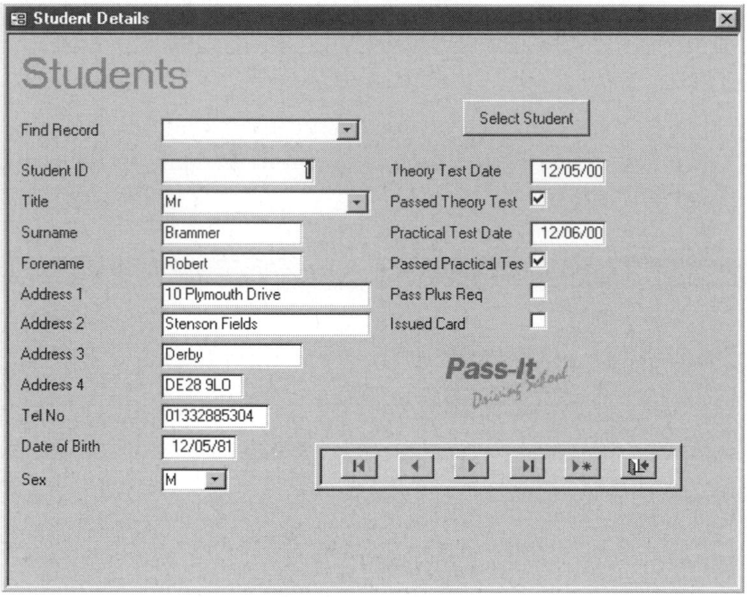

Figure 20.9

Open all your forms in turn and edit them so that controls are aligned, evenly spaced and the right size (see Figure 20.10).

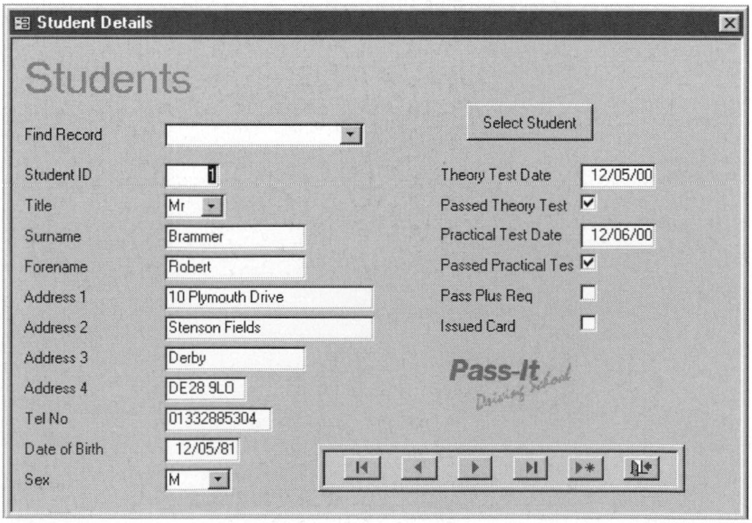

Figure 20.10

Splashscreens

A 'splashscreen,' like the one shown in Figure 20.11, loads when the system loads. It appears for a few seconds before the switchboard loads.

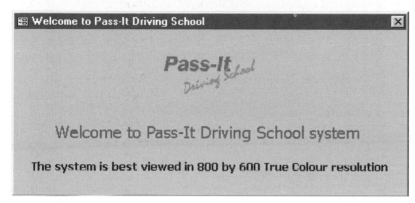

Figure 20.11

Set up a splashscreen as follows:

1. At the Database Window click on **Forms**. Click on **New**. Click on **Design View**. Do *not* select a table or query and click on **OK**.

2. A blank form appears. Enlarge it so that it is roughly 12 cm by 5 cm (see Figure 20.12).

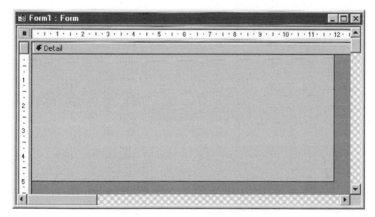

Figure 20.12

3. Use the Toolbox to add the image and to add two labels to display the text as shown in Figure 20.13.

4. Double click on the Form Selector and set the Form properties to remove the **Scroll Bars**, **Record Selector**, **Navigation Buttons**, **Dividing Lines** and **Max Min buttons**. Set the Border Style to **Dialog**. Set the Caption to **Welcome to Pass-It Driving School**.

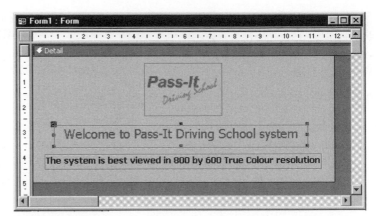

Figure 20.13

5. Save the form as **splashscreen**.

6. Go into Form View. Click on **Window**, **Size to Fit Form**. Your form should look like the one shown in Figure 20.14

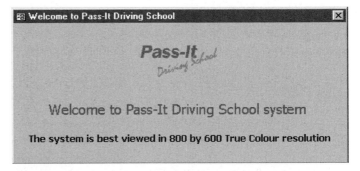

Figure 20.14

7. Close the form. At the Database Window click on Macros and create a new macro to close the splashscreen form.

   ✎ The first Action is Close. The Object Type is Form. The Object Name is splashscreen.

   ✎ The second action is to open another form – the Switchboard (see Figures 20.15 and 20.16).

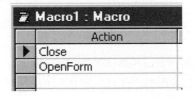

Figure 20.15

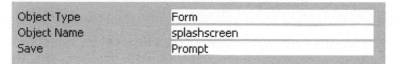

Object Type	Form
Object Name	splashscreen
Save	Prompt

Figure 20.16

8. Save the macro as **Splash**.

9. Load the splashscreen form in Design View and double-click on the Form Selector to view the Form properties. Click on the **Event** tab and set the **TimerInterval** property to **3000**. This is in milliseconds, so it would mean 3 seconds.

10. Click on the **OnTimer** property and select the **Splash** macro. You may need to go back to the TimerInterval property to adjust your timing a little to get it just right (see Figure 20.17).

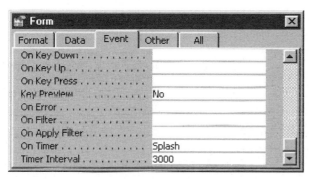

Figure 20.17

11. Save the form. Load the form in Form View mode and test that it stays on the screen for three seconds before switching to the Switchboard.

12. Click on **Tools**, **Startup** to set the startup options to load the splashscreen form when the system loads (see Figure 20.18).

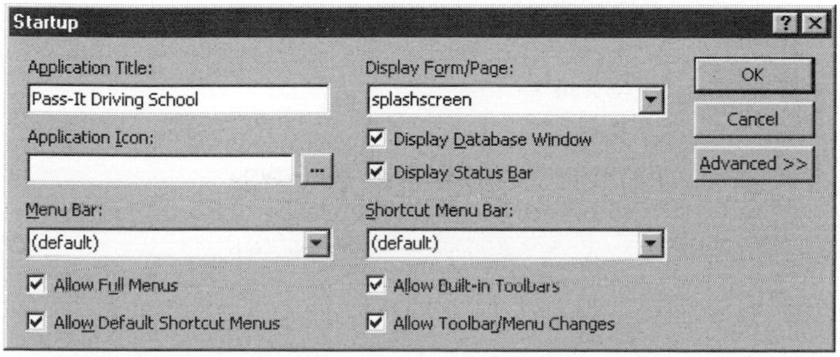

Figure 20.18

▶ Are you sure?

There is an option on the switchboard to exit from the application. It is a good idea to have an 'Are you sure box' in case this button is pressed by mistake (see Figure 20.19).

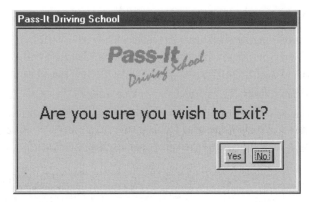

Figure 20.19

To set this up:

1. Open another blank form in Design View.

2. Set the Form properties to remove the **Scroll Bars**, **Record Selector**, **Navigation Buttons**, **Dividing Lines** and **Max Min buttons**. Set the Border Style to **Dialog** Set the Caption to **Pass-It Driving School**.

3. Save the form as **Finish**.

4. Create a macro called **Exit**. The only action is **Quit** with Options set to Exit (see Figure 20.20 and 20.21).

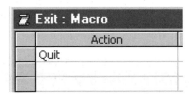

Figure 20.20

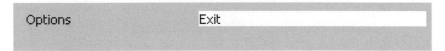

Figure 20.21

5. Create another macro called **NoExit** to close the Finish form.

6. Open the Finish form in Design View. Use the Label icon in the Toolbox to add text similar to the form shown above.

7. Add an image as shown.

8. Add a command button to run the **Exit** macro. Set the text on this button to **Yes**.

9. Add a command button to run the **NoExit** macro. Set the text on this button to **No**.

10. Save the form and close it.

11. Use the Switchboard manager to edit the Exit Application button so that it opens the Finish form in edit mode (see Figure 20.22).

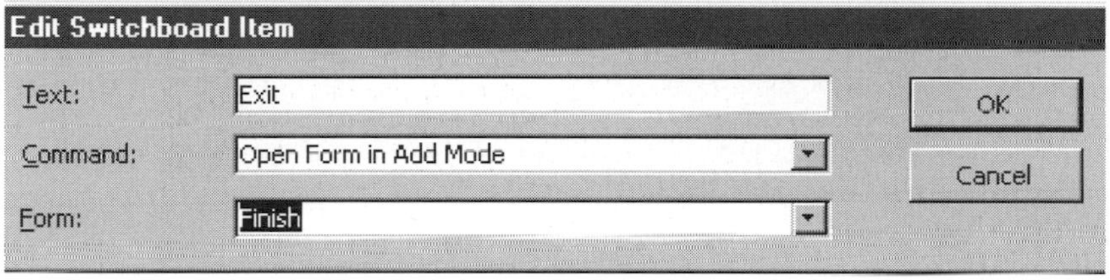

Edit Switchboard Item		
Text:	Exit	OK
Command:	Open Form in Add Mode	Cancel
Form:	Finish	

Figure 20.22

12. Open the Switchboard and test the buttons.

Adding a real time clock to a form

It is possible to add a clock, which updates every second, to an Access form such as the switchboard.

1. Open the switchboard in **Design View** mode

2. Choose the **Text Box** icon in the Toolbox and drag out a text box at the bottom of the switchboard. The text box will be called something like Text30 (see Figure 20.23).

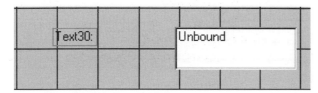

Figure 20.23

3. Click on the label that says the name (Text30) and delete it (see Figure 20.24).

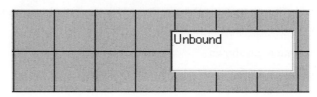

Figure 20.24

4. Click on the text box and click on the **Properties** icon or right click on the text box and choose **Properties**. Click on the **Other** tab and edit the name to **Timer1** (see Figure 20.25).

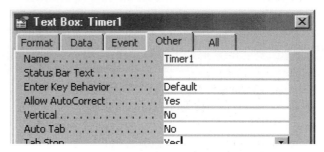

Figure 20.25

5. Click on the **Format** tab and choose the format, **Long Time**.

6. Set the **Font Weight** to **Bold** and **Text Align** to **Center**.

7. With the properties window still displayed, click on the Form Selector.

8. This will display the properties for the form. Click on the **Event** tab and set the Timer Interval to 1000 (this is one second). Timer Interval is the bottom property (see Figure 20.26).

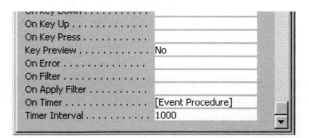

Figure 20.26

9. Choose the **On Timer** property above Timer Interval. Click on the three dots icon and choose **Code Builder**. The Visual Basic Editor loads displaying:

```
Private Sub Form_Timer()

End Sub
```

In the middle line type in:

```
[Timer1]=Now
```

10. Close the Visual Basic Editor and go into Form View mode to test it (see Figure 20.27).

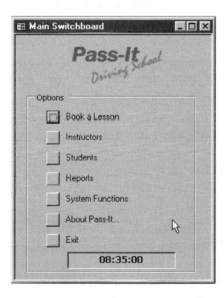

Figure 20.27

Customising menus and toolbars

A fully customised Access system is likely to have customised menus and toolbars. In this section you will learn how to set up a macro to remove or display toolbars, add icons to and remove icons from a toolbar and set up your own toolbar.

Customising toolbars

You can set up the Autoexec macro to remove all toolbars. The Autoexec macro runs automatically when a system loads. For more on the Autoexec macro see Tip 42 page 250.

Removing toolbars means that you can then devote more of the screen to the forms and reports you have set up (see Figure 20.28).

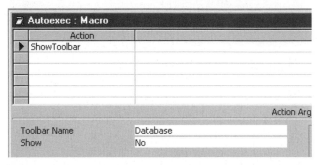

Figure 20.28

Use the **ShowToolbar** action. Select the toolbar from the list and set Show to **No**. You need to use this action several times to remove all the toolbars.

However, before you remove all the toolbars, make sure that your system is fully working. It is very annoying to have to edit the system without any icons.

NB. You can set up a macro to show toolbars only where they are appropriate as shown in Figure 20.29.

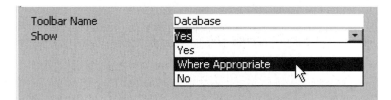

Figure 20.29

Removing or adding single icons

It is possible to add or remove icons from the toolbars. The method is exactly the same as in Microsoft Word and Microsoft Excel, so you may have seen it before.

1. Click on **Tools**, **Customize** or right click on the toolbars and click on **Customize**.

The Customize Dialogue box appears.

2. Click on the **Commands** tab (see Figure 20.30).

3. To remove an icon from a toolbar simply drag it on to the dialogue box.

4. To add an icon, select **All Macros** in the **Categories** box. Find the macro's icon in the **Commands** box and drag it on to the toolbar.

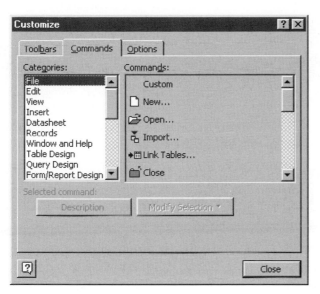

Figure 20.30

For example, to add an icon to run the **About** macro:

1. Click on the Commands tab and scroll down in the **Categories** box until you find **All Macros**.

2. Find **About** in the **Commands** box (see Figure 20.31).

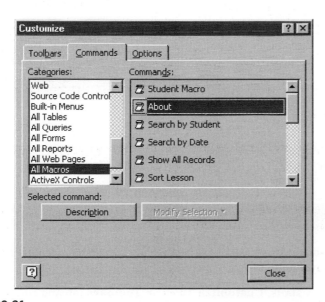

Figure 20.31

3. Drag the **About** icon on to the toolbar (see Figure 20.32).

4. Close the dialogue box.

Figure 20.32

5. You can edit this icon by clicking on **Tools**, **Customize** and then right clicking on the icon (see Figure 20.33).

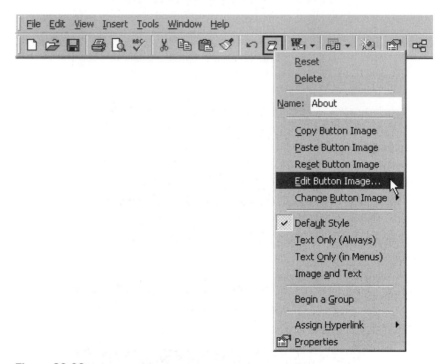

Figure 20.33

6. Select **Edit Button Image** to load a simple painting program to edit the icon or click on **Change Button Image** to show a menu of alternative icons.

Customising menus

Customised menus make finishing touches to a system, extending the system beyond the usual.

1. Click on **Tools**, **Customize**. Click on **Toolbars** tab and click on **New**.

2. Call the new toolbar, **Pass It Driving School**.

A small new blank toolbar has appeared on the screen (see Figure 20.34).

Figure 20.34

3. Click on the blue title bar and drag the toolbar to the toolbar area at the top of the screen (see Figure 20.35).

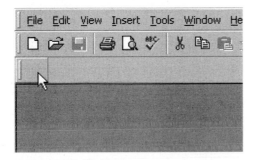

Figure 20.35

4. Click on the **Commands** tab and scroll down in the **Categories** box until you find **New Menu**. (It is the last one in the list; see Figure 20.36).

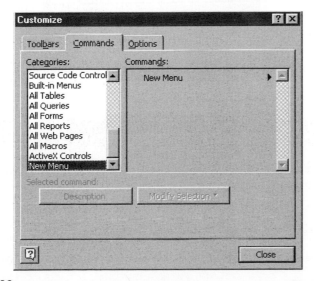

Figure 20.36

5. Drag **New Menu** from the Commands box on to the new toolbar (see Figure 20.37).

Figure 20.37

6. Right click on the words **New Menu** and change the name as shown in Figure 20.38.

Figure 20.38

7. Click on the word **Navigate** and a small blank menu drops down (see Figure 20.39).

Figure 20.39

8. Click on **All Forms** in the **Categories** list in the dialogue box.

9. Find **Lesson Booking Form** in the Commands list and drag it on to the blank menu (see Figure 20.40).

Figure 20.40

10. Click on **Navigate** to make the menu drop down. Right click on **Lesson Booking Form**.

11. Change the name to Book a Lesson as shown in Figure 20.41.

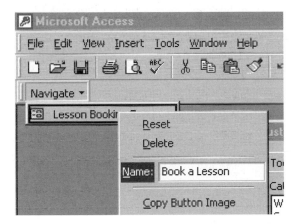

Figure 20.41

12. Close the dialogue box.

13. Test that the new menu loads Lesson Booking Form.

You can add more items to your menu and more menus to your toolbar. Include links to your forms and reports.

It is a good idea to include links to the Database Window and have on-line help in your customised menu. Click on **Windows and Help** in the **Categories** box. Drag the **Database Window** and **Microsoft Access Help** icons on to your menus (see Figure 20.42).

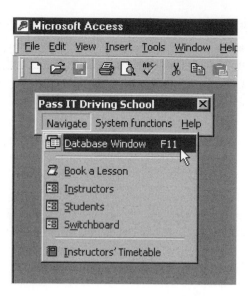

Figure 20.42

When your new menu bar is complete, click on **Tools**, **Startup** and change the start up menu bar as shown in Figure 20.43.

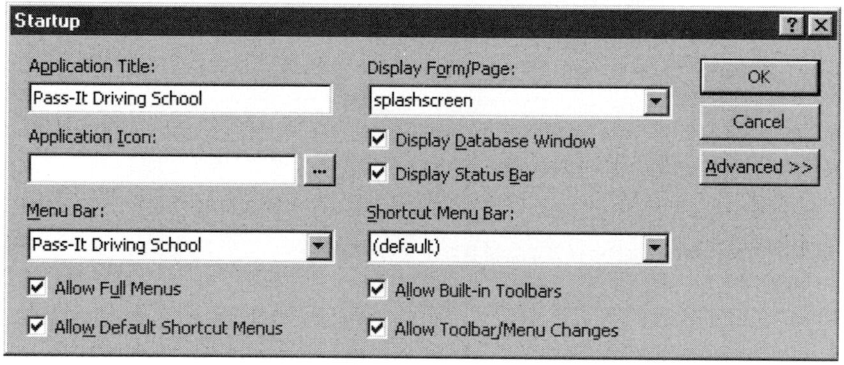

Figure 20.43

Don't forget that to disable the startup options, hold down the SHIFT key as you load the file.

Documenting a system

An ICT project is much more than just setting up the system using Microsoft Access. You must also include documentation covering the analysis of the system, its design, its implementation, testing, a user guide and evaluation.

The following pages show you how to document your system by looking at *some* of the documentation provided with the Pass It system.

Remember: The documentation here is not supposed to be complete but each section offers examples, pointers and hints to what is considered good practice.

■ Pass-It Driving School System

Contents

1 Problem statement
2 Analysis
   (a) Interview with user
   (b) Current system
   (c) End-user requirements
   (d) Data flow diagrams
   (e) Input, processing and output requirements
   (f) Data dynamics
   (g) Sub-tasks
   (h) Resources available
   (i) Evaluation criteria
3 Design
   (a) Possible solutions
   (b) Chosen solution
   (c) Database design
   (d) Data dictionary
   (e) Query designs
   (f) Processing designs
   (g) Screen layouts
   (h) Testing plan
   (i) Time plan
4 Implementation report

5 Testing
    (a) Test results
    (b) User testing
6 User guide
7 Evaluation

Always number the pages and produce a contents page.

1. Problem statement

This should be a clear description of the problem to be solved, the purpose of the new computerised system.

My user will be Mr Doug Jones owner of 'Pass-It Driving School,' a local driving school, which offers driving tuition to learner drivers.

Mr Jones is interested in improving his record keeping, particularly how he stores details of lessons that have been booked and issues information to instructors. At present all these details are stored on paper.

The system will store many different types of information including:

- details of all the students and instructors

- details of lessons booked for each day

Mr Jones needs to know which students have lessons each day, with which instructor and at which times. Details of pick-up points and drop-off points will also need to be stored. Data must be able to be entered and retrieved easily.

2. Analysis

This involves investigating what is required from the new system and what facilities are available. It would probably include:

- details of discussions with the user, usually in an interview;

- details of the current system including existing documents;

- the end user requirements;

- data flow diagrams showing how data moves through the system;

- imput, processing and output requirements;

- data dynamics in the system;

- hardware and software available including version numbers, their capabilities and limitations;

- details of the user's current IT skill level and training needs;

- evaluation criteria for evaluating the success of your system.

Remember: the output from this section will be used as the input for the next section.

(a) Interview with user

The interview with the user is designed to find out the needs of the user. The sort of questions that are likely to be asked are:

- How do you store this information at present?

- What details do you store?

- What is the procedure when someone rings up to book a lesson?

- What is the procedure when someone passes their driving test?

- How long do you keep the information for?

- Do you ever have to refer back to previous lesson details?

- Have you much experience of using computers?

- What computer facilities do you have at present (if any)?

(b) Current system

Figure 21.1 is a page from the Pass-It Driving School booking diary.

Bookings are made by phoning the office and details are entered by hand. Cancellations are made in the same way by simply crossing out the bookings. The column headings show the instructors' initials.

Issuing instructors' timetables is done by photocopying the sheets and giving them to the instructor.

This is presenting problems:

- Searching for available time slots can be a lengthy process.

- Issuing timetables is inefficient and, of course, once issued they may still change with late additions and cancellations. At present they have to be rewritten by hand.

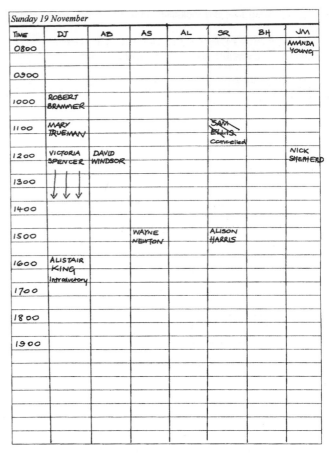

Figure 21.1

At this point you should be in a position to include a summary of the current system, including the information and processes involved.

(c) End-user requirements

The main aims of my new system are to:

- reduce the amount of paper work required from the instructor; as the system will create reports and lists of necessary information;

- have an easy-to-use system;

- speed up the time it takes to make a lesson booking;

- find information about a student quickly;

- keep passed records;

- improve the organisation of the driving school by allowing information to be readily available;

produce reports on lessons and income;

produce a membership card for each student from a link within the system.

(d) Data flow diagrams

Before designing the system you need to analyse in detail how data flows through the system using data flow diagrams (DFDs).

DFDs use the symbols shown in Figure 21.2.

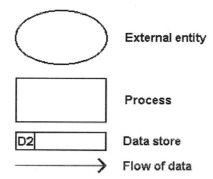

External entity

Process

D2 **Data store**

Flow of data

Figure 21.2

The first stage is to draw a simple diagram called the Context Diagram. This simply shows the system at the centre and all the external entities providing data to or getting information from the system.

In the case of the driving school the external entities are the instructors and the students. Try to show all the data flowing between these entities and the system. Figure 21.3 is the Level 0 data flow diagram.

Level 0 Context Diagram

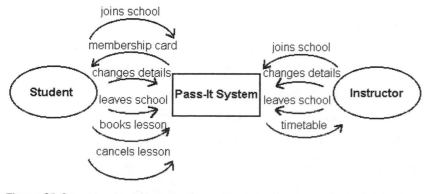

Figure 21.3

The next stage is to add more detail to the data flow diagram by breaking the system down into sub-tasks. In this case the four sub-tasks are student administration, booking a lesson, instructor administration and general administration. Note that each sub-task is numbered.

Draw separate data flow diagrams for each sub-task (although it may help to link these diagrams where necessary). In each diagram link the system to the data stores – where the data is stored. All data stores are also numbered.

Figure 21.4 is the Level 1 data flow diagram. Note that an external entity may appear more than once in a data flow diagram. The diagonal line inside the oval external entity shape shows that the entity appears elsewhere.

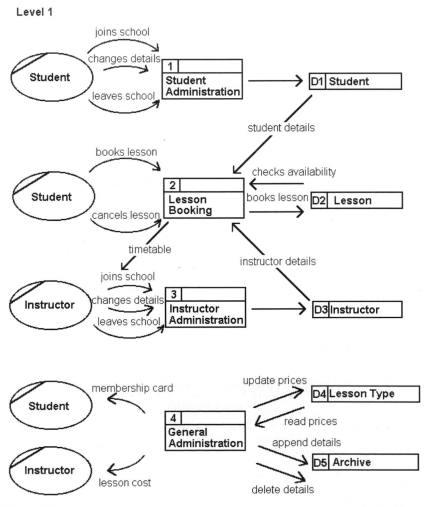

Figure 21.4

The next stage is to take each sub-task and break it down further into the various processes involved. Each process is again numbered and the numbering relates to the Level 1 numbers, e.g. sub task 1 may be split into three processes 1.1, 1.2 and 1.3.

Figure 21.5 is the Level 2 data flow diagram, showing examples for the first two sub-tasks.

Level 2

Process 1 Student Administration

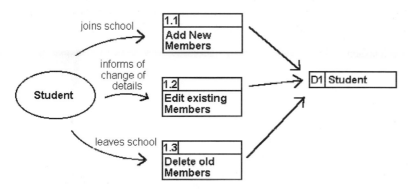

Process 2 Lesson Booking

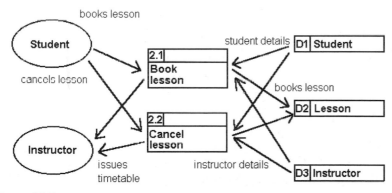

Figure 21.5

(e) Input, processing and output requirements

▓ DATA STORES

Student file
Lesson file
Instructor file
Lesson type file
Archive file

◼ INPUT REQUIREMENTS

Student details
Instructor details
Lesson details

◼ PROCESSING REQUIREMENTS

Student joins school
Edit student details
Student leaves school
Book a lesson
Cancel a lesson
Instructor joins school
Edit instructor details
Instructor leaves school
Calculate lesson prices
Issue membership cards
Update prices
Delete unwanted records

◼ OUTPUT REQUIREMENTS

Timetables for instructors
Student details from ID
Instructor details from ID
Income report

(f) Data dynamics

This section is about the movement of data after an event such as leaving a club, moving from one school year to the next or passing a driving test. Does the data need to be updated? How long will it be kept? Will it be deleted or stored somewhere else in the system?

After a user passes the theory and the practical test their details will not be deleted from the system as they may go on to take the Pass Plus course.

However their data will be transferred from the student data store to a separate data stored from where it can easily be retrieved.

Similarly all lessons over a year old will be stored in a separate data store. After another year this information will be deleted altogether.

Instructors are self-employed. They may leave the company and come back at another time. In which case their details will not be deleted completely but sent to a different data store.

(g) Sub-tasks

You are now in a position to derive a list of sub-tasks within the specification.

The sub-tasks of the new system are:

1. Student Administration
   1.1 Add a new student
   1.2 Edit an existing student
   1.3 Delete an old student

2. Lesson booking
   2.1 Book a lesson
   2.2 Cancel a lesson

3. Instructor Administration
   3.1 Instructor joins school
   3.2 Edit instructor details
   3.3 Instructor leaves school

4. General administration
   4.1 Update prices
   4.2 Calculate lesson prices
   4.3 Issue membership card
   4.4 Delete unwanted records

(h) Resources available

Include details of the hardware resources, software resources and human resources including current skill level and training needs.

(i) Evaluation criteria

You must state clearly how you are going to evaluate your solution when it is finished.

You need to present a clear list of performance indicators, for example:

- The ease of use of the system

- The look and feel of the system (user interfaces)

- Quality of output from the system (the reports)

- Features in the system that will save time

The accuracy of output from the system

The speed of certain functions in the system

Don'ts

- Don't list as many criteria as you can in the hope of gaining more marks.
- Don't make vague statements such as' it will be quicker', 'it will be easier to use'.

Dos

- Only choose criteria that you can back up with evidence.

Some Performance Indicators might be:

PI1. The system will be able to reduce the time taken on the phone when dealing with a booking. It will eliminate the need to search through the folder of daily booking sheets looking for an available slot. Lesson availability will be instant to the caller.

PI2. I will ensure all user interfaces are easy to use with common layouts, icons and styles. During the early development of the system and when the system is complete I will liaise with the user, noting problems and areas for improvement.

3. Design

The design section should include plans for each sub-task.

Your design plans should be done away from the computer. Design plans are probably best done by hand.

Good designs will include details of:

- possible solutions: consider different ways of solving the problem;
- the chosen solution: describe the reasons for the chosen solution;
- the problem broken down into sub-tasks;
- entity relationship diagrams;
- relationship diagrams;
- data dictionary including validation and input masks;
- screen layouts;
- processing and query designs;
- time plan with estimated time allocation for each phase or Gantt charts;

design for data-capture sheets, outputs etc. as appropriate;

testing plan.

(a) Possible solutions

In this section you should consider different possible ways of solving the problem, including advantages and disadvantages. Consider:

improving the manual system;

a Microsoft Access solution;

a solution using alternative software;

an alternative solution within Microsoft Access.

Relate the solution to the problem. Part of two possible solutions are given below.

■ SOLUTION USING MICROSOFT EXCEL

Microsoft Excel is a spreadsheet program for Windows 95/98/ME.

Advantages

The software is easy to use and easy to learn.

The package is part of the standard Microsoft Office package.

Data can be searched using Auto filter.

...

Disadvantages

Every time I book a lesson I will have to enter repeated data which is inefficient

...

■ SOLUTION USING MICROSOFT ACCESS

Microsoft Access is a relational database management system for Windows 95/98/ME.

Advantages

Relationships can be created between tables, linking fields and eliminating redundant data and inconsistency.

⟋ The package is fully customisable.

⟋ Forms and reports can be created in an appropriate style reflecting the company image.

...

Disadvantages

⟋ Microsoft Access is not easy to learn.

...

(b) Chosen solution

You now need to give clear reasons stating exactly why you have opted for the chosen solution.

I have decided to select Microsoft Access 2000 as the software in which I will create the new system for the following reasons:

⟋ Relationships between tables will eliminate redundant data.

⟋ The system will be customised to suit the user.

⟋ The system will be fully automated with the use of macros. This means that users do not need to learn how to use Access.

...

(c) Database design

From the analysis you can see that there will be four main tables:

⟋ Student table

⟋ Lesson table

⟋ Instructor table

⟋ Lesson type table

There will also be tables to archive data.

The tables will be related as shown in Figure 21.6.

All relationships are one-to-many as shown in Figure 21.7.

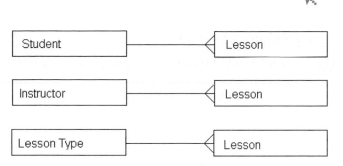

Figure 21.6

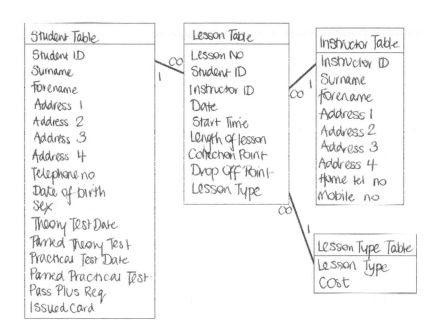

Figure 21.7

(d) Data dictionary

Student Table

Field Name	Data Type	Other information
Student ID	Autonumber	Primary Key field
Title	Text	Lookup: Mr, Mrs, Miss or Ms Field Size 6
Surname	Text	Field Size 20
Forename	Text	Field Size 20
Address 1	Text	Field Size 30
Address 2	Text	Field Size 30
Address 3	Text	Default "Derby" Field Size 20
Address 4	Text	Format > Field Size 10
Tel No	Text	Field Size 15
Date of Birth	Date/Time	Format: Short Date
Sex	Text	Lookup table: Must be M or F Field Size 1
Theory Test Date	Date/Time	Format: Short Date
Passed Theory Test	Yes/No	
Practical Test Date	Date/Time	Format: Short Date
Passed Practical Test	Yes/No	
Pass Plus Req	Yes/No	
Issued Card	Yes/No	

Instructor Table

Field name	Data type	Other information
Instructor ID	AutoNumber	Primary Key field
Title	Text	Lookup Mr, Mrs, Ms, Miss Field Size 6
Surname	Text	Field Size 20
Forename	Text	Field Size 20
Address 1	Text	Field Size 30
Address 2	Text	Field Size 30
Address 3	Text	Default 'Derby' Field Size 20
Address 4	Text	Format > Field Size 10
Home Tel No	Text	Field Size 15
Mobile No	Text	Field Size 15

Lesson Type Table

Field name	Data type	Other information
Lesson Type	Text	Primary Key field. Field Size 25
Cost	Currency	

Lesson Table

Field name	Data type	Other information
Lesson No	AutoNumber	Primary Key field
Student ID	Number	Long Integer
Instructor ID	Number	Long Integer
Date	Date/Time	Format: Short Date
Start Time	Date/Time	Format: Short Time
Length of Lesson	Number	Integer Set validation between 1 and 8
Collection Point	Text	Default value: Home Address
		Field Size 30
Drop-Off Point	Text	Default value: Home Address
		Field Size 30
Lesson Type Standard, Pass	Text	Lookup set values as Introductory, Plus and Test Field Size 25

(e) Query designs

Query Name	Underlying table(s)	Criteria
Search by Student ID Query	Student	Parameter Query Student ID = [Enter the ID number]
Full Details Query	Student, Instructor, Lesson	–
...		

(f) Processing designs

Macro Name	Actions
Archive lessons	Run the Old Lesson Append Query Run the Old Lesson Delete Query Run the Over One Year Delete Query
...	

(g) Screen layouts

You need to present designs for all important screen layouts such as forms, reports and switchboards. Figures 21.8 and 21.9 give two examples.

The system switchboard must have:

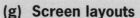 the company logo;

 links to other forms;

 links to reports;

 links to system functions.

It will look like Figure 21.8.

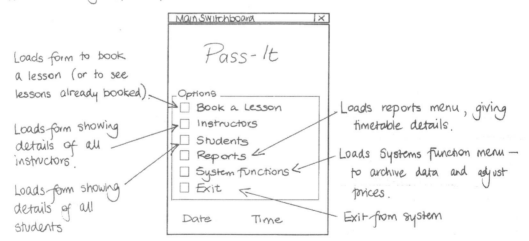

Figure 21.8

Design dos
- Present your plans in a format such that a reasonably competent person could take them and make a start on setting up your system.
- Make them legible and neat. This person must be able read them.

Design don'ts
- Don't use screen dumps from the actual system as part of your design plans.

The lesson booking form will look like Figure 21.9.

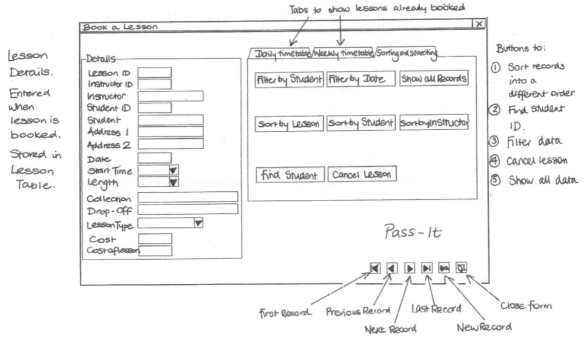

Figure 21.9

▤ IMPLEMENTATION PLAN

In order to create my system I will need to break it down into smaller tasks, which I
can implement in stages as follows:

1. Create a table to store Student details.
2. Create a table to store Instructor details.
3. Create a table to store Lesson Types.
4. Create a table to store Lesson details.
5. Set up the relationships between the tables.
6. Set up a query to search for a student's details.
7. Set up a query to search for a student's lessons.
8. Set up a query to search for an instructor's lessons on any date.
9. Set up a query to search for full lesson details.
10. Set up a query to search for see next week's lessons.
11. Set up a query to calculate income.
12. Create a form to enter new student, edit student details, delete old students.
13. Create a form to enter new instructor, edit instructor details, delete old instructors.
14. Create a form to enter lesson type details.
15. Create a form to book a lesson and cancel a lesson.
16. Create a report to display instructor details.

17. Create a report to display student details.
18. Create a report to issue membership cards.
19. Create an income report.
20. Create a macro to update prices.
21. Create a macro to archive/delete unwanted records.
22. Create a switchboard, which will contain various buttons which will be connected to all the different functions of the system allowing easy control for the end user.

(h) Testing plan

Testing is an integral part of developing an IT system and your design should include a test plan, saying exactly what you will test and how.

Tests should:

- be numbered;

- state the purpose of the test;

- specify the data to be used, if any;

- outline the expected result;

- cross-reference to clear hard copy usually in the form of a screen dump;

- provide evidence of the actual results plus any comments;

- outline any corrective action needed or taken.

Where appropriate, test data should include typical data and if possible, extreme, invalid or awkward data.

Test	Purpose	Test Data	Expected outcome	Actual outcome	Corrective action
...					
4. Search by Student ID Query	To test that the query provides the correct data	7	Details for Mary Trueman appear		
...					
15. Instructors report	To test that the instructors report output fits on to a page and is legible	Whole file	Full details of each instructor appear in the report		

Test	Purpose	Test Data	Expected outcome	Actual outcome	Corrective action
17. End user test initial Student Instructor and Lesson form	Ease of use for the user.	User to run through all options	Comments for future action.		
...					
21. Test Student lookup combo box on the student form.	To check it returns correct details for a student on file and see how it handles a student entered not on file.	Name of Student Jenkins Name of Student Clough	Details for Jenkins shown Details for Clough not shown.		

Test plan dos

- ◼ To find errors you have to try and provoke failure. Try to make your system go wrong!
- ◼ Remember that you are testing whether the data is processed correctly, not just whether a button works or not.

Test plan don'ts

- ◼ Don't forget. The purpose of testing is to find errors.

(i) Time plan

Present a detailed time plan for the whole of your project either as a calendar of events or as a Gantt chart.

Weeks beginning	Process
29 Oct	Decide on project. Write up problem statement, Interview user
05 Nov – 19 Nov	Analyse problem – establish requirements, draw data flow diagrams, establish sub-tasks
26 Nov – 03 Dec	Start design work, write up possible and chosen solutions, present interface designs to the user
10 Dec	Improve designs on user's comments, produce testing plan
	...
14 Jan	Create tables. Enter test data
21 Jan	Create relationships. Create queries
	...

4. Implementation report

This section should contain clear evidence that you have implemented each part of your system.

The information presented here should reflect your specification and design plans.

Screen dumps and/or fully-labelled printouts need to be used to support and provide evidence of work done.

This is your chance to sell yourself and all the techniques you have used in your project. Include:

⟡ printouts of all tables, queries, forms, reports and macros;

⟡ screen shots where appropriate, e.g. the relationship window;

⟡ a concise commentary on how you set up the system.

Task 1 Create a table to store Student details

The first task that was required was the creation of the tables to contain the system's data. This involved setting up the fields, setting the validation and input masks and choosing the primary key (see Figure 21.10).

Field Name	Data Type	Description
Student ID	AutoNumber	Student's ID number
Title	Text	
Surname	Text	
Forename	Text	
Address 1	Text	
Address 2	Text	
Address 3	Text	
Address 4	Text	
Tel No	Text	
Date of Birth	Date/Time	
Sex	Text	
Theory Test Date	Date/Time	
Passed Theory Test	Yes/No	
Practical Test Date	Date/Time	
Passed Practical Test	Yes/No	
Pass Plus Req	Yes/No	
Issued Card	Yes/No	

Figure 21.10

I set up the Student table with the fields as shown above. I set student ID as the Primary Key Field.

I used the Lookup Wizard to set my own values for the Title field. I chose Mr, Mrs, Ms and Miss. This makes entering data easier (see Figure 21.11).

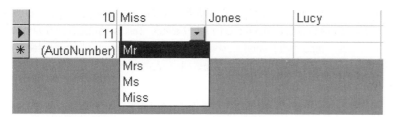

Figure 21.11

I didn't set any validation rules because they weren't necessary but I did set an Input Mask on all Date/Time fields which again makes entering data easier as shown in Figure 21.12.

	10	Miss	Jones	Lucy	31/03/00
𝒪	11	Mr	George	Charles	▌ / /
✳	(AutoNumber)				

Figure 21.12

Task 5 Set up the relationships between the tables

In the Database Window I opened the Relationships window and added the tables Student, Instructor, Lesson and Lesson Type (see Figure 12.13).

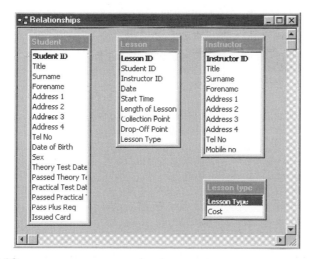

Figure 12.13

To set the links I dragged each key field from the tables Student, Instructor and Lesson Type and dropped them on the same field in the Lesson Table. All relationships were set as one to many.

I set Referential Integrity each time to avoid invalid data being entered. When I linked the Student ID fields also I checked Cascade Deletes. This is so that if and when I delete a student record all related lessons taken by that student will be deleted from the lesson table. This is shown in Figure 21.14.

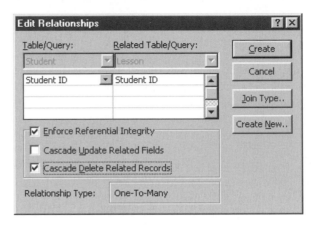

Figure 21.14

The screen shot in Figure 21.15 shows all the relationships set as one to many and the layout saved.

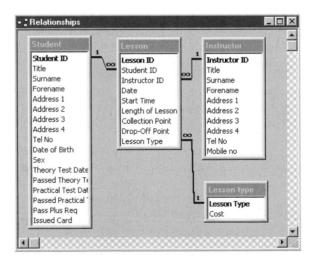

Figure 21.15

Task 16 Create a report to display instructor details

To generate this report I used the wizard and the AutoReport: Tabular option. I based the report on the instructor table (see Figure 21.16).

Instructor

Instructor ID	Title	Surname	Forename	Address 1	Address 2	Address 3	Address 4	Home Tel	Mobile
1	Mr	Jones	Doug	57 Swanmore Road	Etwall	Derby	DE34 5FG	01332122541	07720521
2	Mr	Batchelor	Arnold	13 Gairloch Close	Etwall	Derby	DE34 5FG	01332552147	07980352
3	Mr	Smith	Andrew	5b Sunrise Road	Littleover	Derby	DE45 4ED	01332521452	07980525

Figure 21.16

The layout wasn't really what I wanted. The report only just fitted the page and a number of headings were not in the right place. So I went into Report Design View and made the changes (see Figure 21.17).

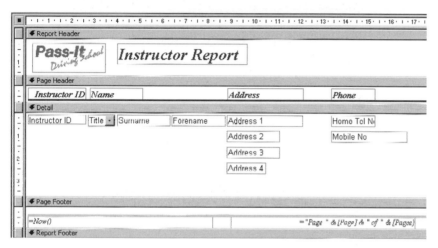

Figure 21.17

- I removed some of the column headings and grouped them as Name, Address and Phone.

- I grouped the text boxes under the appropriate headings.

- I added the Driving School Logo and edited the title to Instructor Report.

- I realigned all labels and data.

The finished report appeared as in Figure 21.18.

Instructor Report

Instructor ID	Name			Address	Phone
1 Mr	Jones		Doug	57 Swanmore Road	01332 122541
				Etwall	07720 521478
				Derby	
				DE34 5F	
2 Mr	Batchelor		Arnold	13 Gairloch Close	01332 552147
				Etwall	07980 352145
				Derby	
				DE34 5F	
3 Mr	Smith		Andrew	5b Sunrise Road	01332 521452

Figure 21.18

Implementation dos

- Be clear and concise
- Use screen dumps to support you explanation.
- Describe all the steps in setting up your system.
- Describe clearly the features of the software you have used.
- Describe any validation you have included.

Implementation don'ts

- Don't undersell the work you have done and remember exam board moderators can only give credit for what they can see.
- Don't submit work set up by the wizards and claim you did it on your own!
- Don't reproduce large tracts of Access manuals.

---

5. Testing

Include:

- details of test data;

- actual results of testing with expected results and evidence – printouts or screen shots;

- corrective actions taken as a result of testing;

- evidence of full end-user involvement in testing.

(a) Test results

Test	Purpose	Test Data	Expected outcome	Actual outcome	Corrective action
...					
4. Search by Student ID Query	To test that the query provides the correct data	7	Details for Mary Trueman appear	Details for Mary Trueman Appear. See Test Result 4	None needed
...					
15. Instructors report	To test that the instructors report output fits on to a page and is legible	Whole file	Full details of each instructor appear in the report	Full details of each instructor appear in the report but some columns are not wide enough. See Test Result 15.	Widths of columns adjusted so that all the text fits in. Headings moved also.. See Test Result 15a
...					
17. End user test initial Student Instructor and Lesson form	Ease of use for the user.	User to run through all options	Comments for future action.	See user comments under Test Result 17.	Action taken later in finishing touches to the system.
...					
21.Test Student look-up combo box on the student form.	To check it returns correct details for a student on file and see how it handles a student entered not on file.	Name of Student Jenkins	Details for Jenkins shown	Details shown correctly.	None needed
		Name of Student Clough	Details for Clough not shown.	Not accepted Access gives error message.	Advice given in user guide.

■ TEST RESULT 4

Student ID	Surname	Forename	Address 1	Address 2	Address 3
7	Trueman	Mary	156 Station Road	Allestree	Derby

Search by Student ID Query : Select Query

Figure 21.19

■ TEST RESULT 15

udent ID	Title	Surna	Forena	Address 1	Addres	Addres
1	Mr	Brammer	Robert	10 Plymouth D	Stenson F	Derby
2	Mr	Jenkins	Steven	7 Woodfield Cl	Etwall	Derby
3	Miss	Fowler	Sarah	19 Sea ViewR	Mickleove	Derby
4	Mr	Beswood	Michael	25 Lundie Clos	Allestree	Derby
5	Miss	Williams	Chalotte	21 Church Str	Littleover	Derby
6	Mr	Windsor	David	86 Milford Roa	Allenton	Derby
7	Miss	Trueman	Mary	156 Station Ro	Allestree	Derby

Figure 21.20

■ TEST RESULT 15A

ID	Name			Address		
1	Mr	Brammer	Robert	10 Plymouth Drive	Stenson Fields	Derby
2	Mr	Jenkins	Steven	7 Woodfield Close	Etwall	Derby
3	Miss	Fowler	Sarah	19 Sea ViewRoad	Mickleover	Derby
4	Mr	Beswood	Michael	25 Lundie Close	Allestree	Derby
5	Miss	Williams	Chalotte	21 Church Street	Littleover	Derby
6	Mr	Windsor	David	86 Milford Road	Allenton	Derby
7	Miss	Trueman	Mary	156 Station Road	Allestree	Derby

Figure 21.21

■ TEST RESULT 17

After designing the initial forms I asked Mr Jones to sit with me and go through the main features on each. I also wanted him to comment on the ease of use, general layout and appearance of the form.

He made the following comments:

- All forms excellent in design and colour schemes used.

- The tool tips over the control buttons were a little unfriendly First Record, Add a record etc.

- Some of the boxes for entering data were far larger than was needed e.g. Student ID., Lesson No., Title. Mr Jones found this a little confusing when entering data. See screen dump in Test Result 21.

Action taken:

↗ Tool tips over all buttons were made more user friendly, e.g. Add a Record changed to Make a Booking.

↗ Form sizes adjusted accordingly.

↗ Text boxes for a number of fields made smaller. For example, on the student form below Student ID and Title reduced to fit typical data (see Figure 21.22).

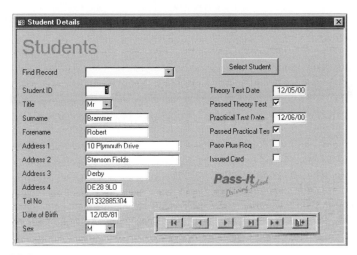

Figure 21.22

■ TEST RESULT 21

The Student form showing details for Jenkins displayed correctly (see Figure 21.23).

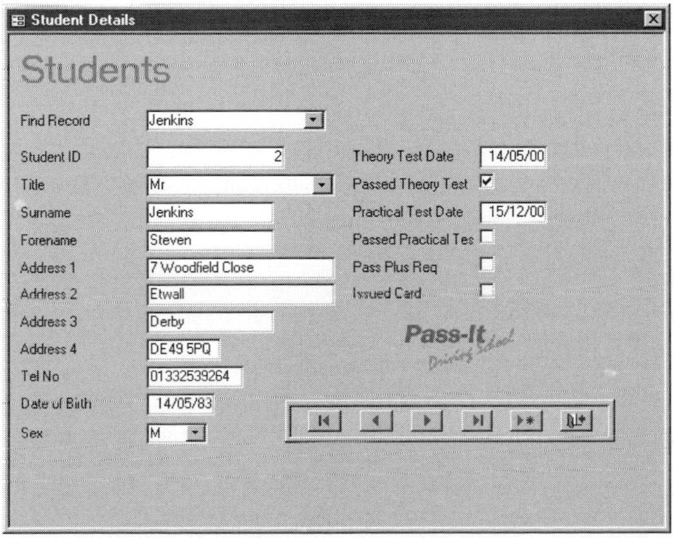

Figure 21.23

When details for student Clough are entered (or any student not on file) Access will not accept and issues this error message (see Figure 21.24).

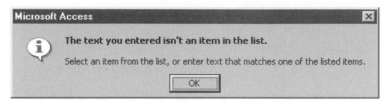

Figure 21.24

(b) User testing

Doug Jones used the system a few times to test it. He made the following observations:

He found it easy to book lessons quickly as he needs to do when dealing with phone enquiries and it was easy to find details of students. He found no major errors in the system but commented on some minor issues.

He thought the system was generally user friendly but he had problems fitting reports to a page. Reports came out on two pages and it was not easy to alter the report to one page.

I will correct this by using landscape format for reports.

Doug said that the system should offer quick information on Lessons already booked further ahead than just the day of the call and for the coming week. This is something I will need to investigate improving.

Doug thought the design of all forms was excellent. He commented on their professional look but he noticed that the forms were generally all different sizes. He found this annoying.

He also said that some of the boxes for data entry were too large for the data to be entered. I will need to resize the forms and review the size of text boxes.

6. User guide

A user guide is just that – a guide for the **user** or **users** of your system.

It should include details of:

- the purpose of the system;

- the minimum system requirements needed to run your system, e.g. Pentium 200 with 64 Mb of memory;

how to get started;

the main menu options;

how to perform each of the routine tasks that make up your system;

common problems or error messages and possible solutions;

security measures, backup procedures and passwords needed.

■ User guide to the Pass-It Driving School System

Introduction

The system allows the user to store details of students and instructors and make bookings for lessons. The system also offers a number of reporting features to deal with bookings, student records and instructor timetables.

System requirements

You require a minimum of a Pentium 500 PC with 64Mb of memory. Microsoft Office 2000 needs to be installed including the component Access 2000.

The system initially uses 6322 Kb of disc space (see Figure 21.25), although this is small by the standard of today's hard drives. A laser printer is recommended to ensure fast, high-quality output.

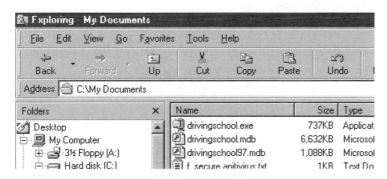

Figure 21.25

For users with an older PC and Office 97, there is an Access 97 version of the system which only takes up 1088 Kb and takes up much less disc space.

■ How to install the system

The system is supplied in compressed format on a 1.44Mb floppy disc. The file is called **drivingschool.exe** and is self-extracting. It can be installed to your hard drive as follows:

1. Insert the floppy disc containing the system.

2. On the Desktop create a New Folder by right clicking the mouse button. Name the folder **Pass It**.

3. Click on the My Computer icon and then the Floppy drive A icon.

4. Drag the file called **drivingschool.exe** onto the folder **Pass It**.

5. Click on the Pass It directory and then double-click on **drivingschool.exe**.

The self-extractor will ask you which folder to install the file in (see Figure 21.26).

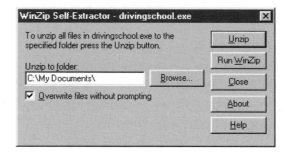

Figure 21.26

Getting started

To boot up the system double click the file icon called **Drivingschool** (see Figure 21.27).

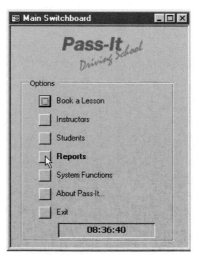

Figure 21.27

The system displays the switchboard giving the user seven options.

1. **Book a Lesson**

2. **Instructors**

3. **Students**

4. **Reports**

5. **System Functions**

6. **About Pass-It**

7. **Exit**

Booking a lesson

1. To book a lesson, click on the **Book a Lesson** button.

The Book a Lesson form loads.

2. Click on the Make a Booking button for a new booking (see Figure 21.28).

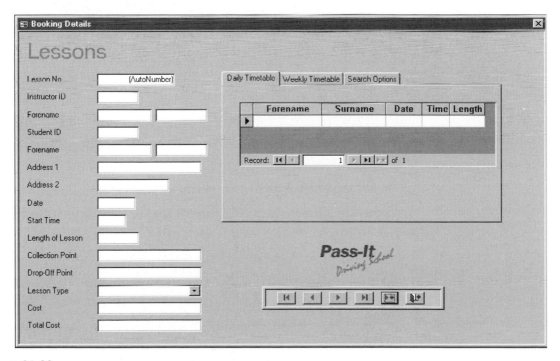

Figure 21.28

3. Enter the Instructor ID in the Instructor ID box.

4. Enter the Student ID in the Student ID box.

5. If you do not know the Student ID number, click on the Search Options tab.

6. Click on Find Student.

The Student form will load (see Figure 21.29).

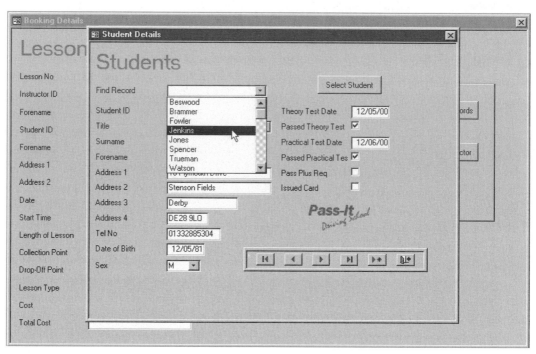

Figure 21.29

7. Click on the Find Record drop down arrow. The students are in alphabetical order of surname.

8. Select the student's name.

9. Click on Select Student to paste the details into the booking form (see Figure 21.30).

10. Enter the date of the lesson.

11. Click on the Daily Timetable tab. Check what times have been booked already with that instructor that day.

12. Enter all the details. Click on the Make a Booking button to confirm the booking.

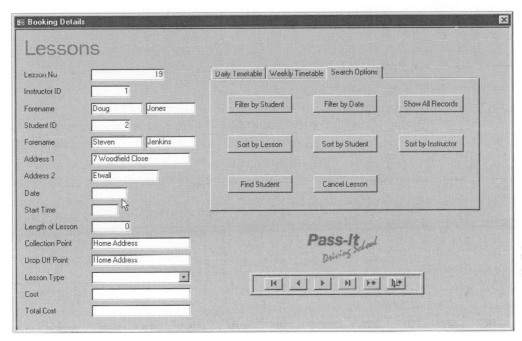

Figure 21.30

Further development

It is likely that the user guide for this system would go on to include:

◢ details of the other user options such as:

◢ how to cancel a lesson;

◢ editing student details;

◢ editing instructor details;

◢ adjusting prices;

◢ producing membership cards;

◢ issuing timetables;

◢ procedures for archiving student and lesson details;

◢ possible problems and troubleshooting;

◢ instructions for backing up the system during daily operation both
when and how.

User guide dos

■ It should contain simple, clear, step by step instructions to using your system.

■ It should be jargon free and well illustrated.

■ It might form or be part of on-line help built into the system.

User guide don'ts

■ It should not be a guide to using the software but a guide to your system.

■ Don't include large tracts of text from user manuals and try to avoid using jargon.

---

7. Evaluation

This section requires the student to report on the degree of success of their project.

Dos

■ Go back to the end user requirements and comment on whether each has been achieved successfully.

■ Return to the evaluation criteria and again comment on each, considering successes, problems and possible solutions.

■ Involve the end user in this process, note problems, limitations and recommend action for further development.

Don'ts

■ Don't moan about the lack of time. Time management is your responsibility.

■ Don't pretend it is all working when some parts are incomplete. Do not be afraid to tell the truth.

■ Don't report on how well you did but focus on how well your system achieved its aims.

Some examples are given below:

End user requirements

UR1. Produce an Instructors' Report to include contact details only

This option was relatively easy to set up using the wizards in Access.
However there were problems fitting it to the page and on reflection it might have been easier to set all reports to landscape. It took a certain amount of time editing to arrange the headings and data to fit the page. Currently the report offers details of all instructors in a continuous list which was not always needed. **See Action Point 1**.

Performance indicators

PI1. *The system will be able to reduce the time taken on the phone when dealing with a booking. Lesson availability will be instant to the caller.*

The system does eliminate the need to search through the folder of daily booking sheets looking for an available slot and therefore does save time. Booking availability was offered in seconds compared with what could be a minute or two looking across a number of sheets trying to find a vacant spot. The system at present only offers quick access to availability on the day of the call and for the coming week. **See Action Point 2**.

PI2. I will ensure all user interfaces are easy to use with common layouts, icons and styles. During the early development of the system and when the system is complete I will liaise with the user, noting problems and areas for improvement.

The user described the design of all forms as excellent. He liked the professional look but was concerned about a few minor irritations he found when working with them. The forms were generally all different sizes. A number of the boxes for data entry were too large for the data to be entered. The control panel on each form whilst looking very professional was a little unfriendly and it was not obvious at first what each button did. **See Action Point 3**.

Future development

■ ACTION POINT 1

I need to investigate designing all reports as landscape. I also need to add an option to the menu which will allow the user to choose the instructor they wish to have a report on. I will need to base the report on the instructor table using a parameter query.

■ ACTION POINT 2

When a student makes a booking, lesson availability can only be viewed on the current day and over the next seven days. Clearly a number of students book lessons over a week ahead or indeed block book the same time each week for a number of weeks. I need to investigate this for further development. Currently the user will have to jot down the booking manually and enter the details off line.

■ ACTION POINT 3

I could:

✦ Design all forms to be the same size. Consider redesigning the system to use the whole screen.

Add text to the buttons in the control panel or consider adding tool tips for each button.

Adjust size of all data entry boxes on each form as required.

■ Presenting coursework to hand in

When your project is finished you should:

produce a front cover; your name, centre and candidate number should be clear;

get your project in order; page numbering and the use of headers and footers is to be encouraged;

produce a contents page which clearly cross references to each section in the project;

bind your project securely; often coursework has to be sent for checking; it needs to firmly attached but ring binders are not encouraged.

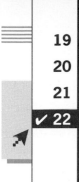

50 Access tricks and tips

Here are 50 tricks and tips that have been found to be more than useful when implementing Access projects.

1   Forcing text in a field to be upper case
2   Changing the appearance of a table
3   Right aligning text in a table
4   Copying data from the previous record
5   Entering the current time into a table
6   Entering the current date into a table
7   Preventing duplicate values in a field
8   Preventing duplicate combinations of data
9   Hiding a table
10   Wildcard searches
11   Finding all the surnames that begin with a letter or combination of letters
12   Finding all the surnames containing a letter or combination of letters
13   Searching for all records this month
14   Using a query to combine two fields
15   Using the DateDiff function
16   What day of the week is a date?
17   Viewing long entries
18   Viewing action queries before running them
19   Searching for records that contain no values
20   Multiple lines in controls
21   Keyboard short cuts
22   Nudging controls
23   Formatting dates on forms and reports
24   Removing the Menu Bar from a form
25   Making a command button the default button
26   Changing the properties of a group of controls
27   Preventing users from adding records to a form
28   Creating read only fields on a form
29   Putting a border around a control
30   Positioning and sizing your form automatically
31   Controlling the position and size of your form from a macro
32   Adding the date or time to a form
33   Starting a form from scratch
34   Drawing a horizontal or vertical line on a form
35   Editing the tab order on a form
36   Setting the focus
37   Filtering data by selection
38   Filtering data by form
39   Changing default print margins in reports

40 Putting the report name in a report footer
41 Formatting text in a Message Box
42 AutoExec macro
43 Disabling AutoExec
44 Removing the Office Assistant
45 Changing the caption text
46 Changing the folder where Access stores your work
47 Password protecting files
48 What if I forget my password?
49 Using help
50 Useful web sites

1. Forcing text in a field to be upper case

You can ensure that data entered into a field is in upper case by setting its Format property.

(a) Go to Design View for the table.

(b) Click on the **Field Name**.

(c) In the Field Properties, enter a greater than symbol (>) in the **Format** property to make the field upper case.

NB. To force a field to be in lower case however it is entered, enter a less than symbol (<) in the Format field property.

2. Changing the appearance of a table

(a) Open a table in **Datasheet View**.

(b) Click on **Format, Datasheet** to change the appearance of the cells and gridlines (see Figure 22.1).

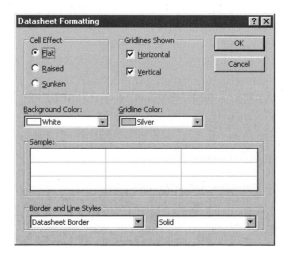

Figure 22.1

(c) Click on **Format, Font** from the menu. Select the required font, size and colour. In Access 97 just choose **Font** from the **Format** menu.

 3. Right aligning text in a table

Open the table in Design View. Select the field you wish to right align. In the Format box of the field properties, enter * (see Figure 22.2).

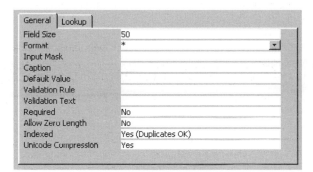

Figure 22.2

 4. Copying data from the previous record

When entering data in a table, you often want to repeat data from the previous record. Do this by simply pressing CTRL and ' (apostrophe).

 5. Entering the current time into a table

Do this by simply pressing CTRL and : (colon).

 6. Entering the current date into a table

Do this by simply pressing CTRL and ; (semi-colon).

 7. Preventing duplicate values in a field

Data in the key field cannot be repeated, for example you could not have two cars with the same Reg. No. You can prevent two records in another field having the same value as follows:

(a) At the Database Window, select the table and click on **Design**.

(b) Select the Field Name and set the Field Property **Indexed** to **Yes** (**No Duplicates**).

8. Preventing duplicate combinations of data

A theatre uses an Access database to store details of seats sold. A seat like A1 may be sold many times. Many seats may be sold for a performance on October 12. But any seat must only be sold once for each performance. How can we prevent seats being sold twice?

The theatre has a sales table. The key field is the **Booking no**. Among the other fields in this table are **Seat No** and **Date**. Once a seat number and date has been entered this combination cannot be entered again.

(a) In the **Design View** for this table click **View, Indexes** from the menu (see Figure 22.3).

Figure 22.3

The Indexes dialogue box is displayed (see Figure 22.4).

Figure 22.4

(b) Add an index name such as **Norepeats** underneath Primary Key. The name you choose does not matter.

(c) In the next column select the first of the two fields which must not be duplicated. Below it select the second field (see Figure 22.5).

(d) Click on **Norepeats** and set the Unique box to **Yes** (see Figure 22.6).

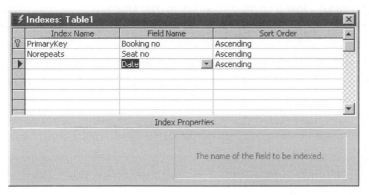

Figure 22.5

Figure 22.6

(e) Test it to make sure you get this error message (see Figure 22.7).

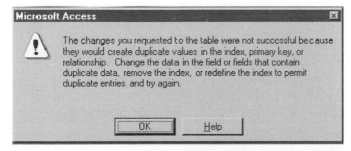

Figure 22.7

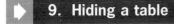 **9. Hiding a table**

You can hide a table from the Database Window.

(a) At the Database Window select the table, then choose **View, Properties**.

(b) In the Properties dialogue box, check the **Hidden**.

(c) Click on **Apply** and then click on **OK**.

The table will not appear in the Database Window.

(a) To show the table, click on **Tools, Options** and click on the **View** tab.

(b) Check **Hidden Objects**, click on **Apply** and then click on **OK**.

The Database Window will now display your hidden table.

10. Wildcard searches

You can use the asterisk (*) as a wildcard in searches and queries.

For example: a query searching on a postcode equal to **DE34*** will find all the postcodes beginning with DE34.

11. Finding all the surnames that begin with a letter or combination of letters

We want to set up a query so that when we enter a letter or combination of letters, the query will return all surnames beginning with those letters. For example, if we enter **Ste** the query would return Stebbins, Stephenson and Stevens etc.

Create a parameter query in the normal way and use the **LIKE** operator and the wildcard symbol (*).Use this statement in the query:

Like [Enter the first letter of the surname:] & "*" (see Figure 22.8).

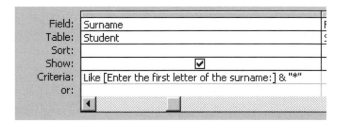

Figure 22.8

12. Finding all the surnames containing a letter or combination of letters

We want to set up a query so that when we enter a letter, we get all the surnames containing that letter (or combination of letters) ? Use this statement in the query:

Like '*' & [Enter the letter in the surname:] & "*"

13. Searching for all records this month

Suppose I want to find all records of driving lessons this month.

(a) Create a new query based on the Lesson table in the Pass-It Driving School.

(b) In the Date column of the QBE Grid, type the following in the Criteria row:

`Year([Date])=Year(Now()) and Month([Date])=Month(Now))`

 ## 14. Using a query to combine two fields

You can join together the text together from two fields using &.

For example, use a calculated field in a query to get a person's full name by entering the following in a new column in the QBE grid.

`Full Name: [forename] & " " & [surname]` (see Figure 22.9).

Field:	Student ID	Surname	Forename	Full Name: [forename] & " " & [surname]	
Table:	Student	Student	Student		
Sort:					
Show:	☑	☑	☑	☑	
Criteria:					
or:					

Figure 22.9

When you run the query it combines Surname and Forename as shown in Figure 22.10.

Student ID	Surname	Forename	Full Name
1	Brammer	Robert	Robert Brammer
2	Jenkins	Steven	Steven Jenkins
3	Fowler	Sarah	Sarah Fowler

Figure 22.10

 ## 15. Using the DateDiff function

Use the DateDiff function in a calculated field in a query or form to work out the difference between two dates. One of those dates could be today's date.

For example, it can be used to work out someone's age from their date of birth or how many weeks to someone's driving test, e.g.

`=DateDiff("yyyy",[date of birth],now())` gives the age in years.

Use "m" to calculate date differences in months, "ww" to calculate in weeks and "d" to calculate in days.

e.g. = DateDiff("d",[practical test], now())

▶ 16. What day of the week is a date?

How can we find out what day of the week a date in a query is? You can use the Lesson table in the Pass-It system to test this.

(a) Open a query based on the Lesson table in **Design View**.

(b) Scroll across to the **Date** field in the QBE grid. Select the next field and click on **Insert, Columns**.

(c) Enter this expression in the Field row of the new column:

Day of the Week: [Date] (see Figure 22.11).

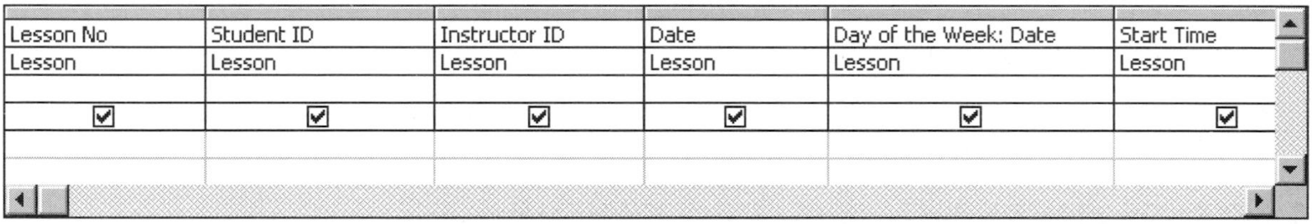

Lesson No	Student ID	Instructor ID	Date	Day of the Week: Date	Start Time
Lesson	Lesson	Lesson	Lesson	Lesson	Lesson
☑	☑	☑	☑	☑	☑

Figure 22.11

(d) Right click on this field and select **Properties**.

(e) In the Format box type **dddd** (see Figure 22.12).

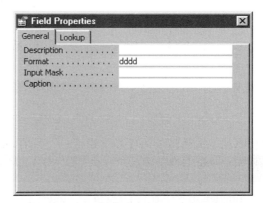

Figure 22.12

(f) Run the query to test it. You should get the results as in Figure 22.13.

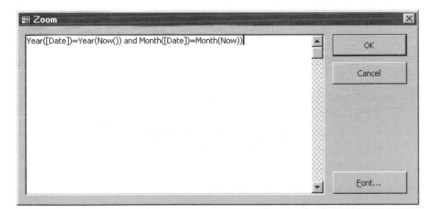

Figure 22.13

 ## 17. Viewing long entries

Often data is too long to fit in the space available, e.g. in a table, query design grid or properties window.

To see the whole of the text, select the cell and press SHIFT and **F2**.

This displays the Zoom box with the text. You can edit and enter the text from the Zoom box (see Figure 22.14).

Figure 22.14

 ## 18. Viewing action queries before running them

You can see the results of an action query before running it. Once you've created your query in the query design grid, you can run the query by clicking on the **Run** icon.

You can't undo any changes made by an action query so, instead of clicking **Run**, click on the **View, Datasheet View** from the menu. This will display a preview of your action query's results without permanently committing those changes.

19. Searching for records that contain no values

In the Pass-It system, suppose you wanted a list of Instructors who didn't have a mobile phone. You need to set up a query using the **Is Null** operator.

(a) Open a query based on the Instructor table.

(b) In the Criteria cell for the Field Name: Mobile No enter **Is Null** (see Figure 22.15).

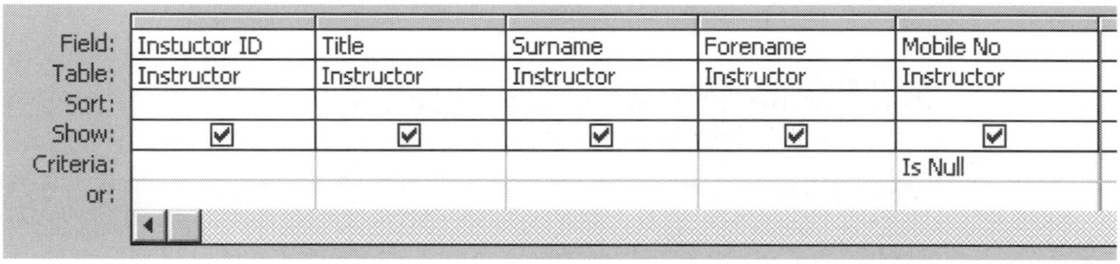

Field:	Instuctor ID	Title	Surname	Forename	Mobile No
Table:	Instructor	Instructor	Instructor	Instructor	Instructor
Sort:					
Show:	☑	☑	☑	☑	☑
Criteria:					Is Null
or:					

Figure 22.15

The operator **Is Not Null** would return all records containing any value.

20. Multiple lines in controls

If you need to enter more than one line of text into a label on a form, press CTRL + ENTER or SHIFT + ENTER to go on to the next line.

Of course the label needs to be high enough to fit the extra lines.

21. Keyboard shortcuts

You can control check boxes and option buttons from the keyboard. Press the TAB key to select a check box or option button, then press the spacebar to toggle the control on and off.

22. Nudging controls

It is often much easier to align controls on a form by using the keyboard to 'nudge' the object into place.

Highlight the control, hold down the CTRL key and then use the arrow keys to move the control in the required direction. In the same way you can resize controls by holding down the SHIFT key and using the arrow keys to resize the control.

23. Formatting dates on forms and reports

You can use the Format function to display different dates in different formats or different date components on a form or a report.

For example, suppose you have a field called Date.

Set up a new text box called Day of the Week and set the Control Source property to:

`=Format([date],"d")` (see Figure 22.16).

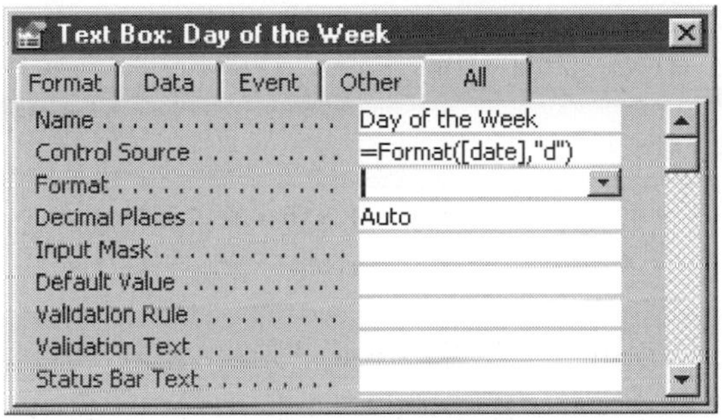

Figure 22.16

This will display the date's day, e.g. 31 if the date was 31/10/00.

`=Format([date],"m")` displays the month number, e.g. 12.

`=Format([date],"yy")` displays the abbreviated year number, e.g. 01.

`=Format([date],"mmm")` displays the abbreviated month name, e.g. Dec.

`=Format([date],"mmmm")` displays the full month name, e.g. December.

`=Format([date],"yyyy")` displays the full year number, e.g. 2001.

You can also combine the formats to create your own format, e.g.

`=Format([date],"dmmmyy")`

which would display the day, the abbreviated month, and a two-digit year value, with no spaces in between each component.

You can also display a literal character, such as a comma and space in a date to make it 17 June 2001. Just use this format:

`=Format([date], "d mmmm" ", " "yyyy")`

 24. Removing the Menu Bar from a form

The Menu Bar is the area across the screen that says File Edit View etc. To remove the menu bar when a form is loaded:

(a) Load the form in Design View and choose the Form Properties.

(b) Click on the **Other** tab and set the **MenuBar** property to =1 (see Figure 22.17).

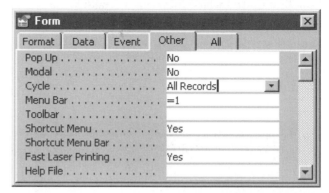

Figure 22.17

25. Making a command button the default button

You can choose a command button by clicking on it or pressing ENTER if no other button has the focus.

(a) Open the form in Design View.

(b) Right click on the button you want to respond to ENTER and choose **Properties**.

(c) Click the **Other** tab and set the **Default** property to **Yes** (see Figure 22.18).

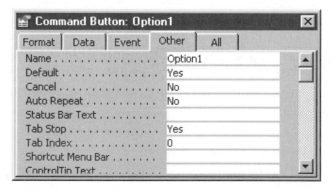

Figure 22.18

When you open the form pressing RETURN will run the command button action.

26. Changing the properties of a group of controls

(a) Open the form in Design View.

(b) Select the first control whose property you wish to change. Hold down SHIFT and select the other controls you wish to change.

(c) Right click on any of the controls and choose Properties.

(d) The Properties window opens with the title **Multiple Selection**. From here any property you select will be applied to all selected controls (see Figure 22.19).

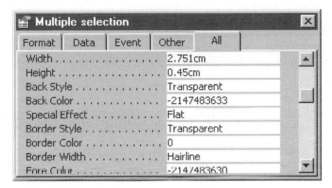

Figure 22.19

27. Preventing users from adding records to a form

Load the form in Design View and choose the Form properties.

Click on the **Data** tab and set the **Allow Additions** property to **No**. When the form is opened the New Record icon is greyed out.

28. Creating read only fields on a form

Sometimes you may wish to make a field available but not allow it to be changed by the user.

(a) In Design View, select the field and click on the Properties icon. Click on the **Data** tab (see Figure 22.20).

(b) Set the **Enabled** property to **No** and the **Locked** property to **Yes**. The field will not be greyed out but the user will not be able to change it.

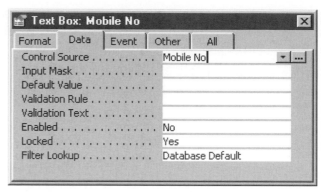

Figure 22.20

29. Putting a border around a control

Borders and other effects can be attached to controls using control's properties.

(a) Right click the control or label in Design View and select **Properties** (see Figure 22.21).

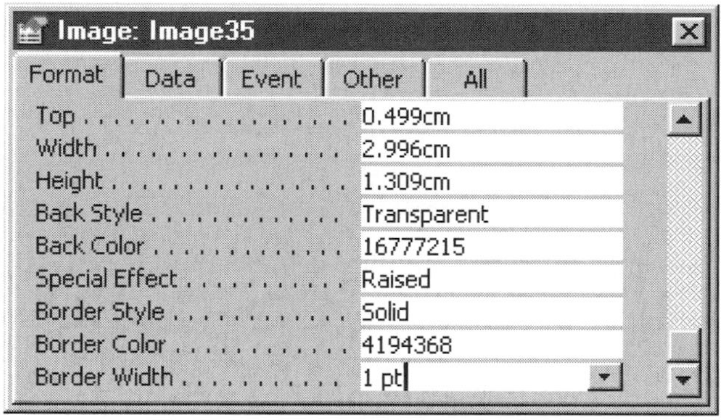

Figure 22.21

(b) Click the **Format** tab and set the **Border Style** to **Solid** instead of **Transparent** (see Figure 22.22).

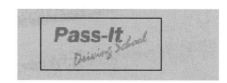

Figure 22.22

(c) Set the **Border Color** and **Border Width** as required.

(d) Set the **Special Effect** property to **Raised** (see Figure 22.23).

Figure 22.23

▶ 30. Positioning and sizing your form automatically

It is easy to position your form using its Form properties. Set the properties as follows. Your form will open centred and sized to display a complete record.

(a) Open the form in Design View.

(b) From the menu choose **View, Properties**.

(c) Click the **Format** tab in the Properties Window.

(d) Set the **Auto Center** property to **Yes**.

(e) Set the **Auto Resize** property to **Yes** (see Figure 22.24).

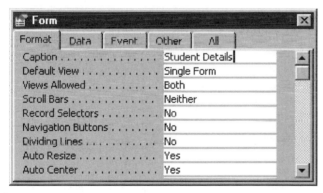

Figure 22.24

▶ 31. Controlling the position and size of your form from a macro

(a) Create a new macro and add the Action **Open Form** from the drop down list. In the Arguments select the Form Name for the form you wish to open (see Figure 22.25).

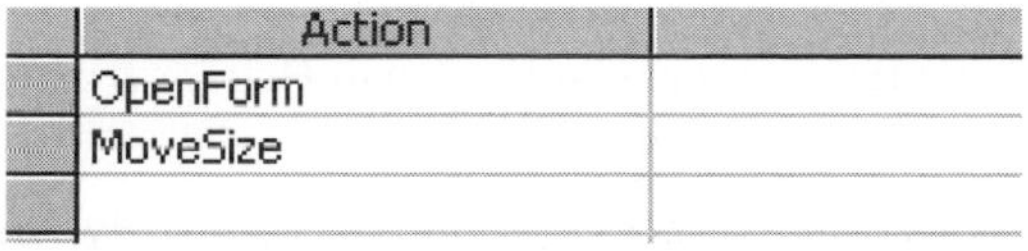

Action	
OpenForm	
MoveSize	

Figure 22.25

(b) Add the Action **MoveSize** and set the options as required (see Figure 22.26).

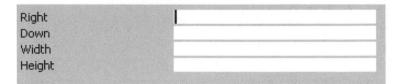

Right	
Down	
Width	
Height	

Figure 22.26

Right is the distance from the left of the window.

Down is the distance from the top of the window.

Width is the window's width.

Height is the window's height.

32. Adding the date or time to a form

(a) Open the form in Design View.

(b) From the menu choose **Insert, Date and Time** (see Figure 22.27).

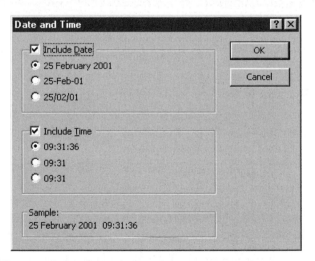

Figure 22.27

(c) Check the Date and/or Time format you want displayed and click on **OK** (see Figure 22.28).

(d) The Date/Time field appears in the Form Header from where it can be dragged to the required position.

(e) Switch to Form view to see the result (see Figure 22.29).

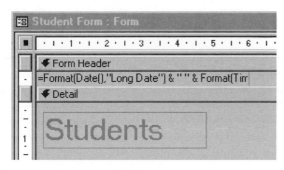

Figure 22.28

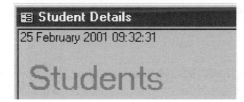

Figure 22.29

33. Starting a form from scratch

Throughout the study units we used the wizards to set up our forms. Of course, as ever, you could choose to ignore the wizards and set up the form manually.

(a) In the Database window, select **Forms** and then click on **New**.

(b) Select Design View and base the form on the Student table as shown in Figure 22.30.

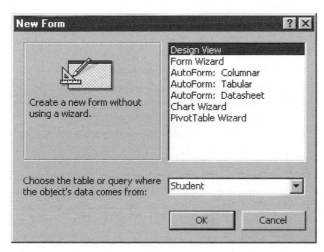

Figure 22.20

(c) The blank form will open in Design View with the **Field List** for the Student table.

(d) Drag and drop the fields needed as required (see Figure 22.31).

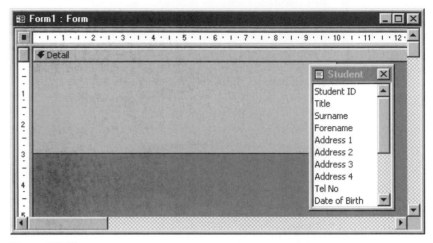

Figure 22.31

NB If the Field List is not displayed then choose **View, Field List** from the menu.

If you accidentally delete a control during the customisation of your form, display the Field List and drag and drop the field from the Field List on to the form.

34. Drawing a horizontal or vertical line on a form

There is a **Line** tool for drawing lines on a form in Design View. If you want to draw a line and make sure that it is horizontal or vertical, hold down the SHIFT key. This forces the line to be horizontal or vertical (see Figure 22.32).

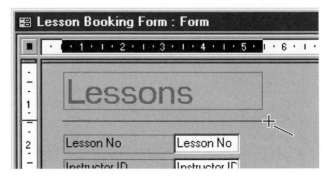

Figure 22.32

35. Editing the tab order on a form

If you press the TAB key when viewing a form, Access tabs you through the controls in the order in which you added them. You can change this order easily.

(a) Open the form in Design View and Click on **View, Tab Order** (see Figure 22.33).

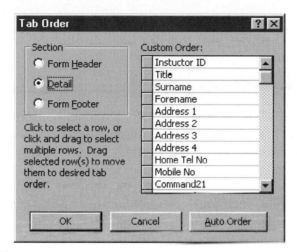

Figure 22.33

(b) The Tab Order dialogue box opens with all the controls listed. Select the required control and drag it to the right place.

 36. Setting the focus

SetFocus allows you to move the focus to a specified control on a form. This means that the user input is directed into the correct box.

Suppose you want to set the focus of the Lesson Booking Form to the Instructor ID control.

(a) Open the form in Design View.

(b) Right click on the **Form Selector** and choose **Build Event...**

(c) Click on **Code Builder** and click on **OK**.

(d) Enter the text below:

    [Instructor ID].SetFocus

(see Figure 22.34).

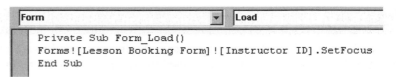

```
Private Sub Form_Load()
Forms![Lesson Booking Form]![Instructor ID].SetFocus
End Sub
```

Figure 22.34

▶ 37. Filtering data by selection

A filter enables you to search quickly for records in a table. For example, you can find all lessons with Instructor ID 1.

(a) From the Database Window, open the **Lesson** table.

(b) Click on a number 1 in the Instructor ID column. (It doesn't matter which one you choose.)

(c) Click on the **Filter by Selection** icon or click on **Records, Filter, Filter by Selection** (see Figure 22.35).

Figure 22.35

You will now see only the records for Instructor number 1 (see Figure 22.36).

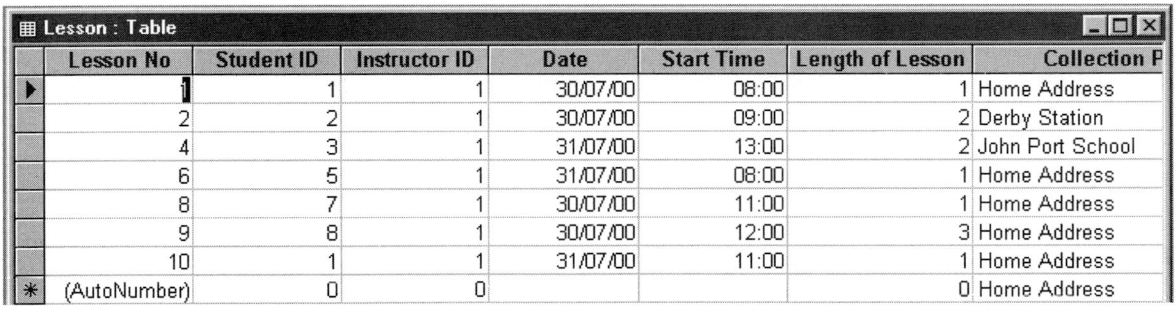

Lesson No	Student ID	Instructor ID	Date	Start Time	Length of Lesson	Collection P
1	1	1	30/07/00	08:00	1	Home Address
2	2	1	30/07/00	09:00	2	Derby Station
4	3	1	31/07/00	13:00	2	John Port School
6	5	1	31/07/00	08:00	1	Home Address
8	7	1	30/07/00	11:00	1	Home Address
9	8	1	30/07/00	12:00	3	Home Address
10	1	1	31/07/00	11:00	1	Home Address
* (AutoNumber)	0	0			0	Home Address

Figure 22.36

(d) To remove the filter click on the **Remove Filter** icon or click on **Records, Remove Filter/Sort** (see Figure 22.37).

Figure 22.37

38. Filtering data by form

Filter by form enables you to carry out more complex searches for records in a table. For example, you can find all the lessons that are on 30/07/00 AND have Instructor ID 2.

(a) Open the **Lesson** table in the Pass-It system.

(b) Click on the **Filter by Form** icon or click on **Records, Filter, Filter by Form** (see Figure 22.38).

Figure 22.38

(c) Click in the **Date** column. A drop-down box appears. Choose **30/07/00**.

(d) Click in the **Instructor ID** column and choose **2**.

(e) Click on the **Apply Filter** icon on click on **Filter, Apply Filter/Sort** (see Figure 22.39).

Figure 22.39

(f) Click on the same icon to clear the filters.

Note: you can find lessons lasting more than one hour by starting a **Filter by Form** and typing >1 in the **Length of Lesson** column.

Blank fields can be found by typing **Is Null** into a filter by form. The opposite is to type **Is Not Null**.

39. Changing default print margins in reports

At the Database Window, click on **Tools, Options**. Click on the **General** tab to set the print margins.

40. Putting the report name in a report footer

To add the name of your report to the footer, add a text box in the footer of your report and enter:

`=CurrentObjectName`

To put in the filename including the path, enter:

`=CurrentDb.Name`

41. Formatting Text in a Message Box

You can format text to bold in a Message Box using the @ symbol.

For example, in the No Data macro used in the Pass-It system set the message as follows:

`There is no data in this report@Please close the report and start again@`

(see Figure 22.40).

Figure 22.40

Run the macro and the Message Box is displayed as above.

42. AutoExec macro

A macro saved as **AutoExec** automatically runs when the database is opened. You can control startup options from this macro.

(a) Create a new macro with the following Actions and Arguments.

Action	Argument	Comment
Echo	No	Hides events
Hourglass	Yes	Pointer displayed as hourglass
RunCommand	WindowHide	Hides the Database Window
OpenForm	Student	Opens the student form
RunCommand	DocMaximise	Maximises the current window

(b) Save the macro and call it **Autoexec**.

NB. Use F11 to display the Database Window again.

 43. Disabling AutoExec

If you don't want the AutoExec macro or the Start-up options to run, hold down the SHIFT key when you open the database.

 44. Removing the Office Assistant

The Office Assistant is an on-screen animation that is supposed to be helpful. Many people find it annoying when it suddenly appears without any apparent reason (see Figure 22.41).

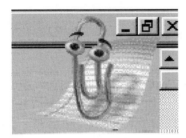

Figure 22.41

To turn off the Office Assistant when it appears:

(a) Right click on the Office Assistant.

(b) Click on Options.

(c) Uncheck Use the Office Assistant.

45. Changing the caption text

The caption appears at the top of the screen. It normally says Microsoft Access (see Figure 22.42).

Figure 22.42

You can customise the caption to include your own text, but clicking on **Tools, Startup...** and entering the text in the Application Title box (see Figure 22.43).

Figure 22.43

Your caption will now appear (see Figure 22.44).

Figure 22.44

46. Changing the folder where Access stores your work

(a) From the menu choose Tools, Options.

(b) In the **Options** dialogue box click the **General** tab.

(c) In the Default database folder enter the new path name;
e.g.**C:\Windows\Desktop** will save your work to the Desktop.

Many other Access startup options can be set from this window (see Figure 22.45).

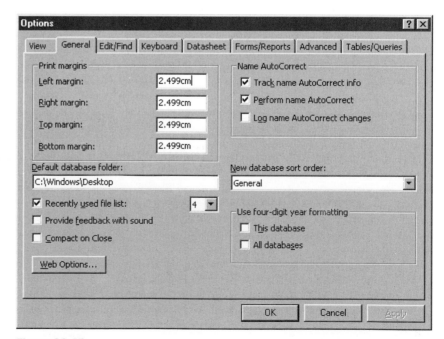

Figure 22.45

47. Password protecting files

It is easy to add a password to an Access file to prevent unauthorised access but be careful. If you forget your password, you won't be able to open your database.

(a) Click on the **Tools, Security, Set Database Password** (see Figure 22.46).

Figure 22.46

(b) In the **Password** box, type your password.

(c) In the **Verify** box, confirm your password by typing the password again, and then click **OK**.

The password is now set. Passwords are case-sensitive. The next time you open the database, a dialogue box will be displayed requesting the password.

Note: You won't be able to set a password if another user on your network has your database open.

To remove a password, click on **Tools, Security, Unset Database Password**.

This command is only available if a password has been set. In the **Unset Database Password** dialogue box, type your password and click on **OK**.

48. What if I forget my password?

In a word, don't.

But if you have, remember that passwords are case sensitive so check that caps lock is turned off.

If this doesn't work, there are companies that produce software to recover such files. You can download them from the Internet. They are *not* free. Try sites like http://www.lostpassword.com/.

This just proves that Access passwords aren't as secure as you might expect.

49. Using help

On-line help is available by pressing F1. Type in the keyword and search for advice.

Access 2000 also has an 'Answer wizard' which enables you to type in a question and get help.

50. Useful web sites

There are many Internet sites offering tips and hints in using Access. As with all Internet sites, the quality varies; good sites can be hard to find and sites are appearing and disappearing all the time.

Go to any search engine and search on *Access Hints*. Here are just a few examples:

http://www.microsoft.com/office/ is full of information tips, tricks, and how-to articles and frequently asked questions for Microsoft Office programs like Access.

http://support.microsoft.com/ has a knowledge base search to search for technical support information and self-help tools for Microsoft products.

http://www.access-programmers.co.uk/Tips.htm is a Microsoft Access help centre providing many tips and a discussion forum and ideas.

http://www.smartcomputing.com/ has lots of pages of articles about Access including a search facility.

Allen Browne's tips for MS-Access users offers lots of tips. http://www.wa.apana.org.au/~abrowne/homepage.html

Tony's Main Microsoft Access Page has lots of Access links. http://www.granite.ab.ca/accsmstr.htm

Uncle Jim's Microsoft Access Tips claims to have twelve pages with over one thousand helpful tips for Access users of all levels. http://www.geocities.com/SiliconValley/Code/5046/access.html

Appendix

Contents

- Access glossary of terms
- Important Access toolbars
- Keyboard shortcuts in Access
- Taking screen shots
- Coursework requirements of the different examination boards

Access glossary

Action query	An **action query** is a query that copies or changes your data. There are four types of action queries: delete, update, append, and make-table.
Append query	An **append query** is an action query that adds the records from a query to the end of an existing table.
AutoExec	The **autoexec** macro is a macro that runs automatically when a file is opened.
Autoformat	An automatic format that can be selected when creating a form or report with a wizard. You can apply an autoformat to an existing form or report by clicking on the AutoFormat icon.
AutoNumber	A field data type that automatically gives a unique number to each record as it is created.
Bound control	A text box or other control on a form or report that gets its contents from a field in the underlying table or query.
Button	A **button** or **command button** is a control on a form or report. Click on the button to perform an operation, e.g. run a macro or apply a form filter
Calculated control	A **calculated control** on a form or report is a control that displays the result of a calculation rather than stored data.
Calculated field	A **calculated field** defined in a query displays the result of a calculation rather than stored data.
Cascading delete	When a record in the primary table is deleted, all the related records in related tables are also deleted. This will only work if referential integrity is enforced between the tables.

Cascading update	When a record in the primary table is changed, all the related records in the related tables are updated. This will only work if referential integrity is enforced between the tables.
Check box	A **check box** is a small box on a table, form or report that can either be selected or not selected. Clicking on a check box puts a little tick in the box. This is called **checking**. Clicking again to remove the tick is called **unchecking**.
Combo box	A **combo box** is a control on a form. Clicking on the combo boxes displays a list of choices available to the user. One of these choices can be selected or the user can type in data. It can also be called a drop-down box.
Command button	see **Button**.
Continuous form	A **continuous form** is a form that displays more than one record on the screen in Form view. You can set a form to continuous using the form's Default View property. A **single form** only displays one record on a form.
Control	An object on a form or report such as a text box, check box or command button. A control can display data or perform an action.
Control Tip Text	A brief description of a control that is displayed when the mouse moves the cursor over the control.
Crosstab query	A query that calculates a sum, average, or count on records and then groups the result by two types of information.
Default property	A property of a control, so when a new control of that type is created, this property will have the same value.
Default value	The **default value** is the value of a field that is automatically entered when a new record is created. For example, in a customer table, a company doing a lot of business in Derby can set the default value for the town field to **Derby**.
Delete query	A **delete query** is a query that deletes records from one or more tables matching the query criteria.
Design view	The mode that allows you to design a table, query, form, report or macro. You can create new objects or modify the design of existing ones.
Dialogue box	A **dialogue box** (or in American English a dialog box) is a box on the screen that enables the user to select choices and/or enter data.
Drop down box	See **combo box**.
Dynaset	A **dynaset** is simply the table resulting from a query.
Event	An **event** is an action that takes place when a certain object is selected, for example, clicking on a command button. Microsoft Access can be programmed to run an event procedure when an object is selected.
Event procedure	An **event procedure** is a procedure automatically executed in response to an event such as clicking on a button.

Expression	An expression is similar to a formula – it can combine values, fieldnames and operators into a single value in a form, report or query. For example: =[Length of Lesson]*[Cost].
Expression Builder	A tool in Access used to create an expression. The Expression Builder includes a list of common expressions that you can select from.
Field	A **field** is a data item stored in a column in a table, storing details such as forename, surname, etc.
Field data types	The possible data types for a field in a table.
Field list	A small window listing all fields in the record source in the design view for a query, form and report.
Field selector	A small bar in Datasheet view that you click on to select an entire column.
Filter	A **filter** selects only certain records based on certain criteria, such as all lessons for student whose ID number is 5.
Focus	The active control in a form. The control that is ready to accept data input.
Form	A **form** is a user-friendly way of displaying data from a table or query. It can also be used to enter data or as a switchboard. A form is fully customisable to suit the user.
Form Design View	The **Form Design View Window** is the window which is used to design forms.
Form Footer	Space at the end of a form. It is used to display, for example, instructions for using the form, command buttons, or unbound controls to accept input.
Form Header	Space at the start of a form. It is used to display, for example, a title, instructions for using the form or command buttons.
Form properties	Features of a form that affect its appearance. Form properties are set in form Design view using the properties window.
Form selector	A box in the top-left corner of a form in Design view. Click on this box to select the form. Double-click on this box to open the form's property window.
Form view	A window that displays the form. One or more records can be displayed. Data can be edited and new data added.
Front end	A **front end** is the name given to a user-friendly interface that appears on the screen when the file is loaded. Usually it will give the user a menu of options. It can also be called a switchboard.
Global menu bar	A customised menu bar that replaces the built-in menu bar in all windows in your application.
Index	An **index** is used to speed up sorting of a table. The key field of a table is automatically indexed.
Input mask	An **input mask** controls which characters can be entered into a field; for example, what format they are and how many characters are allowed.

Key field	The **key field** or primary key is a field which is unique for each record and is used to identify records.
Label	A **label** is a control on a form or report that displays descriptive text, such as a title or a caption.
Linked table	A table in a file outside the open database from which Microsoft Access can access records.
List box	A **list box** is similar to a combo box; a list box displays the choices available in a list format. The user can scroll down to see additional choices.
Lookup field	A field that displays data as a drop-down lists. It is either • a list that looks up data from an existing table or query or • a list that stores a fixed set of values.
Macro	A **macro** is a program that stores a series of Microsoft Access commands so that they can be executed as a single command. Macros automate complex tasks and so save time by reducing the number of steps required to carry out a common task.
Macro group	A collection of related macros that are stored together under a single macro name.
Make-table query	An action query that creates a new table based on the results of a query.
Module	A collection of Visual Basic procedures stored together as one named unit.
Navigation buttons	Buttons in Datasheet view and Form view windows enabling you to move through the records.
OLE object	An object that allows object linking and embedding. An object from another program, for example, a JPEG image can be linked or embedded in a field, form, or report
OLE Object data type	A field data type used to insert objects created in other applications in a Microsoft Access database.
One-to-many relationship	A relationship linking two tables. In the first table, the data appears once. This is usually the key field such as a video code in a table of videos. In a second table, such as the loans table the video code will appear many times as the video can be borrowed many times.
Option button	An **option button** on a form is used for choosing from a list of options. You can select only one option button at a time. Also called a radio button.
Option group	An option group is a group of controls on a form such as option buttons. Only one option in an option group can be chosen.
Page Footer	Space at the bottom of a page of a printed form or a report. It is used to display the date, page number, report summaries or any information you want at the bottom of every page.

Page Header	Space at the top of a page of a printed form or a report. It is used to display titles, column headings, or any information you want at the top of every page.
Parameter query	A parameter query is a query in which a user can enter one or more criteria values on which to select records.
Primary table	The **primary table** is the main table in the database. It will be the 'one' part of a one-to-many relationship.
Print Preview	The **Print Preview** window is particularly useful in designing reports as it shows what the printed report will look like.
Property	A characteristic of an object such as a form or a control that can be set using the Properties window.
Properties window	The **properties window** or **properties sheet** is the window in which you can view and edit the properties of tables, queries, fields, forms, reports and controls.
QBE	Query by Example. The method of setting up a query using query design view.
QBE Grid	A grid at the bottom of the query design view window, used for setting criteria.
Query	A **query** is a question about the data stored in your tables. It can bring together data from multiple tables and serve as the source of data for a form or report. See also Action query
Query Design view	The **query design view window** is the window which is used to design queries.
Record selector	The **record selector** is a small box or bar to the left of a record in Datasheet view or Form view that you can click on to select the entire record.
Record source	In a database, the record source is the table or query that provides the underlying data for a form or report.
Referential integrity	Rules that preserve the relationships between tables when you enter or delete records.
Relationship	A relationship is a link between common fields in two tables.
Report	A **report** is a way of presenting data in a customised printed format. The information in a report comes from an underlying table or query, but the user can control the appearance of item in a report.
Report Design view	The **report design view window** is the window which is used to design reports.
Report Footer	Space at the end of a report. It is used to display summaries and grand totals.
Report Header	Space at the start of a report. It is used to display titles, dates or report introductions.
Report selector	A box in the top-left corner of a report in Design view. Click on this box to select the report. Double-click on this box to open the report's property window.

Row selector	The **row selector** is a small box at the left of a row that when clicked selects an entire row in table or macro Design view.
Select query	A select query asks a question about the data stored in your tables and returns a result set in the form of a datasheet.
Scroll bar	The **vertical scroll bar** appears on the right hand side of the screen, to enable the user to move up and down a table, form or report.
	The **horizontal scroll bar** at the bottom right of the screen, enables the user to move to the right or left in a table, form or report.
SQL	Structured Query Language. A language used to set up queries. It is easier to set up queries using QBE.
Status bar	A horizontal bar near the bottom of the screen that displays useful information about a selected command or an operation in progress, e.g. the status bar shows whether CAPS LOCK has been pressed.
Subform	A form contained within another form or a report.
Subform/Subreport control	A control that displays a subform in a form or a form/subreport in a report.
Subreport	A report contained within another report.
Tab order	The order in which the focus moves in a form from one field or button to the next as you press the tab key.
Table	A **table** is a collection of data about a specific topic. A database will consist of several tables.
Table Design view	The **table design view window** is the window which is used to design tables.
Text box	A control on a form or report that allows you to enter text.
Toggle button	A control that acts as an on/off button in a form or report. Click once to turn the item on. Click again to turn it off.
Toolbar	A **toolbar** is a row of icons, usually but not always at the top of the screen. Additional toolbars can be added to suit the user.
Toolbox	A toolbar used to place controls on a form or report in Design view.
Unbound control	A control that is not connected to any field in the underlying table or query.
Unbound object frame	A control you place on a form or report to contain an unbound object. An unbound object is an object, for example a picture, whose value isn't derived from data stored in the underlying table or query.
Update query	An action query that changes a set of records according to criteria specified by the user.
Validation	Checking data when it is entered to ensure that it is sensible.
Validation rule	A rule that sets conditions on what can be entered in a field.
Visual Basic	**Microsoft Visual Basic** is Microsoft Access's own programming language.

What's This icon	An icon on the Help menu. After you click on the What's This icon, the mouse pointer changes to the question-mark pointer. You can then click on an item to get help on it. Note You can add your own What's This button to your forms and reports by using the **WhatsThisButton** property.
Yes/No data type	A field data type you use for fields that will contain only one of two values, such as Yes or No and True or False.
Zoom box	The **Zoom box** is a box for entering expressions or text, where the original box is not big enough to see all the text.

Access Toolbars

The Access toolbars that you are most likely to use are shown below:

Database

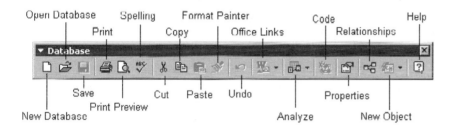

Table Design

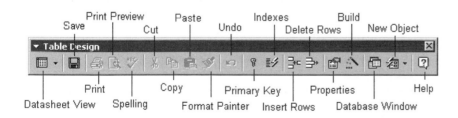

Table Datasheet

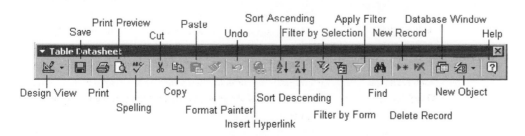

Query Design

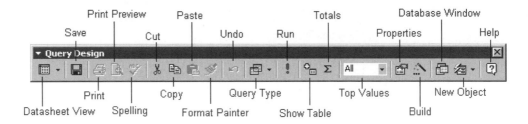

Query Datasheet

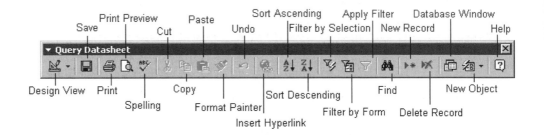

Form Design

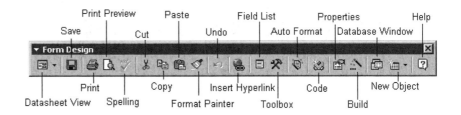

Form View

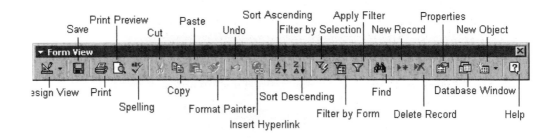

Formatting Form/Report

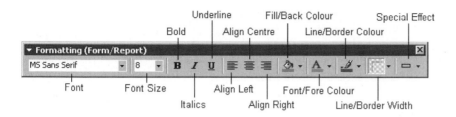

Report Design

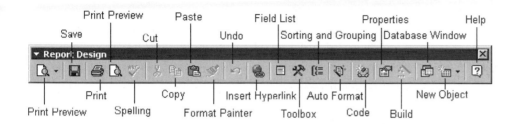

Report Print Preview

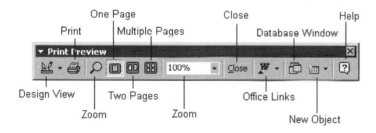

Toolbox

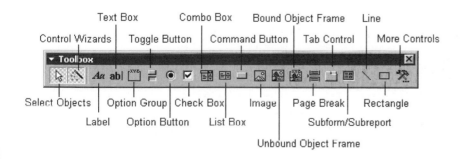

Macro Design

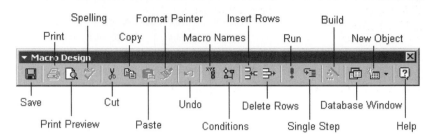

Keyboard shortcuts in Access

There are several keyboard shortcuts to help you move around the screen in Access and perform other common tasks. Here are some of the most useful.

Keystroke	Action
HOME	Move cursor to the beginning of a field
END	Move cursor to the end of a field
PAGE DOWN	Move down one page
PAGE UP	Move up one page
CTRL + −	Delete current record
CTRL + ' (apostrophe)	Copy a field's value from the previous record to the current record
CTRL + :	Enter current time
CTRL + ;	Enter current date
CTRL + + (plus sign)	Add new record to table
CTRL + C	Copy
CTRL + F	Find
CTRL + F6	Cycle between open windows
CTRL + H	Find and Replace
CTRL + N	Open a new database
CTRL + O	Open an existing database
CTRL + P	Print the current or selected object

Keystroke	Action
CTRL + S or SHIFT + F12 or ALT + SHIFT + F2	Save a database object
CTRL + V	Paste
CTRL + W or CTRL + F4	Close the active window
CTRL + X	Cut
CTRL + Z	Undo
CTRL + PAGE DOWN	Moves right one page
CTRL + PAGE UP	Moves left one page
CTRL + SHIFT + 2	Copies of the contents of a cell above into the current cell
CTRL + SHIFT + spacebar	Selects the entire datasheet
CTRL + SPACEBAR	Selects current column
F1	Displays help
F4 or ALT + DOWN ARROW	Displays a selected combo box
F5	Switches from Form Design View to Form View
F6	Switches between the upper and lower parts of a window, e.g. in Table Design View
F7	Checks spelling
F11 or ALT + F1	Brings the Database window to the front
F12 or ALT + F2	Open the **Save As** dialogue box
SHIFT + ENTER	Instant save
SHIFT + SPACEBAR	Selects current row
SHIFT + F2	Zoom
TAB	Exits a combo box or list box
ALT + ENTER	Displays a property sheet in Design View
ALT + F11	Switch to Visual Basic Editor and back
ALT + F4	Quit Microsoft Access, close a dialogue box, or close a property sheet

Taking screen shots

Screen shots of your system in action are vital both to prove that the system is working properly and to include in the user guide and technical instructions.

Using Windows Paint

To get a screen shot in Windows, press the **Print Screen** key on the keyboard. This puts the whole screen into the Windows clipboard.

You can then use **Edit, Paste** to paste the screen shot into your work.

The steps are:

1. Press the **Print Screen key** to capture the screen shot.

2. Switch to **Windows Paint**.

3. Click on **Edit, Paste**.

4. You may be told your image is too big and asked if you would like to expand the image. Click on **Yes**.

5. Save the image. (In *Windows 98* or later, you can save the image as a much smaller file by saving it as a **jpg** or a **gif**.)

6. Insert this image in your document.

If you only need to display part of a screen shot you will need to **crop** it. Cropping means cutting unwanted parts from the top, bottom or sides of a picture. Cropped pictures are smaller and so use less disk space.

Using PaintShopPro

Image manipulation software like PaintShopPro is ideal for screen shots, offering different options such as easy cropping and reducing to 16 or 256 colours to reduce the file size.

In PaintShopPro, the first step is to set up how the Screen will operate.

1. Click on **Capture, Setup**. PaintShopPro will open the **Capture Setup Dialog Box** shown in Figure A.1.

2. Click on the required **Capture** type.

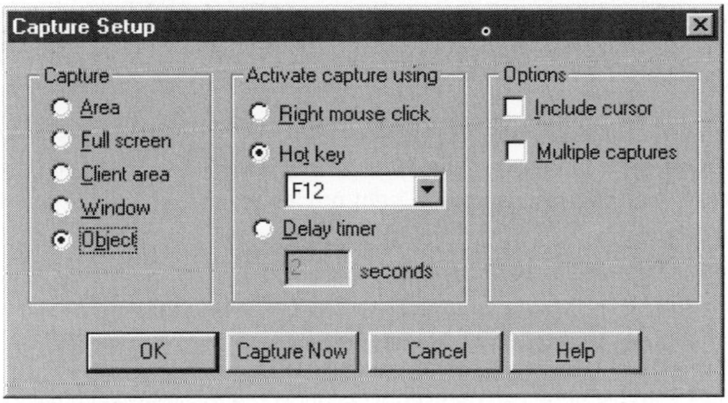

Figure A.1

The capture type determines which area of the screen will be copied.

Area	Select a rectangular portion of the screen
Full Screen	Copy the entire screen
Client Area	Copy the input area of the active window
Window	Copy the entire active window
Object	Copy a window feature or group of features

3. Click on the way you want the screen capture to operate.

Captures can be activated by using the right mouse button, setting up a Hot Key or setting a timer delay.

There is an option to include the cursor or not. If you choose to include the cursor make sure it is in the correct position before activating the capture.

4. Click on the **OK** button to close the dialog box and save the capture set-up settings.

To activate the screen capture choose **Capture now** from the Capture Setup box or Start from the capture menu.

■ Coursework specifications

■ Introduction

The following section offers guidance on these issues:

⚐ structure of the new AS and A2 qualifications.

⚐ pointers to the examination board modules/units supported in this book.

⚐ assessment criteria currently used by the different examination boards.

■ Course structure

All three examining boards, AQA, OCR and Edexcel offer Advanced Subsidiary (AS) and Advanced (A) Level qualifications in Information and Communications Technology (ICT). The AS level is a qualification in its own right or can be the first half of the A level. With all the boards, the AS course consists of 3 units, two are examined by written papers and the third unit is a coursework submission. The full A level is made up of the AS units plus three more units called A2. The first two A2 units are again examined by written papers and the third unit is again coursework.

The information in this book can be used to support the following coursework units assessment where students are required to provide an ICT solution based on the use of **appropriate applications software**.

■ AQA

■ MODULE 3 (AS) ✓

This module counts for 40% of the AS level mark and 20% of the A level mark. Candidates are expected to tackle a task related problem using the facilities of one piece of **generic software**.

■ MODULE 6 (A2) ✓

Candidates are required to research a realistic problem for which there must be a *real end-user*. The solution may be provided by **generic application software**

This module is 20% of the A level mark.

■ OCR

■ UNIT 2513 (AS) ✓

This unit consists of structured practical ICT tasks set by the board. Candidates are required to base a solution on the use of an **appropriate applications package**. This unit of assessment counts for 40% of the AS level mark and 20% of the A level mark.

■ UNIT 2516 (A2) ✓

This unit requires candidates to identify a well-defined problem, involving a third party user and to generate a solution using **applications software** as chosen by the candidate. This module is 20% of the A level mark.

Edexcel

Unit 3 (AS) consists of two coursework tasks worth 40% of the AS assessment.

Task 1 (16%) ✗ is a written report/study of an ICT administration process.

Task 2 (24%) ✓ requires the student to produce and document an ICT solution to a significant problem using a standard **commercial application generator**

Unit 6 (A2) consists of two coursework tasks worth 40% of the A2 assessment.

Task 3 ✗ is a written report on ICT issues.

Task 4 ✗ requires the student to produce and document an ICT solution using event-driven object-based programming.

Assessment criteria

▷ AQA AS Module 3

The project is marked out of a total of 60.

Specification	13 marks
Implementation	20 marks
User testing	12 marks
Evaluation	6 marks
User documentation	9 marks
TOTAL	60 marks

Specification (13 marks)

11–13   You have:
- produced a detailed requirements specification for the identified problem, matching end-user(s) stated needs
- clearly stated the input, processing and output needs, which match the requirements specification
- completed effective designs to enable independent third-party implementation of the solution
- determined an appropriate test strategy and devised an effective test and full testing plan; the testing plan includes the test data and expected outcomes and directly relates to the requirements specification

8–10   You have:
- produced a detailed requirements specification for the identified problem, matching end-user(s) stated needs
- stated the input, processing and output needs, which match the requirements specification
- Completed designs though they lack detail and thus do not allow independent third-party implementation of the solution or are inefficient in relation to the problem stated
- determined a test strategy and devised testing plans but these are limited in scope and do not relate to the requirements specification stated

4–7   You have:
- produced a requirements specification for the identified problem, although it does not fully match end-user(s) stated needs or lacks detail and clarity
- stated the input, processing and output needs, although these do not fully match the requirements' specification or are not sufficiently clear
- attempted design work although this is incomplete and does not reflect an efficient solution to the problem stated
- determined a test strategy although this is either incomplete or does not relate to the requirements specification stated; the testing plan is either vague or missing

1–3
- The requirements specification is vague or missing
- The input, processing and output needs are only vaguely considered or are absent
- There is little or no design effort
- The test strategy and testing plans are vague or missing

0   You have produced no work

Implementation (20 marks)

16–20   You have:
- developed an effective solution operable in the proposed environment by the intended end-user
- used appropriate data capture and validation procedures, data organisation methods, output contents and formats and user interface(s)
- fully employed generic and package specific skills in an effective and appropriate manner
- fully justified the selection of hardware and software facilities in relation to our designed solution designed

11–15   You have:
- developed a solution which is operable in the proposed environment by

the intended end-user although it has some inefficiencies
- produced evidence of the use of appropriate data capture and validation procedures, data organisation methods, output contents and formats and user interface(s)
- fully employed generic and package specific skills but not always in an effective and appropriate manner
- justified the selection of some of the chosen hardware and software facilities in relation to the solution developed

6–10   You have:
- developed a partial solution, but those aspects completed are useable by the intended end-user
- produced evidence of the issue of some data capture and validation procedures, data organisation methods, output contents and formats and user interface(s)
- employed generic and package specific skills but not always in an effective and appropriate manner
- only vaguely justified the selection of some of the chosen hardware and software facilities in relation to the solution developed

1–5   You have:
- developed a very limited solution which is not practically operable in the proposed environment by the intended end-user
- used few, if any, data capture and validation procedures, data organisation methods, output contents and formats and user interface(s)
- used the generic and package specific skills in a simplistic way and/or not always applied them appropriately
- not justified the selection of chosen hardware and software facilities in relation to the solution developed

0   You have not implemented the system

Testing (12 marks)

9–12   You have:
- followed the devised test strategy and test plan in a systematic manner using typical, erroneous and extreme (boundary) data
- fully documented the results of testing with outputs cross-referenced to the original plan
- clearly documented corrective action taken due to test results

5–8   You have:
- followed the test strategy and devised plan in a systematic manner but using only normal data
- partially documented the results of testing with some evidence of outputs cross-referenced to the original plan
- produced some evidence of corrective action taken due to test results

1–4   You have:
- followed the test strategy and devised plan in a limited manner using only normal data
- produced little or no documentation of the results of testing
- given little or no indication of corrective action required due to test results

0   There is no evidence of testing

Evaluation (6 marks)

4–6   You have:
- fully assessed the effectiveness of the solution by meeting the detailed requirements specification and shown full awareness of the criteria for a successful information technology solution
- clearly identified the limitations of the system

1–3   You have:
- partly assessed the effectiveness of the solution in meeting the original requirements specification and shown only partial awareness of the criteria for a successful information technology solution
- been vague about, or failed to mention, the limitations of the solution

0   There is no evidence of evaluation

User documentation (9 marks)

7–9   There is extensive user documentation for the solution which covers all relevant aspects including normal operation and common problems and is appropriate to the needs of the end-user

4–6   A user guide is present which describes the functionality of the solution and is appropriate to the needs of the end-user

1–3   A limited user guide is present which describes only the basic functionality of the solution

0   There is no evidence of user documentation

AQA A2 Module 6

The project is marked out of a total of 90.

Analysis   18 marks
Design   16 marks
Implementation   15 marks
Testing   15 marks
User guide   8 marks
Evaluation   10 marks
Report   8 marks
Total   90 marks

Analysis (18 marks)

15–18 You have:
- identified an appropriate problem in conjunction with your end-user and independently of the teacher
- provided a clear, statement covering both the context and the nature of the problem
- clearly identified and delimited a substantial and realistic problem, and recognised the requirements of intended user(s) and the capabilities and limitations of the resources available
- specified and clearly documented all the requirements
- fully identified the information flow and data dynamics of the problem
- indicated in your analysis an appreciation of the full potential of the appropriate hardware and software facilities available and also, if appropriate, their limitations
- identified the user's current IT skill level and training needs
- identified qualitative and quantitative evaluation criteria in details and completed your analysis without undue assistance

10–14 You have:
- identified an appropriate problem with reference to your end-user and independently of the teacher
- provided a clear outline statement covering both the context and the nature of the problem
- identified a substantial problem and recognised many of the requirements of intended users and many of the capabilities and limitations of the resources available
- provided documentation which is intelligible but lacking in some respects

10–13 You have:
- indicated in your analysis which software will be used but it may not be obvious how the software will be used
- partly identified the information flow and data dynamics of the problem identified reasonable evaluation criteria

- required some assistance to reach this stage
- alternatively, identified a relatively straightforward problem and proceeded unaided, covering most or all of the points required for 15-18 marks

6–9   You have:
- needed some guidance from the teacher to identify an appropriate problem with an end-user
- provided a simple outline statement
- selected a substantial problem and attempted to identify many of the requirements of intended users and many of the capabilities and limitations of the resources available but needed assistance in analysing the problem
- identified only a limited subset of the information flow and data dynamics of the problem
- provided documentation but it is incomplete
- alternatively, identified a fairly simple problem and recognised most of the requirements of intended users and most of the capabilities and limitations of the resources available
- needed assistance in analysing the problem; with documentation that is complete in most respects

3–5   You have:
- required considerable guidance from the teacher to identify an appropriate problem with an end-user
- provided a superficial outline statement
- identified a fairly simple problem and recognised some of the requirements of intended users and some of the capabilities and limitations of the resources available
- provided few, if any, indications of what must be done to carry out the task
- given little indication of how the software will be used
- not identified the information flow and data dynamics of the problem
- provided weak and incomplete documentation
- needed much assistance in analysing the problem

1–2   You have:
- identified a simple problem or been given a straightforward problem
- given only minimal recognition of either the requirements of intended users or capabilities and limitations of the resources available
- provided poor documentation and needed substantial assistance

0   No analysis is present

Design

■ GENERATION OF POSSIBLE SOLUTIONS AND SOLUTION DESIGN

The design phase includes bringing together the results of the analysis and gathering and ordering information related to the background of the problem into the generation of a range of possible solutions which meet them. This may be alternative types of package or alternative solutions within a package. The solution design should be specified so that a competent person can implement it. There should be a clear specification of how each of the sub-tasks identified in the analysis is to be solved.

The detailed design (16 marks)

13–16 You have:
- considered a relevant range of appropriate approaches to a solution in detail, given compelling reasons for final choice of solution which have been fully justified, and fully considered likely effectiveness
- specified a completely detailed solution which a competent third party could carry out, clearly breaking down the proposed solution into sub-tasks with necessary indications of how these are to be solved, and specified and clearly documented all the requirements
- included a well-defined schedule and work plan, showing in detail how the task is to be carried out and what is required in a comprehensible manner; this can include layout sheets, record structures, spreadsheet plans, design for data-capture sheets etc. as appropriate
- devised an effective and full testing plan with a comprehensive selection of test data and reasons for the choice of the data clearly specified
- completed this stage without assistance

9–12 You have:
- considered a relevant range of appropriate approaches to a solution, giving reasons for your final choice of solution and reasonably considering likely effectiveness
- specified a solution so that a competent third party could carry it out but with some difficulty, and breaking down the proposed solution into sub-tasks with some indication of how these are to be solved, specifying and clearly documenting some of the requirements
- included a schedule and work plan showing how the tasks are to be carried out, showing what is required in a reasonable manner; this can include layout sheets, record structures, spreadsheet plans, design for data-capture sheets etc. as appropriate
- devised a testing plan with some tests clearly specified
- completed this stage without undue assistance

6–8 You have:
- provided a limited range of approaches which may have required some assistance; the reasons given for the final choice are weak and likely effectiveness has not been discussed in detail
- given sufficient detail so that you, but not another person, can replicate the solution at a later date; an attempt has been made to break down the solution into sub-tasks with some indications of how these are to be solved; the documentation is clear but lacking in some respects
- provided a schedule and work plan but these are limited
- presented a testing plan
- completed this without undue assistance

3–5 You have:
- considered only one approach which may have required considerable assistance, giving only vague reasons for the formal choice and without discussing likely effectiveness
- given sufficient detail so that the candidate, but not another person, can replicate the solution at a later date but with some difficulty; an attempt has been made to break down the solution into sub-tasks but with insufficient indications of how these are to be solved; the documentation is lacking in many respects
- provided a schedule and work plan but these are poorly thought out
- supplied a poor testing plan
- required possibly substantial assistance

1–2 You have:
- given little or no consideration to approaches to the solution and no or invalid reasons for final choice of solution
- chosen a superficial outline of the solution so that you are unable to replicate the solution at a later date; little attempt has been made to break down the problem into sub-tasks; schedule and work plan are vague or missing; testing plan is vague or missing; documentation is poor and substantial assistance may have been required

0 No detail of chosen solution given

Implementation (15 marks)

11–15 You have fully implemented the detailed design unaided, in an efficient manner with no obvious defects, fully exploiting all the appropriate facilities of the software and hardware available; documentation is clear and thorough

6–10 You have:
- implemented the essential elements of the design reasonably effectively and largely unaided; implementation has exploited some of the relevant features of the software and hardware available; documentation lacks detail or may be missing completely
- alternatively, fully implemented a simple design

1–5   You have only partially implemented the design; the implementation has exploited few of the relevant features of the software and hardware available; the documentation lacks detail or may be missing completely

0   There is no implementation

Testing (15 marks)

11–15   You have shown insight in demonstrating effective test data to cover most or all eventualities and provided clear evidence of full end-user involvement in testing. The system works with a full range of test data (typical, extreme, erroneous); the test outputs are annotated fully

6–10   You have demonstrated a range of appropriate test data perhaps with some assistance and some evidence of end-user involvement during testing. The system works with a limited range of test data; the tests outputs are annotated to a limited extent

1–5   There is little evidence of testing and only limited involvement of the end-user in testing. It does not meet the design specification

0   There is no evidence of testing

User guide (8 marks)

6–8   You have produced a comprehensive, well illustrated user guide that deals with all aspects of the system (installation, backup procedures, general use and troubleshooting)

4–5   You have produced an illustrated user guide that deals with general use of the system but only vaguely considers the other areas required for 6-8 marks

1–3   A user guide is produced that deals with general use of the system

0   No user guide is present

Evaluation of the project (10 marks)

9–10	You have considered clearly a full range of qualitative and quantitative criteria for evaluating the solution, fully evaluated your solution intelligently against user requirements, and provided evidence of end-user involvement during this stage
6–8	You have discussed a range of relevant criteria for evaluating the solution, evaluated your solution against user requirements in most respects, identified some, but not all, performance indicators, and specified any modifications to meet possible major limitations and/or enhancements, maybe with assistance
3–5	You have only partially evaluated the system against the original specification and user requirements. This may be because the original specification was poor. Few, if any, performance indicators have been identified. Discussion concerning the limitations or enhancements to the system are largely absent or have required some prompting
1–2	You have made little attempt at evaluation. No performance indicators have been identified. Discussion concerning the limitations or enhancements to the system are absent or limited and have required considerable prompting
0	No attempt at evaluation has been made

Preparation of the report (8 marks)

7–8	You have produced a well-written, fully illustrated, organised report, describing the project accurately and concisely
5–6	You have produced a well-written report but it lacks good organisation. Alternatively the report is well-organised but of limited quality
3–4	Your report is of generally poor quality but shows evidence of organisation. There are deficiencies and omissions
1–2	Your report is poorly organised and presented with few or no diagrams. There are a considerable number of omissions
0	No report is present

OCR Module 2516

The project is marked out of a total of 120.

Definition and analysis	25 marks
Design	21 marks
Development, testing and implementation	35 marks
Documentation	24 marks
Evaluation	15 marks

(a) Definition, investigation and analysis (25 marks)

i. Definition – nature of the problem solved (5 marks)

You should not expect the examiner to be familiar with the theory and practice in the area of the chosen system.

You should give a brief description of the organisation (e.g. firm or business) involved and the current methods used in the chosen areas that may form the basis of the project, and a clear statement of the origins and form of data. At this stage the exact scope of the project may not be known and it may lead to an interview with the user.

1. A vague description of the organisation
2. Some description of both the stages of study and organisation involved
3. A good description of either the area or organisation with some description of the other.
4. A clear description with one element missing (for example, origins of the data).
5. An excellent description with all elements present

ii. Investigation and analysis (20 marks)

This section is the 'systems analysis'. The question is not how a system performs detailed tasks, but rather how the project progresses from the original data to the results. You should describe how user requirements were ascertained (possibly by long discussions with users; question and answer sessions should be recorded and outcomes agreed). A clear requirements specification should be defined. Alternative outline solutions should be discussed and evaluated against one another

16–20

Excellent user involvement with detailed recording of the user's requirements. Alternative approaches have been discussed in depth. All other items must be present, showing a thorough analysis of the system to be computerised. A detailed requirements specification has been produced

11–15

Good user involvement and recording of the interview(s). Most of the necessary items have been covered including a detailed discussion or alternative approaches. However, one or two items have been omitted. A requirements specification is present but with some omissions

6–10	Some evidence that an attempt has been made to interview the user and some recording of it has been made. Attempts at some of the other items have been made. An attempt has been made to develop a requirements specification
1–5	Some elements have been discussed but little or no user involvement

(b) Design (21 marks)

i. Nature of the solution (13 marks)	A detailed systems design (including diagrams as appropriate), should be produced and agreed with users. Proposed data structures should be described and design limitations included. Design of the user interface is of paramount importance and should be documented in detail in the form of data capture forms, input formats (with examples of screen layouts if necessary), and output formats should be included where relevant. A detailed summary of the aims and objectives should also be included. These are the design specifications which should be agreed with the user
11–13	A clear set of objectives with a detailed and complete design specification, which is logically correct. There are also detailed written descriptions of any processes/modules and a clear, complete definition of any data structures. The specification is sufficient for someone to pick up and develop an end result using the software and hardware specified in the requirements specification
6–10	A clear set of objectives have been defined; a full design specification is included but there may be some errors or logical inconsistencies, e.g. validation specified may be inadequate or field lengths incorrect
3–6	The major objective of the new system has been adequately summarised, but omissions have been made. There is a brief outline of a design specification, including mock-ups of inputs and outputs, task model described (including any diagrams). However, there is a lack of completeness with omissions from the task model, inputs and outputs. Data structures have been identified but there may be inadequate detail
1–2	Some vague discussion of what the system will do with brief diagrammatic representation of the new system

ii. Intended benefits (3 marks)	There should be some discussion of the relative merits of the intended system and of the previous mode of operation. This may include any degree of generality beyond the original scope of the system. One mark should be awarded for each valid benefit up to a maximum of three marks
iii. Limits of scope of situation (5 marks)	This may include volume (sizing limitations), limitations imposed by the interface and/or limitations of the facilities used. For full marks there must be some estimate of the size of storage space required for the implemented system implemented system
4–5	A detailed description of the system limitations has been given, including the estimate of,the size of the files required for the implemented system
2–3	The major limitations of the system have been adequately summarised, but omissions have been made
1	A vague discussion of what the system limitations are

(c) Software development, testing and implementation (35 marks)

i. Software development and testing (18 marks)	■ A technical description of how the solution relates to the design specification produced and agreed with the user should be included. It is your responsibility to produce evidence of your development work and for producing a test plan for the system. It is vital to produce test cases and to show that they work. To do this,. it is necessary not only to have test data, but to know what the expected results are with that data ■ An attempt should be made to show that all parts of the system have been tested, including those sections dealing with unexpected or invalid data as well as extreme cases. Showing that many other cases of test data are likely to work – by including the outputs that they produce – is another important feature. Evidence of testing is essential. Comments by teachers and others are of value, but the test plan must be supported by evidence in the report of a properly designed testing process. The examiner must be left in no doubt the system actually works in the target environment. This evidence may be in the form of a hardcopy output (possibly including screen dumps), photographs or VHS video
14–18	Technical evidence is provided in the form of printouts. Data structures are illustrated as part of the listings where appropriate, detailing their purpose. There is a full set of printouts showing input and output as well as data structures. All hardcopy evidence is fully

annotated and cross-referenced. A full test plan, with evidence of each test run is present in the report, together with the expected output. The test plan should cover as many different paths through the system as is feasible, including valid, invalid and extreme cases. Marks may be lost for lack of evidence of a particular test run or lack of expected results

| 9–13 | Evidence of tailored software packages/tailored interface software/tailored client software are provided in the form of printouts. Data structures are illustrated as part of the listings where appropriate, detailing their purposes. There is some annotation evident to illustrate how the package was tailored for a particular purpose or to indicate the purpose of sections of code in a program listing. The developed solution partially fulfils the design specification. There should be at least eight test runs together with a test plan and hardcopy evidence. However, the test plan has omissions in it and/or not all the cases have been tested (i.e. have no evidence of testing) |

| 5–8 | Evidence of tailored software packages/tailored interface software/tailored client software etc. are provided in the form of printouts. Data structures are illustrated as annotation evident to illustrate how the package was tailored for a particular purpose or to indicate the purpose of sections of code in a program listing. The developed solution has logical flaws and does not fulfil the design specification. There is little evidence of testing with a badly developed test plan with clear omissions. There is no description of the relationship between the structure of the development work and the testing in evidence |

| 1–4 | Evidence of tailoring of a software package or integration of interface software is tailored into a system and is provided in the form of printouts but with no annotation or relationship to a test plan or test run. The developed solution does not fulfil the design specification. A collection of hardcopy test run outputs with no test plan, or a test plan with no hardcopy evidence may also be present. A teacher may award up to 2 marks if they have shown the system working satisfactorily and there is no hard evidence in the project report |

| ii. Implem-entation (10 marks) | It is recognised that the user organisation (preferably 'third party'), I may not fully implement the system, although this is the ultimate aim. However, to score any marks in this section there must be some evidence that the person for whom the system was written has seen the system in operation. This can be done in a number of ways: such as by inviting the user to see the product and by your ability to demonstrate the system, or by taking the system to the user involved. There should be an implementation plan written, including details of system changeover, training required and details of user testing |

8–10	A clear and detailed implementation plan, including detailed stages of user testing. All aspects of user testing, user acceptance, implementation and system changeover have been documented. There is written evidence available from the user that the system has been fully tested
5–7	A good implementation plan with details of training required. There is written evidence available from the third party user indicating that they have seen the system in operation
1–3	Details of system changeover have been documented with some recognition that the user(s) will require training. Some evidence of user testing is given, usually by questionnaire or written comments by fellow students or others who were not directly involved in the development of the system
0	No evidence that the third party user has used the system. No written implementation plan
iii. Appropriateness of structure and exploitation of available facilities (7 marks)	Some discussion of the suitability of methods and any product (e.g. hardware or software) used for the particular system should be included. Some recognition and discussion of the problems encountered and actions taken when appropriate should also be included . A log of such problems should be kept. Suitability for subsequent maintaniability and extendibility
4–7	A complete discussion of the hardware and software available and how they were suitable in solving the given problem, together with a good, informative explanation of the problems encountered and how they were overcome
1–3	Some attempt at discussing either the suitability of the hardware and software or the problems encountered

(d) Documentation (24 marks)

i. Technical (10 marks)	■ Much of the documentation will have been produced as a by product of design and development work and as a part of writing up the report to date. However, a technical guide is a standalone document produced to facilitate easy maintenance and upgrade of a system. The contents of the guide should, where relevant, include the following: data structures used and/or database modelling and organisation including relationships, screens, reports and menus; data dictionary, where appropriate; data flow (or navigation paths through the interface); annotated software details in the form of printouts; detailed flowcharts/transition diagrams as necessary; details of

	any functions, procedures, macros etc. and any formulae used. All parts of the guide should be fully annotated since this is very important for subsequent development of the system. The specifications of the hardware and software on which the system can be implemented should be included
	■ Since the system in the technical guide will differ from one project to another, professional judgement as to what would be necessary for another analyst to maintain and develop the system has to be made
7–10	No major omissions, with all parts fully annotated. Marks will be lost for inadequate items of documentation, e.g. non-specification of hardware on which the system can be implemented. For full marks the guide should be well presented rather than just a collection of items
3–6	One or two major omissions, but the rest is fully annotated
1–2	Some items are present but little annotation
ii. User (14 marks)	Clear guidance, as friendly as possible, should be given to the user for all operations that they would be required to perform. These would include input format with screens display, print options, back-ups (file integrity routines), security of access to data and a guide to common errors which may occur. (Note: you will not he required to copy out large volumes of any underlying software's user-guide, but to produce a non-technical and easy-to-follow guide for someone with little computer knowledge.) Some mention here of the relationship between items of software and the data they deal with may be relevant. The user guide should be well-presented with an index and, where necessary, a glossary of the terms used. Alternatively, an electronic guide could be based around hypertext links (screen dumps will be required)
10–14	A full user guide with all options described, well presented (possibly as booklet), with an index and a glossary. No omission of any of the options available (including backup outlines, guide to common errors). Marks may be lost for inadequate descriptions of some options. For full marks, good on-screen help should exist
5–9	All but one or two options fully described, e.g. back-up routines not mentioned. In the main the options are easy for the user to follow with screen displays
1–2	An incomplete, badly produced guide. No screen displays/interface mock-ups. Some options briefly described but difficult for the user to follow

(e) Evaluation (15 marks)

i. Discussion of the degree of success in meeting the original objectives (6 marks)	This discussion should demonstrate your ability to evaluate the effectiveness of the completed system. The original objectives stated in requirements specification should be matched with achievements, taking into account the limitations. User evaluation is also essential and should arise from a questionnaire or, preferably, direct user evaluation. For full marks it is important that the user provides sets of data as they are likely to occur in practice, and that the results arising from such data be given. This data is typical data rather than test data and it may show up faults or problems that your own test data failed to find
4–6	A full discussion, taking each objective mentioned in (b) (i) and explaining the degree of success in meeting them, indicating where in the project evidence can be found to support this or reasons why they were not met
1–3	Some discussion about a number of objectives, but some omissions or inadequate explanation of success or failure
0	No discussion present
ii. Evaluate the users' response to the system (5 marks)	It is important that the user is not assumed to be an expert in computer jargon, so some effort must be made to ensure that the system is user-friendly. It will be assumed that the user will have considerable knowledge of the underlying theory of the business being computerised. Clarity of menus, clear on-screen help and easy methods of inputting data are all examples of how the system can be made more user-friendly. Here marks are awarded for the degree of satisfaction that the user indicates in the acceptance procedure. Could the system, or its results, be used? Was the system specification achieved? Do any system faults still exist? You should evaluate users' response to the final version of the system
4–5	A fully user-friendly system has been produced. The user indicates that the system fully meets the specification given in section (a), and there are no known faults with the system
2–3	The system is, in the main, user-friendly, but there is room for improvement (e.g. no on-screen help has been provided). The user indicates that the system could be used but there are some faults, which need to be rectified
1	Some effort has been made to make the system user-friendly, but the user still has difficulty using the system

(iii) Desirable extensions (4 marks)	As a result of completing the system, you have identified the good and bad points of the final system highlighting limitations and necessary extensions to the system, indicating how the extensions could be carried out. You have:

1. identified the obvious good points of the system, and possibly some bad points or limitations.

2. clearly identified good and bad points and any limitations

3. clearly identified good and bad points of the system, limitations and the possible extensions.

4. clearly portrayed the good and bad points of the system indicating the imitations, possible extensions and how to carry out the extensions

Edexcel

Edexcel Task 2 will consist of a practical, documented ICT solution to a significant problem that focuses on one of the areas of:

 modelling

communications

modem user interface

multimedia

data logging involving significant file processing

database manipulation

It is expected that such a task will involve the advanced use of one or more commercial/ industrial standard application generators. **In general, it will not be expected for you to employ programming skills.** You will want to use the best software to which you have access in a manner that is most appropriate to the task in hand. Thus it is the intention that the following marking guidelines could be applied in most situations. You will be expected to produce documented evidence under the specified ten sections.

Marking of Task 2

The assessment guidance gives three mark ranges to correspond to what may e considered as a foundation task (F), an intermediate task (1) and a higher task (H). The teacher examiner will have to exercise judgment as to what level of task the student has attempted.

Section	Assessment criteria	Mark ranges		
		F	**I**	**H**
Specification	Clear description of the task to be attempted. Particular references to the potential users and type of processing required. Statements that justify an ICT approach to the task and some consideration as to possible wider implications	0–3	3–6	6–9
Facilities	Discussion of the suitability of specific hardware and software required as they relate to the demands of the task in hand	0–1	1–2	2–3
Analysis	Evidence that a thorough investigation of the background to die ask has taken place in relationship to the potential users of the product. This should include, where appropriate, an analysis of any existing systems that are to be replaced and indications of from where the evidence has been gathered. Description of the complete data requirements of the proposed system and indications of the sources of these data	0–3	3–6	6–9
Design	Top view of the proposed system showing the sources of the information, the information flow paths, the general nature of the processing required related to appropriate application generators and any remedial process that may be built in (data validation). Complete designs of all proposed input and output interfaces; for example: screen designs, report structures (of input signals if a real-time application). Complete designs of any required processing structures such as file structures, database structures, spreadsheet functions, hypertext connections, OLE sources and destinations	0–3	3–6	6–9
Implementation	Detailed evidence of the implementation of the design. It is important that the relationship between the design and the implementation is clear, and this may include reporting any iteration between design and implementation that often takes place (prototyping). It could be an advantage to implement a system in a modular fashion and ensure that the documentation reflects this approach as it may assist in the awarding of deserved marks. Annotated hard copy should be produced where appropriate	0–3	3–6	6–9
Testing	It is good practice to perform technical testing as integral with implementation. Nevertheless, to help you maximise credit for testing, it is sensible for you to give evidence, in a separate section, of what tests you have designed and tried out. You should include evidence of results that show that the components of their implementation work as expected	0–3	3–6	6–9
Documentation for the systems administrator	Documents that will assist a systems administrator install, test and troubleshoot the implemented system.	0–1	1–2	2–3

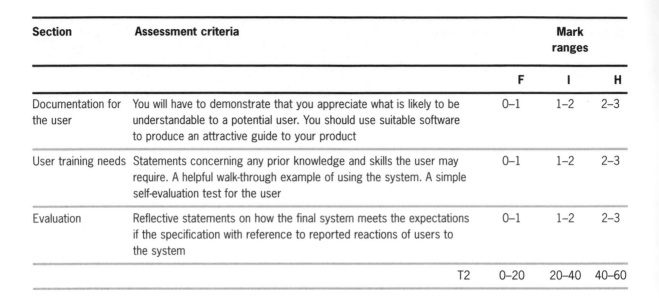

Section	Assessment criteria	Mark ranges		
		F	**I**	**H**
Documentation for the user	You will have to demonstrate that you appreciate what is likely to be understandable to a potential user. You should use suitable software to produce an attractive guide to your product	0–1	1–2	2–3
User training needs	Statements concerning any prior knowledge and skills the user may require. A helpful walk-through example of using the system. A simple self-evaluation test for the user	0–1	1–2	2–3
Evaluation	Reflective statements on how the final system meets the expectations if the specification with reference to reported reactions of users to the system	0–1	1–2	2–3
	T2	0–20	20–40	40–60

Examining board qualifications

Full specifications for the qualifications are available at these web sites:

www.aqa.org.uk

www.ocr.org.uk

www.edexcel.org.uk

Index

Action queries 166–74, 237
Analysis 194–202, 273–4, 287
And query 47
Append queries 166, 167, 168–9, 174
Archiving data 167
Are you sure box 182–3
Autoexec 250–1
AutoForm 64, 67, 138, 141
AutoReport 98–9, 111

Borders 242
Buttons, on forms 83

Calculated fields 62, 155–65, 235–6
Caption text 251–2
Cascade Delete 36, 37, 38
Cascade Update 38
Clock, adding 183–5
Combo boxes 87–92
Command buttons 83–6, 150, 240
Comparison operators 34, 47
Control Source 159
Controls 72–5, 238, 241, 242
    panels 86-7
Counting records 161–2
Criteria, multiple 48–9
Current system 195–6

Data
    dictionary 206–7
    dynamics 200
    entry 22–8
    types 9, 11–12, 29–30
Data flow diagrams 197–9
Database Window 6–7, 8
Date function 49–50
DateDiff 235–6
Default values 18, 32
Delete queries 166, 167, 170–2, 174
Design 202–11, 275–6, 280–1, 287
Design View, reports 101–2, 104–5
Documentation 193, 272, 283–4, 287
    analysis 194–202
    design 202–11
    implementation 212–16

problem statement 194, 279–80
    testing 216–20
Duplicate values, preventing 231

Evaluation 226–8, 272, 278, 285–6, 288
    criteria 201–2

Fields 3
    calculated 62, 235–6
    key 13, 14
    linking 142, 146, 149
    names 9, 11–12
    properties 9, 14–21, 30, 32–3
Filtering 150–2, 248–9
Forms 4–5, 64, 243–8
    captions 93
    combo boxes 87–92
    command buttons 83–6
    control panels 86–7
    dividing lines 93
    Form Design View 70–80
    Form Wizard 65–9, 85, 136, 137
    formatting 76–8
    graphics 81–3
    properties 92–3
    record selectors 93
    scroll bars 93
    tidying up 178
    views 68–9
    see also SubForms
Front ends 124
    see also Switchboards

Glossary 255–61
Graphics, in forms 81
Group footer 158
Grouping data 115–18

Help 191, 254

Icons, changing toolbar 186–8
Implementation 209–10, 270–1, 276–7,
        282–3, 287
Input masks 19–20, 23, 31–2

Input requirements 199–200
Is Null operator 238

Key fields 13, 14
Keyboard shortcuts 238, 264–5

Layout preview, reports 104–5
Linking fields, SubForms 142, 146, 149
Lookup table 15–17, 21, 23, 28
Lower case, forcing 230

Macros 5, 121–4, 150, 151, 153, 163–5,
        172, 174, 180–1
Menu Bar, removing 239–40
Menus, customising 188–92
Message boxes 123, 250

Nudging 238

Or query 49
Output requirements 200

Pagebreaks, forcing 119–20
Parameter queries 51–5, 111, 234
Passwords 253
Performance indicators 202, 227
Primary key 13, 14
Print Preview, reports 100–1, 104–5
Processing requirements 200

Queries 4, 94–6, 235
    action 166–74, 237
    append 166, 167, 168–9, 174
    delete 166, 167, 170–2, 174
    design 39–44, 207
    multi-table 56–63
    parameter 51–5, 111, 234
    select 4, 39–50
    update 167, 173

Real time clock 183–5
Record selector 93
Records 3, 24
Referential integrity 36, 37, 38
Relationships 35–8
Reports 5, 98–120
    attaching macros 163–5
    calculations in 155–65
    customising 105–9
    formatting 98
    orientation 103–4
    pagebreaks, forcing 119–20
    queries 111–20
    Report Wizard 109, 115, 155

running totals 162–3
toolbars 102–3
views 99–102, 104–5
with no records 163–4
Right aligning text 231
Running totals 162–3

Screen layouts 208–9
Screenshots 266–7
Search options 150–2, 153
Select queries 4, 39–50
Set Focus 247
Show all records 151
Simple Query Wizard 45, 62, 168, 173
Sorting 46, 152, 158
Specifications, requirement 269–70, 287
Splashscreens 179–81
Start up options 133–4, 192
SubForms 135–49, 142, 143, 146, 148,
    149
Switchboards 125–34
    customising 130–3
    items table 133
    report 131–3
    Switchboard Manager 126–30
    updating 175–7

Tab
    controls 143–5, 150, 161
    order 247
Tables 2, 3–4, 231–2
    design 9–21
    hiding 233–4
    naming 13
Test plan 210–11
Testing 216–20, 271–2, 277, 281–2, 287
Time plan 211
Timer Interval 181, 184
Toolbars 8, 185–8, 261–4

Update queries 167, 173
Upper case, forcing 230
User
    Guide 220–6, 272, 277, 288
    interview 195
    requirements 196–87
    testing 220

Validation rules 21, 23, 32–4

Web sites 254
Wildcard searches 234

Zoom box 237